D1538725

THE MARTINSVILLE SEVEN

Race, Rape, and Capital Punishment

CONSTITUTIONALISM AND DEMOCRACY

KERMIT HALL AND DAVID O'BRIEN, EDITORS

THE

MARTINSVILLE

SEVEN

Race, Rape, and

Capital Punishment

ERIC W. RISE

UNIVERSITY PRESS OF VIRGINIA

Charlottesville and London

THE UNIVERSITY PRESS OF VIRGINIA

Copyright © 1995 by the Rectors and Visitors
of the University of Virginia

FIRST PUBLISHED 1995

Library of Congress Cataloging-in-Publication Data
Rise, Eric W.
   The Martinsville Seven : race, rape, and capital punishment / Eric
W. Rise.
      p.   cm.—(Constitutionalism and democracy)
   Includes bibliographical references and index.
   ISBN 0-8139-1567-8 (cloth)
   1. Martinsville Seven Trial, Martinsville, Va., 1949.   2. Trials
(Rape)—Virginia—Martinsville.   3. Discrimination in criminal
justice administration—Southern States—History—20th century.
I. Title.   II. Series.
KF224.M29R57   1995
347.73'05—dc20
[347.3075]   94-24078
                                                                  CIP

PRINTED IN THE UNITED STATES OF AMERICA

FOR KAREN

CONTENTS

ILLUSTRATIONS

ACKNOWLEDGMENTS

The practice of history is a collegial endeavor, and I welcome this opportunity to thank those who aided the research and writing of this book. I am especially indebted to Kermit Hall, who suggested the topic and guided me through the project with equal measures of criticism and encouragement. The scope of this study has grown considerably since its inception, and Kermit must receive much of the credit for its transformation.

The librarians and archivists whom I encountered during my research performed their duties with courtesy and professionalism. The staffs of the circuit executive's office of the Fourth United States Circuit Court of Appeals, the George Washington University Library, the Patrick Henry Community College Library, the Margaret I. King Library at the University of Kentucky, the Moorland-Spingarn Research Center at Howard University, the Seeley G. Mudd Manuscript Library at Princeton University, the National Archives—Mid-Atlantic Region, the Richmond Public Law Library, the Richmond Public Library, the Schomburg Center for Research in Black Culture, the Earl Gregg Swem Library at the College of William and Mary, the Harry S. Truman Library, the clerk's office of the United States District Court for the Eastern District of Virginia, the University of Delaware Library, the University of Florida Libraries, the University of Virginia Library, the Virginia State Law Library, the Virginia State Library and Archives, the Virginia Commonwealth University Library, the Washington National Records Center, and the Widener University Legal Information Center all provided expert assistance. I would particularly like to acknowledge the courtesies extended by Joe Sullivan at the Library of Congress and Carl DeHart at the Blue Ridge Regional Library in Martinsville. Rick Donnelly and Rosalie Sanderson of the University of Florida's Legal Information Center provided expert guidance in legal research. Melanie Davis in the university's Interlibrary Loan Office unearthed mounds of obscure material. Cary Beth Cryor of the Afro-American Newspapers Archives and Research Center, Joanne Slough of the Richmond Newspapers library, and Pat Ross of the Bassett (Virginia)

Branch Library located most of the photographs that illustrate this volume. Special thanks go to Ashby R. Pritchett, clerk of the Martinsville Circuit Court, who provided me with access to the trial transcripts and other court records, ample work space, and a pleasant research environment during my visits to Martinsville.

Several scholars graciously volunteered information that enhanced the quality of this volume. In the early stages of the project Charles Martin directed me to most of the pertinent archival collections. Jerome Gorman, an anti–death penalty activist in Richmond, sent me photocopies of material he had collected concerning the Martinsville case. Peter Wallenstein shared his files on the justices of the Virginia Supreme Court of Appeals, and Richard B. Sherman supplied some elusive biographical data on Martin A. Martin, the principal attorney in the case. Tim Huebner and John Benske took time from their own research in Virginia to locate some sources. I am especially grateful to Oliver Hill and the late Roland Ealey, who graciously took time out of their busy schedules to explain the legal strategy that the NAACP developed in the Martinsville cases.

Gus Burns, David Colburn, Stephanie Cole, Mary Dudziak, James W. Ely, Jr., Ken Haas, Darlene Clark Hine, Charles Martin, Mike Radelet, John Sommerville, Anne Spitzer, Dave Tegeder, Charlie Thomas, Samuel Walker, Robert Zieger, and several anonymous reviewers read various versions of the manuscript. Their collective advice, representing a broad range of disciplinary and methodological perspectives, greatly improved my scholarship. Frank Scarpitti, former chair of the Department of Sociology and Criminal Justice at the University of Delaware, fostered a scholarly environment that was conducive to the writing of legal history. At the University Press of Virginia, Dick Holway patiently guided me through the process of turning a manuscript into a book. Portions of this study appeared previously in the *Journal of Southern History* 58 (1992): 461–90, which kindly granted permission to reprint those sections.

Finally, I must thank my family, friends, and colleagues for their words of advice and support. The debts of gratitude that I owe are many, but I am particularly certain that I will never be able to repay my parents, Walter and Beverly Rise, who instilled in me a passion for learning, nor my wife, Karen, who has been an unflagging source of encouragement, inspiration, and good humor.

THE MARTINSVILLE SEVEN

Race, Rape, and Capital Punishment

Introduction

During the first week of February 1951, the "Martinsville Seven," a group of young black men convicted of raping a white woman, died in the electric chair of the Virginia State Penitentiary. Never before had a state executed so many men for a single rape incident, nor had a lynching of that magnitude for men accused of rape ever been reported.[1] At a time when African Americans were beginning to assert their civil rights vigorously, the executions provided a stark reminder of the harsh treatment reserved for blacks who violated southern racial codes. Yet concerns other than racial control surfaced throughout the course of the proceedings. The values of due process, crime control, community stability, judicial restraint, and domestic security, as much as a commitment to white supremacy, influenced the outcomes of the trials and the appeals. Thus the conduct of the Martinsville Seven case challenged the traditional view that southern African-American defendants entered a criminal justice system dedicated solely to preserving a society based upon racial inequality.

The stereotypical view of southern justice has been well documented. Black defendants fortunate enough to escape the lynch mob's rope faced trial in southern courtrooms that institutionalized the informal practices of the mob. Racist juries summarily convicted these defendants on false charges of crimes against whites, usually rape, and sentenced them to be executed. Civil rights lawyers seized on these cases to challenge due process violations such as the all-white jury, lack of adequate counsel, and coerced confessions, but southern appellate courts sacrificed constitutional principles in order to preserve a culture which used fear and violence to subordinate African Americans.[2]

A litany of cases in the twentieth century amply supported this view of the southern legal system. In 1932 an Oklahoma jury convicted Jess Hollins of rape and sentenced him to death despite exculpatory evidence. Two years later Ed Brown and two other black Mississippi tenant farmers were convicted of murder on the basis of confessions obtained only after several days of torture and intimidation. Certainly the most notorious incident occurred in 1931 in Scottsboro, Alabama, when nine black teenagers received death sentences for rape on the questionable testimony of the alleged victims, one of whom later recanted her original statements. These incidents suggested that innocent black defendants often fell victim to judges and juries that either ignored due process requirements or, more insidiously, employed the trappings of procedure to mask discriminatory motives.[3]

In many respects the case of the Martinsville Seven fit this pattern. On January 8, 1949, a thirty-two-year-old white woman in Martinsville, Virginia, accused seven young black men of violently raping her. Within two days state and local police had arrested and obtained confessions from each of the suspects. In a rapid succession of brief trials held over the course of eleven days, six separate juries convicted the defendants of rape and sentenced them to death. State and federal appellate tribunals rejected pleas to overturn the convictions on procedural and constitutional grounds. In February 1951, amid protests from civil rights activists, radicals, and death penalty opponents, the seven men died in the electric chair.[4]

Nevertheless, certain striking characteristics distinguished the Martinsville case from classic "legal lynchings," as the summary convictions of innocent black defendants were known. The evidence presented at trial clearly proved that nonconsensual sexual intercourse with the victim had taken place. All seven defendants admitted their presence at the scene, and although some of the men may not have actually consummated the act, Virginia law authorized capital punishment for attempted rape and aiding and abetting a rape.[5] Angry mobs made no attempt to exact extralegal punishment, even though five months passed from the crime to the first trial, nor did large crowds even assemble at the Henry County Courthouse during the trials. The prosecution emphasized the preservation of community stability, not the protection of the virtues of white southern womanhood, as the dominant concern of Martinsville's white citizens. Most important, the trial judge made a concerted effort to mute the racial overtones of the trials. Although white juries decided each case, blacks appeared in every jury pool. Race-baiting by prosecutors and witnesses, a common feature of many similar rape trials, was notably absent in the Martinsville proceedings. By diligently adhering to procedural requirements, the court attempted to try the case, in the judge's words, as if "both parties were members of the same race."[6]

These actions illustrated Virginia's traditional reliance on the legal system to enforce the subordination of blacks. Of all the southern states, Virginia had experienced the fewest lynchings; half of the counties in the commonwealth had never witnessed a lynching. On the other hand, between 1908, when state penitentiary officials assumed authority for performing executions, and 1951, when the Martinsville Seven were executed, only three states—Texas, North Carolina, and Georgia—executed more blacks for rape than Virginia. In 1928 the Virginia General Assembly passed an antilynching statute, not at the urging of humanitarian reformers but at the insistence of law-and-order conservatives who promoted modern law enforcement as the most effective method of preserving racial stability. Virginia prosecutors knew how to enforce the existing racial order within the constraints of new procedural guidelines, eliminating the need for mob violence.[7]

Oliver Hill, one of the attorneys for the Martinsville Seven, cynically described the reasoning of white Virginians: "We don't need to lynch the niggers. We can try them and then hang them." But racial prejudice alone cannot explain the proceedings. The unique nature of the Martinsville case also stemmed from the competition between the values of due process and crime control that characterized the administration of justice after World War II. The societal dislocations that accompanied the end of the war created a fear of disorder and lawlessness and led to a call for stricter treatment of criminal behavior. The fear of black criminality was exacerbated by the eruption of race riots in Detroit, New York, Los Angeles, and other American cities. Law enforcement agencies became more professionalized and placed increased emphasis on crime prevention. Mob action declined as the citizenry placed greater trust in the local police force and judiciary to control crime and violence and maintain domestic and racial stability.[8]

At the same time proceedings such as the Scottsboro case had prompted the federal courts to promulgate procedural rules that would prevent "legal lynchings" in southern courtrooms. In cases arising from the Ed Brown and Scottsboro episodes, for instance, civil rights attorneys convinced the United States Supreme Court, under the due process clause of the Fourteenth Amendment, to outlaw coerced confessions and to mandate the appointment of defense counsel in capital cases. A procession of similar cases led Justice Hugo Black to remark in another confession case, *Chambers v. Florida* (1940), that abuses of due process by the states appeared to fall unduly on "the poor, the ignorant, the numerically weak, the friendless, and the powerless," categories that included a disproportionate number of African Americans. After World War II southern courts and police recognized that adherence to minimal due process requirements immunized them from appellate censure and granted them wide latitude to enforce local standards of orderly behavior.[9]

Ironically, the success of the due process campaign by such groups as the National Association for the Advancement of Colored People (NAACP) made it more difficult to save defendants such as the Martinsville Seven from execution. Procedural reforms curbed the egregious abuses of authority that resulted in the conviction of innocent African Americans, but they did little to help defendants who conceded their guilt but protested unusually severe sentences. This anomaly struck particularly hard at black defendants convicted of rape because of the historically harsh penalties reserved for black men who assaulted white women. Between 1600 and 1949, 588 African-Americans had been executed for rape in the South while only 48 whites had suffered the death penalty for the same offense. The juries who heard the Martinsville cases, therefore, delivered death sentences that reinforced the traditional racial mores of a southern community within the legal constraints mandated by federal law.[10]

Because the perceived injustice in the Martinsville case appeared in the severity of the sentences rather than the conduct of the trials, attorneys for the NAACP, who represented the men on appeal, elected to abandon narrow procedural challenges in favor of a direct attack on the discriminatory application of the death penalty. In fact, the Martinsville case was the earliest instance in which lawyers marshaled statistical evidence to prove systematic discrimination against blacks in capital cases, rather than focusing on procedural errors within a particular case. The shift from due process to equal protection arguments also represented an attempt to link the NAACP's criminal litigation program to the broader goals of the civil rights movement.[11] This tactic, however, struck at the heart of the power of local juries to prescribe punishment for those who disrupted community stability or transgressed codes of acceptable conduct. The state and federal courts that heard the Martinsville Seven's legal appeals refused to invoke the equal protection clause to limit the sentencing discretion of local juries.

One further difficulty arose in representing the Martinsville defendants. The interest of radical civil rights organizations such as the Civil Rights Congress (CRC) made it difficult for the NAACP to challenge the discriminatory administration of justice without appearing to be aligned with Communists and other leftists who aimed similar criticisms at the American legal system. Animosity between the NAACP and Communist legal organizations dated back to the mid-1920s and received its widest publicity in the struggle over the Scottsboro defense. After 1945 the enmity between the United States and the Soviet Union and the fear of domestic communism exacerbated these tensions. Yet despite the historical antagonism between the NAACP and radical groups, many Americans assumed that they maintained close ties. Many southern politicians attributed the emergence of widespread civil rights activism to Communist agents who had inspired growing demands for black equality. The simultaneous appearance after World War II of blacks, foreigners, and radicals who vigorously asserted their rights and liberties, they intimated, could hardly be a coincidence. At the very least, other cold warriors declared, the NAACP fueled radical criticisms of the American social and economic order by calling into question the operation of the prevailing legal order.[12]

The executions of the Martinsville Seven, more than any other case, demonstrated the power of the southern legal system to enforce informal codes of racial behavior. Not even the Scottsboro case, the cause célèbre for a generation of combatants against racial injustice, carried the same force, because all of the defendants escaped execution, and four of the men avoided prosecution altogether. In the Martinsville case, by contrast, appellate courts uniformly endorsed the procedures used to sentence seven men to death for a crime which involved no homicidal intent; moreover, those procedures were the product of lawsuits filed earlier by civil rights attorneys on behalf of other black defendants. Because the guilt of the defendants was never seriously challenged, the strictly legal issues related to equal protection for black defendants eclipsed the humanitarian motives associated with freeing the wrongfully accused. This difference forced NAACP attorneys to initiate broad attacks on systemic racism in the legal process while simultaneously distancing themselves from radical civil rights organizations that consistently sought to discredit American government and society. The strategies and tactics of the NAACP, which had met only limited success in saving innocent blacks from execution, proved even less effective when applied to guilty defendants during a period of domestic tension informed by xenophobic anticommunism and the related fear of rising black activism.

1

A Rape in Martinsville

On the afternoon of January 8, 1949, Ruby Stroud Floyd walked through the backyard of her home in Martinsville, Virginia, hurried across U.S. Highway 58, the road to Danville, and entered the predominantly black neighborhood of east Martinsville known as Cherrytown. Although the thirty-two-year-old housewife had only moved to Martinsville four years earlier, when her husband, Glenn Floyd, accepted a position as manager of the United Dollar Department Store, she was no stranger to this section of town. Not only had many of the residents purchased used clothing or homegrown vegetables from her, they also knew her as the "Watchtower Woman" because of her extensive missionary work for the Jehovah's Witnesses.[1]

Despite her familiarity with the area, Mrs. Floyd had never been to the home of Ruth Pettie, who owed her six dollars for a secondhand suit and a pair of shoes. She knocked on the door of Rosa Martin's house to ask for directions; when no one answered she walked next door to Dan Gilmer's house. After speaking briefly to Gilmer's wife, Nannie, in the kitchen, Mrs. Floyd went outside and asked Gilmer if he knew where Mrs. Pettie lived. Gilmer stopped work on the henhouse he was building, took a nail from his mouth, and scratched a crude map of the route to the Pettie home, which was about a mile away. Gilmer noticed that it was getting dark, however, and recommended that she wait until the following day because on "Saturday night the people like to celebrate and have a nice time. If I was you I wouldn't go." Mrs. Floyd insisted on continuing, however, and Rosa Martin's eleven-year-old son, Charlie, agreed to accompany her.[2]

At approximately the same time, four young black men stepped from the lobby of the Rex Movie Theater in Baldwin's Block, Martinsville's black business district, into the chilly winter air. One of them suggested that they get something to drink, and Howard Hairston pulled a pint of apricot brandy from his back pocket. They also stopped at a liquor store to buy two bottles of muscatel, which they drank underneath the water tank along the Danville and Western Railroad tracks, which passed through Martinsville's black neighborhoods. After finishing both bottles they purchased a third at Gardner's Esso service station, but since they were getting hungry, they decided to save it for later. Three of them went to Frank Hairston's house to eat supper, while Booker T. Millner went home to fetch his overcoat. Detecting the smell of liquor on her son's breath, Ida Millner warned Booker: "I don't want you to go out any more. You're drinking." Booker promised his mother that he was only going next door to Howard Hairston's house, but as soon as he got there he met the others and left with them for the railroad tracks.[3]

As the men continued drinking wine and apricot brandy, they spotted Ruby Floyd and Charlie Martin approaching them. Mrs. Floyd asked them where Ruth Pettie resided, and Booker Millner directed her to the second house on the right-hand side of the road. She thanked the men, and as she walked away, Joe Henry Hampton told the others that the woman "looked good enough to hug." They half-heartedly advised Hampton to leave her alone; since he was more intoxicated than any of them, they assumed that he was merely joking. About ten minutes later Mrs. Floyd and Charlie returned. As she passed, Hampton remarked, "That woman's got some pretty legs," and ran behind her calling, "Wait, honey." As he put his arm around her waist, she pulled away and began running. The other men called for Hampton to stop as he followed her out of sight.[4]

Shortly after six o'clock Francis DeSales Grayson burst through the front door of Ethel Mae Redd's house. Grayson, his wife, and five children had only recently moved to Martinsville and were living in Mrs.

Redd's small home. John Clabon Taylor and James Luther Hairston had just stopped to visit with Mrs. Redd, and Grayson breathlessly informed them that "some boys got a lady up on the track." He had not been able to get a good look at the woman, and he asked the others to come with him to find out who she was. Hairston hesitated, questioning the wisdom of the idea, but after a little coaxing all three men left to satisfy their curiosity.[5]

Shortly before Grayson arrived, his wife Josephine had left to catch the late bus into town to see her doctor. She was accompanied by Leola Millner, the sister of Booker T. Millner, and John Travis Redd, who was going into town to see a movie. As they walked along the Danville and Western track, Ruby Floyd suddenly emerged from the darkness and wrapped her arms around Mrs. Grayson, sobbing, "Help me, make these boys let me alone." Startled by Mrs. Floyd's entreaties, Josephine Grayson pulled away from her, exclaiming, "Don't tear my clothes off me." Joe Henry Hampton appeared from behind an embankment and grabbed Mrs. Floyd around the waist and dragged her away. She continued to cling to Mrs. Grayson, pulling a button off her coat. As Redd hurried his companions along, they passed Frank Hairston, Booker T. Millner, and Howard Hairston standing beside the railroad tracks as Hampton and Mrs. Floyd disappeared into some nearby woods.[6]

At about half past seven that evening, Mary Wade laid a plate of hot food in front of her husband, Jesse Wade, when a sudden knock at the door startled them. Mary hesitated for a moment, then inquired from behind a locked door who was calling. A sobbing voice replied, "A white lady, open the door quickly." Mary hastily unfastened the latch and opened the door to find Ruby Floyd clad only in her shirt, sweater, and a torn slip. She had scratches on her arms, her hair was tangled, and "her thighs were red-rubbed like." Disturbed by the commotion, Jesse came to the door and noticed that she had bruises on her arms and legs, mud and dirt on her clothes, and pine needles and sticks in her hair. Mary also thought she detected the smell of urine on Ruby's damp clothing. In addition to her dishevelment, Mrs. Floyd also "seemed to be scared to death." Claiming that she had been raped by at least thirteen men, she asked the Wades to call an ambulance immediately. Like most other black residents in the neighborhood, the Wades did not own a telephone, but Jesse Wade armed himself with a pistol and volunteered to escort her to Prillaman's Paint Shop, a nearby store owned by Mayor Nick Prillaman. With Mary and Jesse supporting Ruby Floyd on either side, the trio walked a short distance to the paint store and telephoned the police.[7]

Just before 8:15 P.M., Martinsville police officers T. G. Finney and R. L. Stover, assigned to patrol car no. 3, responded to the call. Neither man had much training in crime scene investigation, and they quickly determined that a more experienced investigator was needed. When they radioed Martinsville police headquarters to confirm that an assault had occurred near Prillaman's Paint Shop, Sergeant Murray V. Barrow, a detective with the Martinsville police force, heard the dispatcher take the call and immediately left the station. When he arrived at the paint store, he found Mrs. Floyd waiting in a squad car with the two uniformed officers. He could see that she was nervous and that her mouth was swollen and her arms and legs were covered with scratches. She also had splinters in her arm, which Barrow guessed had been picked up when she was dragged over railroad ties. Although it was dark, Barrow convinced her to take him to the scene of the attack. She led him along the Danville and Western tracks for about half a mile and indicated that she had been raped just off the track along the eastern right-of-way. Barrow located a patch of ground where the weeds and grass had been "mashed down," and he also found Mrs. Floyd's change purse and watch. She told Barrow that she had been dragged into some nearby woods and raped again, but the darkness made it impossible to detect any evidence under the trees.[8]

When they returned to the paint store, Mrs. Floyd spotted Booker T. Millner and Frank Hairston, Jr., wandering by the building. She told Barrow, "That looks like two of them now." The detective ordered Finney and Stover to arrest them. By this time additional officers had arrived, and Barrow ordered Averette T. Finney, Emory Bolejack, and an Officer Urrie to transport the suspects to the police station while he drove Mrs. Floyd to the hospital.[9]

Neither Hairston nor Millner, both Martinsville natives, had been in serious trouble with the police before. Eighteen years old at the time of his arrest, Hairston had left school in the seventh grade to work at odd jobs at the local Woolworth's department store and the lumber company where his father labored. He also found seasonal work in Martinsville's tobacco warehouses, where he earned about thirty dollars a week. He had no criminal record. Millner, two weeks shy of his twentieth birthday, had been arrested once, in 1947, for being drunk and disorderly and throwing a rock at a car. He was fined sixty dollars and ordered to pay for the damage to the car. He had dropped out of school in the eleventh grade to help support his family. At the time of the arrest he worked at a local cemetery, placing tombstones on graves.[10]

As the patrol car pulled out of the paint shop's driveway onto the Old Danville Road, the officers saw two more black men walking along the road. While Bolejack and Urrie got out to question the men, Finney remained in the backseat with the suspects. Noticing that Hairston had mud and dirt on the knees and cuffs of his trousers, Finney asked him how the stains had gotten there. According to Finney, Hairston replied: "I got that on there getting me a little piece. What's wrong with that? Can't you get a little piece and walk down the road without being picked up?" Although Hairston smelled of liquor, Finney did not think his statements were drunken ramblings because he "could speak clear and walk along all right."[11]

At 9:30 P.M. Sergeant Barrow delivered Mrs. Floyd to the emergency room of the Martinsville General Hospital. Dr. Joseph A. Ravenel, Dr. Paul B. Toms, and a nurse attended her. After checking her clothes for bloodstains, which they did not find, the physicians began a thorough physical examination. In addition to some swelling of her lower lip, they noted multiple scratches and abrasions on her elbows, shoulders, knees, and buttocks, her neck, and her right rib cage. They also found a long scratch running from the outside of her left thigh to her knee, which Ravenel believed had been made by a fingernail. A pelvic examination revealed a large amount of dirt and twigs in her pubic hair. The doctors could not detect any vaginal trauma, but three of the four vaginal smears they examined contained "active, motile sperm," which indicated that "intercourse had taken place within a reasonably short period of time." Mrs. Floyd was extremely upset throughout the examination, frequently screaming out the details of her attack in an incoherent fashion. Ravenel recommended that she stay in the hospital overnight for observation, but she insisted on leaving. At 11:30 the doctor gave her a sedative and allowed her husband to take her home. He also prescribed penicillin and sulfonamides to guard against venereal disease.[12]

After Sergeant Barrow left Mrs. Floyd at the hospital, he went to the police station where Millner and Hairston were being held. Officer Finney told Barrow about the remarks Hairston had made, and Barrow went to the interrogation room to question the men. He saw the mud caked on Hairston's pants and noticed that Millner had only a little mud around the cuffs of his pants. Barrow ordered Millner to strip off his clothes, including his underwear, and he examined Millner's shorts for semen stains. Barrow found no evidence of sexual intercourse, but he told Millner, "I expect I better hold you anyhow." He put Hairston back into the detention cell at the police department and drove Millner to the Henry County jail to await further interrogation.[13]

Because Mrs. Floyd had said that a dozen men had assaulted her, and only two suspects had been apprehended, Sergeant Barrow requested additional manpower from the Department of State Police. In 1924, like many other states in the early twentieth century, Virginia had created a department of motor vehicles to regulate activity on the state's newly built highways. Improvements in transportation wrought by the automobile increased urban criminals' access to rural areas, so in 1932 the General Assembly gave employees of the commissioner of motor vehicles the status of police officers and authorized them to enforce the criminal laws of the state. In addition, the rapid industrialization of areas such as Martinsville gave many rural localities urban traits, including greater criminal activity. Because most local police agencies and sheriff's departments were unequipped to investigate serious crime, the legislature in 1942 created the Department of State Police to assume the duties of law enforcement and public safety previously delegated to the commissioner of motor vehicles.[14]

Around nine o'clock Sergeant James H. Barnes of the Virginia State Police received a call that a rape had occurred near Prillaman's Paint Shop. Officially stationed in Martinsville, Barnes was responsible for policing a four-county area in southwestern Virginia, and he was patrolling Floyd County when he received the call. By the time he completed the mountainous fifty-mile drive to Martinsville, it was after ten o'clock. Learning that two men had already been taken into custody, he drove immediately to the Martinsville police station. After briefly conferring with Barrow about the progress of the investigation, Barnes walked to Hairston's holding cell. Closing the heavy door behind him, he informed Hairston that he did not have to make any statements but that Barnes would like to know the truth about the incident. Hairston, however, claimed that he "didn't know a thing in the world about it." Barnes left the cell and discovered that investigators had located a witness to the crime, Charlie Martin. After questioning Charlie, Barnes led the boy to the detention cell and asked whether he knew the man lying on the bunk. Charlie identified Hairston by name and told Barnes: "He is the one I told you about just now. He was down to the railroad track."[15]

After sending Charlie home, Barnes drove to the county jail to interview Millner. During Millner's brief stay at the police detention cell, however, Hairston had warned him not to speak to the police, and Millner refused to reveal any information. At about 1:00 A.M., January 9, Barnes returned to the police station and roused Hairston from his bunk. This time he took him out of the cell and brought him back to the department's interrogation room where Sergeant Barrow and another officer, D. L. Nance, were already waiting. While Hairston slouched over a bare table cradling his head in his hands, Barnes asked him again to "tell the truth." Hairston later remembered Barnes telling him that although he could not make any promises, "he'd do everything he could to help" him. Hairston remained silent for several minutes, then asked if he could speak to Barnes alone. At 1:45 Barnes emerged from the room with a signed confession.[16]

In his statement Hairston told Barnes that he, Millner, Howard Hairston, and Joe Henry Hampton had been drinking wine beside the railroad tracks when Ruby Floyd stopped to ask directions to Ruth Pettie's house. Hampton had been "the one that decided to catch the woman when she came back," and he was the first to grab her as she returned from her errand. By the time the others caught up to him, "he was doing the act." When Hampton finished, they dragged her to an embankment where Frank Hairston and Millner had sexual intercourse with her. Frank did not see Howard Hairston with the woman, but he assumed that he had assaulted her as well. As he was leaving, James Hairston, John Clabon Taylor, and "a boy they call DeSales" arrived at the scene, but he did not know whether they had anything to do with the attack or not.[17]

Now that Hairston had implicated Millner in the attack, Barnes returned to the jail to see whether Millner would change his story. Barnes informed him that he was charged with criminal assault against a white woman and that any statements he made "would be used either for or against him as the case might be." Upon learning that Hairston had confessed, Millner replied, "If Frank told the truth about it I reckon I just as well tell the truth." He placed the same seven men at the scene that Hairston named in his confession, but unlike Hairston, Millner had only seen Hampton and Hairston with the woman. Barnes repeatedly accused Millner of having intercourse with Mrs. Floyd, but he claimed, "I tried to go to her but I could not." He also told Barnes that he had given Charlie Martin a quarter in exchange for a promise not to tell anyone he had seen him.[18]

While these interrogations continued, Martinsville police officers, Henry County sheriff's deputies, and state troopers scoured the vicinity of the attack, searching for suspects. Throughout the night police picked up black men for questioning, but except for Millner and Hairston all were released after brief questioning by either Barnes or Barrow. After Barnes obtained statements from Millner and Hairston, however, the focus of the investigation narrowed to the seven men named in the confessions. Between 3:30 and 4:00 A.M. Officer A. T. Finney found four of the men sleeping at their homes and brought them back to the police station for questioning.[19]

At about four o'clock in the morning John Clabon Taylor met Sergeant Barnes in the interrogation room. A twenty- one-year-old with a fourth-grade education, Taylor had spent his boyhood in Martinsville, but he later worked for some time as a bellboy in a Virginia Beach hotel. He had been arrested twice by the Martinsville police. In 1944 he had been fined twenty-six dollars for a misdemeanor, and a year later he had faced charges for stealing a truck, which were dismissed by the court. In 1945 Taylor had also been fined five dollars after being arrested in Norfolk for fornication. After he returned to Martinsville, he found jobs as a hospital orderly and a tobacco worker.[20]

Taylor had already been questioned by police during an earlier roundup of suspects, but he had been released after cursory questioning. This time Barnes informed Taylor that he had been charged with criminal assault and that he did not have to answer any questions. Taylor exercised this right, declaring that he "didn't know a thing in the world" about the attack on Mrs. Floyd. He offered that he would be "glad to help" if he could, but he "just didn't know what [Barnes] was talking about."[21]

Rather than pursuing a lengthy interrogation, Barnes decided to see whether any of the other suspects might be willing to make a statement that would implicate Taylor. James Luther Hairston, a twenty-year-old tobacco and furniture worker, was waiting in another room. Although he had also been questioned earlier and released, Hairston proved more susceptible to Barnes's interrogation than Taylor had. As with the others, Barnes informed Hairston that he was charged with criminal assault and that he did not have to answer any questions. Barnes also informed Hairston that other suspects had already been arrested and given statements detailing their roles in the attack. Hairston immediately agreed to talk. At 4:30 Hairston signed a brief statement implicating the same seven men mentioned in the first two confessions. The confession did not provide many details, but Hairston did admit that all seven of the men had "gone to" the woman as she lay on the ground.[22]

Hairston's eighteen-year-old half brother, Howard Lee Hairston, followed him into the interrogation room. Both men had lived with their aunt, Irene Hodge, for several years after their mother died. Like his brother, Howard had never been arrested, and he quickly made a statement after being informed that others had confessed. Unlike the others, he was less specific as to who actually had assaulted the victim. He could not recall who was on top of the woman when he arrived, but "all of them was pulling on each other trying to get to her next." He placed the same seven men at the scene, and he guessed that "all of them went to the lady and tried to [have intercourse]." More than any of the others, however, Howard Hairston directly implicated himself in the attack. As he explained, "When I got a chance I tried to go to her but I could not get it in. I tried several times to get it in but I could not." Although Hairston apparently believed impotence was a defense for rape, such an admission was actually much more damaging than the others' general statements that they had "gone to" Mrs. Floyd.[23]

At ten minutes before six that morning, Barnes interrogated Francis DeSales Grayson. Grayson's background differed markedly from those of the other suspects. At thirty-seven years of age, he was sixteen years older than the next eldest suspect, John Clabon Taylor. A United States Army veteran who had served during World War II, Grayson was married and the father of five children. While the other suspects had all grown up in Martinsville, Grayson was a native of Maryland who had also lived in North Carolina and New Jersey before moving in 1948 to Martinsville. At the time of his arrest he worked for the American Furniture Company, one of the area's largest employers, and he had never been convicted of any crime.[24]

Initially, Grayson denied any knowledge of the crime and refused to answer any of Barnes's questions. When Barnes informed him that "some of the other boys have told us their part in this case," however,

Grayson reconsidered his silence. After mulling his situation for a couple of minutes, he told Barnes, "I'll tell you the truth about it." According to his statement, he had been walking along the Danville and Western tracks when he heard a woman begging a man to let her go. He continued home but later returned with James Hairston and John Taylor to the scene, where they joined four men in assaulting the woman. Grayson was not sure who had initiated the attack or in what order they had assaulted her, but "it looked like all of them went to her before I left." Like Howard Hairston, Grayson also used an admission of impotence to defend himself. After the last attacker finished, he explained, "I tried to go to her but I could not get up a hard. I tried for two or three minutes but was unable to do the job."[25]

By the time Grayson finished making his statement, dawn had broken. Soon the Sunday morning paper would bring news of the attack to the townspeople, and churchgoers would be trading gossip following the early services. Fearing that a mob might soon form on the courthouse lawn, Barnes ordered the men to gather their belongings because "we don't know what the feeling is going to be here and we are going to do everything we can to protect you." Barnes and some other officers then transported the suspects to the Patrick County jail in Stuart, about twenty-five miles west of Martinsville. Meanwhile, the remaining officers continued to search for the seventh suspect, Joe Henry Hampton.[26]

The suspects arrived in Stuart around 7:30 A.M. Before taking them to their cells, Barnes assembled all six men in the Patrick County sheriff's office. Since John Taylor had refused to cooperate, Barnes asked the other five men to describe, in Taylor's presence, "exactly what part [Taylor] had in this case." Before anyone spoke, Taylor interrupted: "Wait a minute. I don't want anyone to tell on me. I was right with them, in it just like they were. I don't want them to tell on me at all. I'll tell the truth."[27] Taylor admitted that he and the six other suspects had assaulted the woman. Apparently aware of Mrs. Floyd's religious activity, Taylor warned "the other boys that that was a Christian woman and it would cause us some trouble. . . . That if she was a drunk we might get by with it but I could tell from the way that she talked that she was a good woman." The other men, however, had reminded him that if they were caught, he would be implicated as well. Faced with this dilemma, Taylor decided to join the others, admitting to Barnes, "I was the last one to get it from her."[28]

Meanwhile, Sergeant Barrow returned to the crime scene to see whether the daylight would yield any more clues. The previous evening Mrs. Floyd had indicated that part of the assault had taken place in a wooded area about fifty yards from the railroad tracks, but the area had been too dark to search. This time, Barrow found a low gully in the woods where it looked like a struggle had occurred. Lying nearby he found a man's gray felt hat. A uniformed officer who accompanied Barrow also discovered an earring.[29]

About eight o'clock that morning, Dr. Ravenel received a call from Glenn Floyd. Floyd told Ravenel that his wife was "pretty much torn up," that she was very upset and had not slept all night. Ravenel admitted Mrs. Floyd to the hospital immediately, where he diagnosed her as suffering from "nervousness and generalized muscular aching along the inner aspect of both thighs." He placed her in a private room, prescribed barbiturates and heat treatment, and restricted visitation to her immediate family.[30]

For the next twenty-four hours law enforcement officers continued the search for the remaining suspect, nineteen-year-old Joe Henry Hampton. More than any of the other suspects, Hampton had good reason to be wary of the police. Hampton's mother had died when he was eight years old, and in 1943 he had moved with his father to the outskirts of Henry County, where he quickly earned a reputation as a truant and a troublemaker. When he was seventeen he was convicted of grand larceny in the Martinsville Circuit Court after he had stolen some money, clothing, and a watch from his father. His probation officer, P. C. Shields, reported "considerable difficulty" in supervising his probation, which was revoked after he repeatedly missed conferences and threatened to move to Ohio. Shields also noted that Hampton had considerable difficulty holding a job and had earned only $121 in the seven months of his supervision.[31]

Early Monday morning, January 10, Hampton approached Mary Wade's house after sleeping in the woods all weekend. Mrs. Wade told him that the police were looking for him and asked him what he had done. Hampton admitted that he and some others had raped a woman because they had "been drinking some old wine and stuff and it just had them all upset." Mrs. Wade advised him to surrender to the authorities "because you couldn't get away," and Hampton agreed to wait on the porch while her husband telephoned the police on his way to work. Around nine o'clock Sergeant Barrow and two other officers drove to the Wades' house and arrested Hampton. Martinsville police chief Harold W. Stultz called Sergeant Barnes and asked him to come to the police station to conduct the interrogation.[32]

According to Hampton's statement he, Millner, Howard Hairston, and Frank Hairston were drinking wine on the railroad tracks on the night of January 8. After giving a "white lady and a little colored boy" directions to Ruth Pettie's house, they "all planned to get her when she came back." Subsequently, Hampton grabbed her while the others "pushed the lady down." As the men fought among themselves "to see who would be the first to get it from her," the woman "was pushing back and trying to keep us from carrying her down the ridge." After they dragged her forty or fifty yards into the woods, the four men raped her, followed by Grayson, Taylor, and James Hairston, who had arrived on the scene. The woman continued to "put up a big scuffle . . . trying to get loose from the boys [and] begging us not to do anything to her." Not only did Hampton's detailed statement corroborate many aspects of Ruby Floyd's story, it also refuted the claims of some of the other suspects that Mrs. Floyd had consented to intercourse.[33]

By this time news of the crime had spread throughout the city. Offenses as serious as gang rape rarely occurred in Martinsville, prompting some concern and uncertainty about the possible public reaction. Circuit court judge Kennon C. Whittle, concurring with Sergeant Barnes's assessment of the prisoners' safety, ordered that they remain jailed outside Henry County "in order that there would be no unfortunate happening in the city." Whittle did not fear any mob violence, he claimed, but he insisted that the state had a responsibility "to protect these men from any trouble that might happen." As he later recalled, "God knows we didn't want anything to happen in the way of a lynching." Consequently, Grayson and Taylor remained in the jail at Stuart; Hampton was taken to Chatham, about thirty miles northwest of Martinsville in Pittsylvania County; and Millner and the Hairstons were confined in the Roanoke city jail, forty-five miles north of Martinsville.[34]

The nature of the crime undoubtedly stirred deep emotions among local citizens. The Henry County jailer later revealed that he was so affected by the viciousness of the attack that had a mob demanded the key to the jail, he would have relinquished it. Nevertheless, a lynch mob never materialized. For one thing, the swift decisions of Barnes and Whittle to separate the prisoners at distant locations increased the difficulty of organizing violence against the men. More important, the speed and efficiency with which law enforcement officials captured the seven men assured the townspeople that the legal system could adequately handle the crisis. Chief Stultz proudly reported that "every man on the department worked long and hard to see that the defendants were brought to justice; and I think it is a credit to them that not one of the seven men remained out of custody for more than a day and a half."[35]

More than a month passed before the seven defendants entered the Martinsville Trial Justice Court for their preliminary hearing. Several factors contributed to the delay. On January 22, as required by Virginia law, Judge Whittle appointed seven attorneys to represent the defendants at trial and all preliminary proceedings. Six days later Joseph C. Whitehead informed the Martinsville prosecutor's office that his client, Joe Henry Hampton, would waive his preliminary hearing. Not until February 1, when the seven attorneys convened to formulate a defense strategy, did the lawyers request a preliminary hearing.[36]

At the same time rumors began to circulate that Mrs. Floyd would drop the charges because of her religious objections to testifying. Commonwealth's Attorney Irvin W. Cubine vehemently denied these reports, informing reporters that "both she and her husband have assured me they have no religious scruples that would keep them from prosecuting the defendants to the fullest under the laws of the Commonwealth."[37]

In fact, medical problems associated with the attack kept Mrs. Floyd out of the courtroom until mid-February. On January 15, after spending a week in the hospital, Mrs. Floyd had gone to North Carolina to recuperate at her mother's house. Ten days later she returned to Martinsville General Hospital complaining of nausea, vomiting, chills, and abdominal pain. She was also running a temperature of 103 degrees. Dr. Ravenel detected some swelling on the left side of her abdomen, but the spot was so tender he was unable to perform an adequate vaginal examination. Mrs. Floyd left the hospital on January 31 after her fever subsided, but four days later her condition worsened and she was admitted to the Duke University Hospital in Durham, North Carolina. In addition to treating her for fever and nervousness, Dr. Baynard Carter ran routine tests for trauma, venereal disease, and pregnancy. The tests were negative for pregnancy and sexually transmitted diseases but he located an "inflammatory mass" on the left side of her pelvis near the uterus caused by the rupture of thin-walled blood vessels. The ureter running from the left kidney to the bladder was also "displaced and dilated." Although the fever fell rapidly after the fourth day of observation, Mrs. Floyd remained in the hospital until February 14, when the danger of rupture and peritonitis had passed.[38]

On February 17, amid an atmosphere of secrecy and tight security, the preliminary hearing began in the Martinsville Trial Justice Court before Judge M. H. MacBryde. The defendants had been secretly transported into the city early that morning, and no public notice of the hearing had been issued. Furthermore, the usual 9:00 A.M. starting time of the court had been postponed for five hours, and the court had been moved from its usual location in city hall to the Henry County Courthouse across the street. Seventeen state, city, and county law enforcement officers guarded the doors of the courtroom.[39]

The Virginia legislature had created the trial justice courts in 1921. The courts not only served as police courts for the trial of misdemeanors and violations of local ordinances, they also performed certain magisterial functions for the circuit court, including the determination of probable cause to hold criminal defendants for trial. Unlike most justices of the peace or rural magistrates in other states, MacBryde and his colleagues possessed at least five years' experience practicing law in Virginia, and they held no other public office during their four-year terms. Like the state police, the trial justice courts brought efficiency and professionalism to the administration of justice in industrializing areas of the state.[40]

The state relied chiefly on the testimony of Sergeant Barnes, Officer Barrow, and Mary Wade to establish probable cause. Mrs. Wade described Mrs. Floyd's disheveled appearance on the night of the attack and stated that she had smelled of beer or urine. She also testified that Joe Henry Hampton had come to her house two days after the crime, admitted to twice raping a woman, and implicated the other defendants as well.[41] Barrow described his part in the investigation and told the court that he had found Mrs. Floyd's change purse and watch near the scene of the attack. Barnes read each of the seven confessions into the record. On cross-examination Stephen Martin, attorney for Howard Hairston, challenged the validity of the confessions, asserting that Barnes had promised the defendants leniency if they confessed. Barnes denied the allegation, however, because he "knew the statement wouldn't be no good under those circumstances."[42]

Legally, the purpose of a preliminary hearing is to allow a magistrate to determine whether there is sufficient evidence against the accused to justify holding the suspects for trial. In practice, the hearing also provides the defense with an opportunity to assess the strength of the prosecution's evidence and the reliability of the state's witnesses. Because the prosecution bears the burden of demonstrating probable cause, the defense may choose to allow the state's case to stand on its merits, or it may actively challenge the evidence.[43] In the Martinsville case the defense attorneys elected to challenge the medical evidence of rape and the reliability of the complaining witness.

In questioning the two physicians who attended Mrs. Floyd after the attack, the defense sought to minimize the severity of her injuries and to demonstrate the inconsistencies in her story. Dr. Paul Toms told Clarence Kearfott, attorney for James Hairston, that the patient's "general condition was fairly good," that she "was not shocked," and that she had "minor abrasions" on her limbs. Kearfott asked Toms whether the "small quantity" of sperm or the "very slight bruise" inside her vagina indicated how many times she had intercourse that evening. Toms replied that such conditions could not provide any reliable indication, but he noted that Mrs. Floyd's memory of the number of men who had intercourse with her "varied . . . from time to time. . . . At one time she said about 12 and another time she said about 10." Dr. Ravenel was more reluctant to characterize the injuries as minor, but he did state that none of the injuries was bleeding "at the time I saw her." He also testified that she had claimed that "anywhere from six to a dozen" men had attacked her in the woods.[44]

The defense called Ruby Floyd as its final witness. This strategy posed some risk, because any statements that Mrs. Floyd made became part of the official record against the defendants. Nevertheless, the defense attorneys apparently believed that if they could expose enough inconsistencies in her story, they might save some of the defendants from criminal prosecution. Even if Judge MacBryde declined to dismiss the cases for insufficient evidence, a poor performance by the victim on the witness stand might persuade the prosecution not to seek the death penalty.

W. L. Joyce, attorney for DeSales Grayson, conducted the examination for the defense. Joyce first questioned Mrs. Floyd's judgment in entering the black neighborhoods of Martinsville on a Saturday night, especially after residents of the neighborhood had advised her not to. Judge MacBryde, however, refused to permit this line of questioning. Second, Joyce elicited an admission from the victim that she had not called for help when she was first accosted on the railroad tracks because "I figured I could get away from them" and "it was too far from anyone's house." But why, Joyce queried, did she not scream for help once they had captured her? At this point Mrs. Floyd, who had remained calm throughout the questioning, began to sob. "I didn't try to holler," she cried, "because they told me they'd kill me if I did."[45]

Joyce also exposed Mrs. Floyd's inability to identify all of her attackers because part of the attack took place after nightfall. Nor could she state definitely how many men attacked her or how many times she had been raped. "I couldn't count the times," she testified. When asked if she recognized anyone in the courtroom, she indicated Joe Henry Hampton as the first attacker and she positively identified DeSales Grayson as the last man to assault her. Asked to name her second attacker, she wavered between James Hairston and Booker Millner, stating only for sure that "it was one of those." Joyce prodded her to select one definitely, and when she failed he asked her, "You don't know which one, do you?" "No, sir," Mrs. Floyd admitted.[46]

Despite the defense team's attempts to call her credibility into question, Mrs. Floyd steadfastly resisted any implications that she had been a willing participant in the incident. She had not screamed, she repeatedly asserted, because the attackers had threatened to kill her. She physically resisted their advances and "begg[ed] all the time to please turn me loose and let me go home." When she managed to briefly escape, she called to passersby for help, but they ignored her entreaties. She did not run from her attackers once they finished, she explained, because "I was completely exhausted. I was almost paralyzed. I just could not run."[47]

Finally, Joyce questioned her "calm and composed" demeanor after she checked into the hospital. Mrs. Floyd denied such a state of mind; she had been "in a nervous condition" and "was all to pieces." But had she not invited company to her hospital room after the attack, he countered, despite her doctors' suggestions that she see no visitors? Not "too much company," she replied, only "friends and relatives— mother and father and people." When Joyce continued to press the issue, W. R. Broaddus, one of the prosecutors, objected that Joyce was attempting to impeach his own witness. Judge MacBryde, who was quickly losing patience with Joyce's tactics, agreed because Joyce had not announced Mrs. Floyd as an adverse witness, a tactic which would have given him latitude to challenge her testimony.[48] In any case, Mac-Bryde continued, he could not understand how her actions at the hospital, hours after the attack, had any bearing on the case. Joyce tried to explain that her state of mind was relevant to her credibility, but MacBryde cut him short. "I'm going to send this on to the grand jury on [the basis of] the confessions," he announced. "You're just wasting time."[49]

MacBryde ordered the men held without bail and directed Chief Stultz to return them to out-of-town jails until the grand jury of the Martinsville Circuit Court had acted. On April 11, almost two months later, the grand jury, composed of four white men and three African-American men, indicted each defendant on one count of rape and six counts of aiding and abetting a rape by the other defendants.[50]

To most of Martinsville's white community, the arrest, pretrial processing, and indictments of the seven suspects represented the best attributes of the administration of justice in the modern South. In stark contrast to stereotypical notions of southern justice, the community did not rely on crude methods of racial control, such as mob violence or kangaroo courts. The legal system continued to enforce codes of racial behavior but through modern police methods and legal processes that emphasized the preservation of community stability and social order.[51]

In Martinsville the local law enforcement establishment preserved community stability by rapidly apprehending the suspects. At the same time Chief Stultz, Judge Whittle, and Judge MacBryde ensured that the suspects were not subjected to mob violence by ordering them removed from local jails and by conducting judicial proceedings with a minimum of publicity. In addition, local officials were not pressured to hurry the legal process to satisfy demands for immediate retribution. More than a month passed between the arrests and the preliminary hearing; nearly another two months passed before the grand jury indicted the suspects.

Most significantly, local authorities did not act as extensions of the mob. Instead they displayed a professionalism which was increasingly characteristic of police departments after World War II. Although one critical observer, reporter Mel Fiske of the Communist-supported *Daily Worker*, cynically commented that police "arrested practically every male over 14 who had mud on his shoes," only the seven men implicated by the victim or the suspects' confessions were actually arrested.[52] Other African Americans were detained only long enough for brief questioning. Officer Barrow launched an immediate search of the crime scene, and he quickly transported the victim to Martinsville General Hospital where physicians obtained physical evidence of rape.

In addition, Chief Stultz relied on the state police to conduct the investigation. While officers on the Martinsville police force received rudimentary professional training, their primary mission emphasized the preventive functions of community patrol and order maintenance. By contrast, Sergeant Barnes had received training in modern methods of scientific crime detection.[53] Consequently, Stultz gave Barnes broad authority to conduct the investigation, and Barnes assumed the most important task: interrogating the prisoners. Not only was Barnes schooled in the law regarding the admissibility of confessions, he was certainly familiar with the most efficient techniques of interrogation. He obtained the first six confessions within the space of six hours and secured Joe Henry Hampton's confession less than two hours after he was arrested.

To the white citizens of Martinsville, the local law enforcement system had restored stability to the community without violence. To African-American observers, however, the proceedings stirred troublesome reactions. Shortly after the preliminary hearing, a reporter from the Richmond *Afro-American*, one of the state's leading African-American newspapers, identified the Martinsville case as one that bore "all the earmarks of the late Scottsboro, Ala. mass trial."[54] Admittedly police officers and judges had supervised the capture of the defendants with apparent regard for their due process rights and with a minimum of racial rhetoric. But while Martinsville's law enforcement community had demonstrated that black suspects could be arrested and arraigned in an equitable fashion, the question remained whether they could be tried and punished in a southern courtroom without reinforcing traditional codes of racial behavior.

2

"A Matter for the
Jury to Decide"

Like many southern localities after World War II, the city of Martinsville was attempting to accommodate rapidly changing economic, demographic, and political circumstances within the context of social customs and cultural beliefs that had taken over a century to develop. Originally dependent on tobacco culture and slave labor, Martinsville turned from agriculture to industry at the turn of the twentieth century and grew into one of the state's leading industrial centers. Traditional patterns of racial deference and paternalism persisted, but community race relations were deemed harmonious both by white citizens and by a prominent black professional class. Yet developments in the 1940s exposed the fragility of this racial harmony. Some African Americans began to challenge the social and political practices that characterized the traditional racial order. An increase in the black population after World War II revealed to many whites the limits of social control through numerical superiority. The trial of the Martinsville Seven, therefore, took place at a time when citizens of both races were reexamining traditional perceptions of racial stability.

Martinsville was founded in 1791 when the Virginia General Assembly authorized the establishment of a town on fifty acres of land in the center of Henry County. The new town, named after the Virginia pioneer and Indian fighter Joseph Martin, was situated 30 miles west of Danville, 60 miles south of Roanoke, 165 miles from Richmond, and 10 miles from the North Carolina border. In 1928 the General Assembly designated Martinsville as a city of the second class after it reached a population of 5,000 people. In 1941, after the census revealed that over 10,000 citizens resided in Martinsville, it was named a city of the first class, which allowed it to establish a circuit court independent from the Henry County circuit court. In 1947 the city added 3,500 people to its population when it annexed six square miles of urbanized area surrounding the central business district.[1]

Martinsville's growth was largely attributable to its successful shift from agriculture to industry. The cultivation and processing of tobacco had sustained the region throughout the nineteenth century, but in 1906 the "tobacco trust," led by the R. J. Reynolds Tobacco Company, purchased most of the county's tobacco factories and discontinued their operation. Over the next four decades, however, a number of prominent manufacturing companies located their factories in Martinsville and Henry County, including the Bassett Furniture Company, Marshall Field's Fieldcrest Mills, and a nylon plant operated by the Du Pont Company. By 1940 Martinsville housed sixteen furniture factories and nine textile factories and ranked sixth in the state in employment, wages, and product value. Only Virginia's largest urban centers ranked higher. Industrial growth even allowed the city to escape the worst ravages of the Great Depression as local factories managed to absorb some displaced rural workers. Martinsville's unemployment rate in 1940 was around 4 percent, almost ten points lower than the national average. By 1950 Henry County had more families with an annual income over $5,000 than any other surrounding county.[2]

African Americans in the Martinsville area did not share in the benefits of economic development. In 1890 almost half of the total population of the city and county had been black. Since then the total population had risen steadily, but the proportion of black residents had declined to 25 percent as African Americans migrated to factories and mills in the North and Midwest. Black workers who did not leave found their employment opportunities limited as new factory jobs went primarily to white workers while blacks labored disproportionately in agricultural and personal service occupations.[3]

Those who remained encountered an inhospitable cultural environment as well. The former tobacco-growing counties along the southern border of Virginia, collectively known as the Southside, had a reputation for racism, nativism, and parochialism. Although Martinsville's industrial character and low density of African Americans distinguished it from the most tradition-bound rural counties in the region, Martinsville citizens regularly voted in a pattern consistent with Southside stalwarts such as South Boston and Prince Edward County. A few of its residents also participated in the renaissance of the Ku Klux Klan during the 1920s. In 1925 a reputed Klansman from Henry County, John David Bassett, challenged the incumbent state treasurer on a "100 percent American" platform. The neighborhoods of Martinsville were stringently segregated, and even the black communities within the city limits lacked passable roads, modern utilities, police protection, playgrounds, sidewalks, and other amenities that the rest of the city received. Martinsville also exhibited the hallmark of racism in Virginia, an abysmal educational system for black children. With a dearth of employment opportunities and a hostile social environment, it was not surprising that many blacks chose to leave the area.[4]

The Henry County Courthouse, built in 1824, epitomized the history of Virginia's Southside. Its red brick exterior, stately columns, and freshly painted white portico idealized the plantation homes whose masters the court had served for most of its existence. Until the turn of the century, on the first Monday of each month, the square in front of the courthouse, which stood at the center of Martinsville, had hosted "court day," when farmers, plantation owners, tobacco traders, and salesmen from throughout the county met to do business, discuss politics, observe the proceedings of the court, and socialize with distant neighbors. A monument to Confederate veterans, placed in front of the courthouse in 1901, greeted lawyers, judges, and litigants as they entered the building. Inside the second-story courtroom, portraits of Patrick Henry and Robert E. Lee surveyed the proceedings from opposite ends of the room. No visitor to the building could ignore the southern traditions embodied in the Henry County Courthouse.[5]

To conduct a trial for interracial rape in those surroundings evoked images of southern courts that avenged the desecration of white southern womanly virtue without regard for due process or equal justice. The Martinsville courts had certainly not been immune from racial sentiment in the past. In 1900, for instance, Charles Hairston, an African American, was sentenced to death without benefit of counsel for the rape of a white girl after every member of the Henry County bar refused to represent him. The judges and lawyers who frequented the courthouse after World War II, however, respected tradition but were not bound by it. The rhetoric of crime control and community stability replaced prosecutorial race-baiting. The paternalistic assumptions of the criminal law were subsumed within a broader regard for preserving law and order. As the city's furniture and textile industries grew to national stature, the courts became more respectful of emerging national standards of what constituted a fair trial. The criminal justice system that emerged in Martinsville after the war reinforced the racial values embedded in the southern legal system, but it restrained the more outrageous forms of racial control.[6]

Since 1944 Judge Kennon Caithness Whittle had presided over this fusion of the old and the new. The fifty-seven-year-old jurist was himself steeped in the Virginia legal tradition. His father, Stafford Gorman Whittle, had served on the Virginia Supreme Court of Appeals from 1901 to 1919. After graduating with a bachelor of laws degree from Washington and Lee University in 1914, Kennon Whittle established a practice in Martinsville with his brother, Stafford Whittle, Jr., specializing in civil and criminal defense. They also represented many of Martinsville's most prominent business interests. From 1922 to 1926 Kennon Whittle gained his first judicial experience as a bankruptcy referee for the Danville division of the United States District Court for the Western District of Virginia. Whittle served on several American Bar Association committees, as a member of the Virginia constitutional convention that repealed the Eighteenth Amendment in 1933, and as president of the Virginia State Bar Association in 1940. A lifelong Democrat, he represented his state at the Democratic National Convention in 1932.

Because of his legal credentials and his fealty to the state Democratic party, the Virginia assembly elected Kennon Whittle to the Seventh Judicial Circuit Court, located in Martinsville, in 1944. The relaxed manner in which he issued rulings from his leather rocking chair behind the bench belied his swift disposition of the cases that came before him. During his tenure on the court, none of his rulings were overturned by appellate courts. In 1951 Governor John S. Battle would appoint Whittle to fill a vacancy on the Virginia Supreme Court of Appeals, and the General Assembly would place him on the court permanently in 1954.[7]

On April 19, 1949, the seven defendants indicted for the rape of Ruby Floyd entered Judge Whittle's courtroom with their attorneys. Before the preliminary hearing in February, Whittle had appointed seven lawyers of remarkably varying levels of experience. State Senator Frank P. Burton, the oldest of the group, represented John Taylor. In 1947 Burton had been elected to the state legislature, and in the following year he chaired the States Rights (Dixiecrat) party in Virginia. The party was comprised of southern Democrats who opposed the civil rights plank of the 1948 Democratic platform. William L. Joyce, De-Sales Grayson's attorney, was regarded by the chief of the probation and parole office in Danville as "one of the foremost defense attorneys in this entire area." Like Burton, Joyce resided in Stuart, where their clients were confined. Joe Henry Hampton, jailed in Chatham, was assigned Joseph C. Whitehead, Jr., a former commonwealth's attorney for Pittsylvania County. The four defendants being held in Roanoke were assigned to four young attorneys from Martinsville—William F. Carter for Frank Hairston, Claude E. Taylor, Jr., for Booker Millner, Clarence Kearfott for James Hairston, and Stephen D. Martin, a federal court magistrate, for Howard Hairston. At forty-one years of age, Carter was the eldest of the Martinsville contingent, while Taylor had been practicing law for less than a year. The lawyers received twenty-five dollars apiece for the three months they represented their clients.[8]

Irvin W. Cubine headed the prosecution team. The forty-eight-year-old prosecutor had practiced law in Martinsville since 1929, spent three years as the city attorney, and became commonwealth's attorney for the city of Martinsville in 1942. Judge Whittle also allowed Cubine to employ two assistants in this case. W. R. Broaddus, Jr., elected to the House of Delegates in 1946, had been Henry County's chief prosecutor for eighteen years. Hannibal N. Joyce, Whittle's former law partner, had served as Martinsville's city attorney from 1937 to 1947. Both Broaddus and Joyce represented some of the city's most prominent business interests.[9]

Before the proceedings began Judge Whittle called all the attorneys into his chambers. From the outset he emphasized that he would insist on strict adherence to propriety and decorum and would not permit the attorneys to stray from the fundamental legal and procedural issues of the case. He reminded counsel of their "duty as lawyers to see that these defendants receive a fair and impartial trial according to the law and evidence," and he asked the attorneys to "play fairly with the

Court." Addressing the defense counsel, he asked the more experienced members of the defense team to assist the younger attorneys in the trial of their clients.[10]

Whittle also addressed the racial issues that would inevitably arise from the case. He emphasized that the defendants should not be treated differently because of their race, but more significantly, he pleaded with the attorneys to downplay the racial overtones so that community stability would not be disturbed. The judge lamented that this "unfortunate" matter was "made even more regrettable due to the fact that these seven negroes are charged with the rape of a white woman." Asserting the positive state of race relations in Martinsville and Henry County, he reminded the attorneys that "we have in our community a negro population of splendid citizens" who "deplore this unfortunate happening as much, or more, than do the citizens of the white race." He continued, "I here and now admonish you that this case must and will be tried in such a way as not to disturb the kindly feeling now locally existing between the races. It must be tried as though both parties were members of the same race. I will not have it otherwise."[11]

Whittle's concern that the trial might breed racial antagonism arose not only from his knowledge of similar cases of interracial rape in other areas but also from specific changes in the conduct of race relations in Martinsville in the past two decades. Like most other white members of the community, Whittle assumed that harmony existed between the races because African Americans were content with having relative autonomy within a limited sphere of activity, including business, religion, and education. Many black professionals who had achieved social prominence or financial success concurred with this positive assessment of local race relations. "The races of our city have more in common than in difference," wrote the Reverend R. T. Anderson, one of Martinsville's most respected black citizens. "The ties that bring them together are stronger than the ties that keep them apart." General satisfaction with racial conditions extended to working-class blacks as well, according to some observers. Race relations in Martinsville were "surprisingly harmonious," reported Lem Graves, a Pittsburgh *Courier* correspondent assigned to cover the trials, despite obvious social and economic inequalities.[12]

Whittle knew, however, that during the late 1930s and 1940s many local African Americans had begun to challenge their subservient position. Throughout the Depression a number of fraternal organizations and social clubs, including a Colored Knights of Pythias lodge, an American Legion post named after a local black soldier killed in World War I, and a Society for the Improvement of the Negro Race, gave blacks the opportunity to organize collectively. In 1940 a group of black teachers protested the inequality of salaries for black and white educators, a situation which was remedied during the 1944–45 school year when the local school board placed all public school teachers in the county on the same pay scale. In 1941 the NAACP chartered a branch in Martinsville with fifty-four members. The local NAACP's biggest victory came in 1944 when it convinced the city registrar to allow all eligible blacks to register to vote. The NAACP also began recruiting attorneys to represent black defendants charged with crimes against whites.[13]

The defendants' attorneys also worried about the effect of the local climate on their clients' chances for a fair trial. Before the trials began Judge Whittle heard the defendants' motion for a change of venue. The crime of which the defendants were accused, the attorneys argued, aroused "great public indignation, feeling and anger" among the citizens of Martinsville. Furthermore, the accounts of the investigation published in the *Martinsville Bulletin,* the city's only newspaper, were so "highly inflammatory" that the "general sentiment of the citizens of the City of Martinsville" had been "so inflamed by the said newspaper accounts" that it would be impossible to "secure a jury or juries in said City free from bias or prejudice." Finally, the fact that the defendants had been "carried under heavy escort and police protection" to out-of-town jails further demonstrated that "it will be utterly impossible to have a fair and impartial trial in the City of Martinsville." Accompanying the petition were copies of eleven articles that had appeared in the *Bulletin* between January 9 and April 11 and eight notarized affidavits from citizens who believed that the seven could not get a fair trial.[14]

The defense called twenty-five witnesses, eight of whom were black, to the stand to support the petition. During questioning the attorneys sought to establish that the brutal nature of the crime and the articles in the *Bulletin* had aroused local sentiment against their clients, that the arrest of the defendants had created racial tensions in the community, and that the removal of the prisoners from the city proved they were in danger.

The first two witnesses represented the poles of argument over the possibility of a fair trial. Cary J. Randolph, commonwealth's attorney for Henry County, testified that he had "observed very little race prejudice at all in this case" and that "as many colored people as white people had expressed themselves as being opposed to this crime." Given the heinous nature of the crime, he had found it "very unusual" that the newspaper coverage was "fairly presented and lacking in any inflammatory matter at all." Randolph admitted, however, that he had heard "considerably more discussion" than usual to the effect that the defendants were guilty and ought to be put to death. In fact, he added, even he on occasion had made the statement, "Well, they ought to get the works." Nevertheless, he believed that an impartial jury could be impaneled in Martinsville. When Will Joyce reminded him that seven separate juries would be required if the trials were separated, Randolph maintained that impaneling the juries would be "more difficult than in an ordinary case, but I think it could be done."[15]

H. P. Williams, a black physician who had practiced medicine in Martinsville for twenty years, was much more skeptical of the defendants' chances for a fair trial in Martinsville. Like Randolph, he remarked that the local people had "acted fairer than [he] expected," and he credited the *Bulletin's* temperate handling of the case as "the reason the flames of animosity haven't been stirred." The serious nature of the offense, however, had created a backlash against the defendants among Martinsville blacks, who feared that "this crime has set up something which may disturb the racial relationship." A fair trial in the city, Williams concluded, would be "pretty hard to do" because "I doubt whether there is anybody in this immediate vicinity who hasn't said to themselves or to their friends . . . what they think ought to be done to people who had done such a crime as that."[16]

Several of the remaining witnesses, including Mayor Prillaman, testified that a change of venue would not be necessary for a fair trial, although one witness, H. Claybrook Lester, admitted that his idea of a fair trial was "that they should be convicted and electrocuted." Most of the witnesses had heard their fellow townspeople express shock at the brutality of the crime, and some had heard them recommend the maximum punishment if the defendants were guilty. The witnesses believed, however, in the words of Harry Fusfeld, "that if the jury was picked with caution they might get a fair trial." An important factor in forming this opinion was the time that had elapsed since the arrests and the absence of mob sentiment. As the Reverend Chevis F. Horne, a white minister, explained, "Aroused feelings never help clear and fair thinking." However, he noted, "the feeling has not been as intensive as I thought it would be." The community had "not come near expressing itself in mob violence." In the three months that had passed since the arrests, the people had become "very calm and very deliberate and rational in their thinking about" the crime.[17]

Another citizen to oppose moving the trials was Dr. Dana O. Baldwin, one of Martinsville's leading black businessmen. Baldwin had moved to the area in 1910 from Philadelphia, where he was working as a dance instructor, to begin practicing medicine as Henry County's first black physician. Baldwin's practice started slowly, but he soon became successful enough to invest in various businesses, including a large shopping center, a hotel, and a twelve-room hospital, the first in the city for blacks. Baldwin's success was routinely touted by Martinsville's white leaders as an example of the freedom of opportunity that existed for all races in the city.[18]

Baldwin testified that a change of venue would not be necessary because the crime had not created "any strained relationship between the races." Although his privileged status may have blinded him to the more serious inequities in the community, he recognized that the autonomy of Martinsville's African-American community, and especially its middle class, existed only within a range of behavior prescribed by white elites. In order to restore racial harmony, if not equality, Baldwin agreed that local community members were competent to police transgressions of the established social and legal code.[19]

Only four witnesses, two of them white, declared absolutely that a fair trial would be impossible in Martinsville. Charles M. Hart, a white man, stated that he had already made up his mind that the defendants were guilty, so that he would "be a little biased" if he served on the jury. He did not think that anyone else could be more impartial. George Galloway, a black janitor, spoke in favor of moving the trials because the defendants' families, who lived in his neighborhood, had complained that the men could not get a fair trial in town. George Boone, a white World War II veteran who had lived in Martinsville for about four years, believed that most of the townspeople had such strong opinions about the crime that if "any mitigating circumstances" surfaced during the trials, they "might not be given the proper weight." Agnes Redd, a black department store worker, went even further. She believed that because of the magnitude of the crime, the men could not get a fair trial anywhere.[20]

Some of the most compelling testimony came from Sergeant Barnes. Barnes stated that "right after [the rape] happened there was quite a lot" of discussion about the crime. Since then interest in the case had died down, but nearly everyone whom he had heard discussing the case had expressed the opinion that the defendants were guilty. However, he had "actually heard people say they didn't think they would get but very little" punishment, and several people had predicted that none of them would receive the death penalty. In any event, most of the discussions had been initiated by "irresponsible" people, so Barnes believed that "plenty of level headed businessmen" would be available to render impartial verdicts. Because Mrs. Floyd and her husband were not natives of Martinsville, he added, "the evidence we heard would have the same effect on people away from here as here." On the possibility of a fair trial, Barnes predicted tellingly, "I can't see where it would be any different here than anywhere else."[21]

On behalf of the commonwealth, Hannibal Joyce submitted 114 identical notarized affidavits from white Martinsville residents who stated that they had heard the case of "alleged rape" being discussed, that no "racial difficulties" had arisen after the incident, and that the defendants could receive "a fair and impartial trial in the city of Martinsville."[22] The state's only witness, *Martinsville Bulletin* editor Kay Thompson, defended his newspaper's coverage of the crime. From the beginning, he testified, his policy had been not to "print anything inflammatory or anything to create any feeling in the case." He noted that the *Bulletin* had not identified the victim or even mentioned her race in the initial reports. He had also used the term "criminal assault" rather than "rape" and had refrained from printing photographs of the suspects and the crime scene, even though they were available. In fact, he reminded the court, even "the Scottsboro case received a greater amount of publicity" in his newspaper than had this case. Because of his restrained approach to covering the crime, Thompson concluded, "no mass prejudice" had arisen against the defendants, making a fair trial possible without moving its location.[23]

At the close of evidence, the defense attorneys inexplicably elected not to summarize their arguments for the court, even though most of the defense witnesses had stated that the defendants could get a fair trial. W. R. Broaddus emphasized this point in his summation for the commonwealth and noted especially the testimony of Dr. Baldwin. Broaddus also argued that the defense had committed a technical error by not petitioning for a change of venire (the pool of persons from which the jury would be selected) before seeking a change of venue. Since the basis of the defendants' motion was that the court would encounter "difficulty in obtaining jurors" from within the jurisdiction, he asserted, the appropriate remedy would be to summon jurors from other cities or counties. William L. Joyce rebutted this argument, claiming that when "the application for a change of venue is based upon the grounds [that] there exists such prejudice and excitement against the accused as to endanger the fairness and impartiality of a trial conducted in the county," a preliminary motion for change of venire was unnecessary. In short, he was not arguing that "a fair and impartial jury cannot be secured" but that "a fair and impartial trial cannot be had" within the city of Martinsville.[24]

Judge Whittle denied the motion for a change of venue. He congratulated the press and the public for "the way they have conducted themselves in this matter." He recognized that the community had not been silent about the case because "it is perfectly natural that people will discuss happenings of this kind." However, "no mass feeling against these defendants" had developed. Securing jurors who had expressed no opinion on the case might prove difficult, "but we will have to cross that bridge when we get to it."[25]

Although most of the testimony had focused on the prejudice created by the brutality of the attack, Whittle did not ignore the possibility that jurors might be biased against the defendants because of their skin color rather than their crime. "Unfortunately," he lamented, "this race question enters into the matter." He assured the attorneys that he would "permit strenuous examination" of all prospective jurors and would "see that any juror that goes in the box will be free from prejudice" of any type.[26]

Two days later, on April 21, 1949, the court convened to begin the trial. At the beginning of the session, William Joyce requested, with the assent of the other defense attorneys, that each defendant be tried separately. Several motives lay behind this request. If the trials were severed, the juries could only hear evidence about the activities of the particular defendant in each case, not the group as a whole. This was especially important for James Hairston, John Taylor, and Joyce's client, DeSales Grayson, because they had allegedly arrived late on the scene.

Testimony about the initial attack on the victim, therefore, would be severely restricted in their cases. In addition, none of the confessions could be used to implicate any defendant except the one who had made the statement. Severance thus meant that the prosecution would have to prove the merits of each case, rather than relying on the residual guilt that the most culpable defendants would cast upon the others. By individualizing the cases rather than emphasizing the seven as a group, the attorneys hoped that some of the defendants might be acquitted or receive lighter sentences than the others. Judge Whittle granted the motion for severance without objection from the commonwealth.[27]

Because of the strength of the case against Joe Henry Hampton, the prosecutors elected to try him first. Hampton was uniformly considered to have been the ringleader of the attack, and some of the most damning evidence concerned Hampton's role in the crime.[28] He was also the only defendant to attempt to elude capture, hiding out in the woods near east Martinsville for two days before surrendering to the police. Finally, he had the most serious criminal record of the seven men, a fact the prosecution would attempt to convey to the jury. If Irvin Cubine could secure a quick conviction and a death sentence against Hampton, he reasoned, the remaining convictions would fall into place. After Hampton he would try the other three men accused of the initial attack—Frank Hairston, Booker Millner, and Howard Hairston—in that order, then DeSales Grayson, John Taylor, and James Hairston. The latter two defendants subsequently agreed to be tried jointly.

A new jury had to be selected for each trial. Every jury pool contained at least two African Americans, and four blacks were called in the trials of DeSales Grayson, John Taylor, and James Hairston. During voir dire Judge Whittle asked the prospective jurors whether any of them were related to the victim or the defendant, whether there was any reason why they could not form an impartial opinion as to the defendant's guilt, and whether they had any conscientious scruples against imposing the death penalty. Most of the black jurors were excused because they did not believe in the death penalty, and several white men were disqualified because they had already determined that the defendants were guilty. The prosecutors did not question anyone, but they exercised their peremptory challenges to exclude several prospective jurors, including the remaining black men. As a result, all-white juries decided each case.

The defense attorneys adopted three criteria for challenging jurors. First, they sought to exclude any members of the Elks Club, which had recently contributed to Mrs. Floyd's medical care, and the Martinsville Retail Merchants' Association, of which the victim's husband was a member. Second, they asked jurors whether the race of the defendants or the victim would influence the verdicts they rendered or the penalty they would impose. Not all of the veniremen were forthcoming in their answers. In Frank Hairston's trial, for instance, one prospective juror stated that he had not expressed an opinion about the appropriate sentence should Hairston be found guilty. William Carter successfully challenged him because he had overheard the man earlier declare that "anybody guilty of such a crime should be" put to death.[29] Finally, as the cases progressed, the defense lawyers inquired whether the verdicts in the previous trials would influence their decisions. This standard made it increasingly difficult to seat a jury. In the final proceeding, for example, forty-seven prospective jurors were questioned before a panel could be seated.[30]

Testimony for the commonwealth was virtually identical at each trial. The prosecution opened with its strongest witness, Ruby Stroud Floyd. Under questioning from Cubine, Mrs. Floyd recounted the full details of the attack, beginning with her stop at Dan Gilmer's house to ask directions. As she and Charlie Martin walked east along the railroad track, she testified, they passed four black men who pointed the way to Ruth Pettie's home. When she returned, the men blocked the path and forced her and Charlie to walk around them. As she passed, Hampton yelled, "Hey, Honey" or "Wait, Honey," and grabbed her from behind. He threw her down next to the track, lay on top of her, and threatened to kill her if she screamed. By then the other men had begun to hold her down and pull off her skirt and underpants. Mrs. Floyd struggled, protesting that she was a Christian woman and that their actions were "against the laws of the land . . . and against the laws of the Bible."[31] Hampton raped her first, penetrating her "more than once," then assisted the others as they assaulted her. As she described to the court, "They were holding my legs, prizing my legs open. Every time I pulled my legs together they said 'Hold them legs up woman.' Every time I tried to move or holler or say anything they'd slap me in the mouth and as each one got on me he put his tongue in my mouth. They kept my mouth covered all the time with their hands and tongues, sucking my tongue and slobbering all over me."[32]

After the initial attack the four men began quarreling among themselves. At that moment a man, a woman, and a teenaged girl, all of them black, passed by the scene. Mrs. Floyd broke away from her assailants and begged the passersby for help, grabbing the woman's coat and pleading for mercy. The woman, later identified as Josephine Grayson, the wife of one of the defendants, "snatched away and said 'Don't tear my clothes off of me.'" By this time the attackers had caught up to her, and they dragged her to an embankment in the woods where they would not be so easily spotted. She continued to struggle, managing to keep her feet free but still unable to escape. Hampton and his accomplices, this time joined by several more men, assaulted her again, "every bit of twelve or fourteen times." At three of the trials she also testified that she had felt something penetrate her rectum.[33] As her other assailants fled, the last attacker, "a heavy set fellow," told her, "Now when I finish with you I'm going to turn you loose." Although she felt "paralyzed from the hips down," she made her way to Mary Wade's house to seek help.[34]

During all of her appearances on the witness stand, Mrs. Floyd appeared highly emotional, at times sobbing so violently that her questioning had to be halted. The trial of Booker T. Millner was postponed for a day because the victim's doctor testified in chambers that her physical and emotional condition "make it inadvisable for her to testify on this day."[35] Most of the defense attorneys subjected her to only light cross-examination, probably because they did not want to elicit any further sympathy for the victim on the part of the jury. Claude Taylor asked only one question, making the point that she was recovering from her injuries, while Stephen Martin declined to examine her at all. Will Joyce did not vigorously cross-examine her, but his frequent objections during the prosecution's direct examination caused Mrs. Floyd to grow noticeably more upset.[36]

Not all of the attorneys treated the victim gently. William Carter kept her on the stand for forty minutes in an unsuccessful attempt to get her to admit that she could not positively identify Frank Hairston as her second attacker. During John Taylor's trial Frank Burton challenged her testimony that Dan Gilmer had not warned her to leave the neighborhood because nightfall was approaching. Through these strategies the defense attorneys not only questioned the victim's ability to identify her attackers in the darkness, they also implied that she bore some responsibility for the attack by frequenting a dangerous neighborhood after dark. It also weakened her credibility when Gilmer later told Burton on the witness stand that he had warned Mrs. Floyd not to continue. For the most part, however, the defense attorneys failed to discredit her testimony in any significant way.[37]

The prosecution called Mary Wade, Ethel Mae Redd, and Charlie Martin to corroborate Mrs. Floyd's testimony. Mrs. Wade told the court about Mrs. Floyd's appearance at her door the evening of the attack and described her disheveled appearance. She noted that the victim's clothing was wet and smelled like either beer or urine. At Hampton's trial she testified that the defendant had come to her house two days after the crime and admitted to raping a woman. After some prodding from Cubine, she also reluctantly stated that when she had asked Hampton why Mrs. Floyd's clothes were damp, he replied that some of the other men had urinated on her.[38]

Charlie Martin placed four of the men at the scene of the crime. He testified that he had accompanied the victim to Ruth Pettie's house and that upon their return Joe Henry Hampton, Frank Hairston, Booker T. Millner, and Howard Hairston had accosted her. After Hampton grabbed the woman, Millner gave Charlie a knife and told him "if anybody come down, to cut them." When Charlie refused, Millner gave him a quarter and warned him that if he told anybody about the attack, he would kill Charlie. Charlie changed his story slightly at Millner's trial, stating that the defendant had given him the knife after the quarter and mentioning nothing about a death threat. After the attackers fled, Charlie testified, he had returned home to tell his mother and, later, the police.[39]

Ethel Mae Redd appeared only at the last two trials to connect De-Sales Grayson, John Taylor, and James Hairston to the crime. According to her testimony Grayson had burst through her door on the night of the crime and told Hairston and Taylor, who had stopped for a visit, that "some boys got a white lady up on the track. Come on let's go up there." One of the others (she could not remember which one) suggested that might not be a good idea, but then all three of them left, presumably to find out what was happening.[40]

The prosecutors closed each case with the testimony of law enforcement officers and medical examiners. Officer A. T. Finney and Detective Murray Barrow detailed the investigation that had led to the capture of the defendants. Sergeant Barnes read the confessions into evidence. Dr. Joseph Ravenel, the physician who had examined Mrs. Floyd, described her symptoms on the evening of the attack. When she arrived at the hospital, he testified, she had a swollen lower lip and abrasions on several parts of her body. A pelvic examination revealed active sperm in the vagina, but he could not guess how many men had had sexual intercourse with her. Throughout the examination she had appeared "pretty well excited" and "extremely nervous," and she had returned to the hospital the following morning complaining of muscular aches. Since then she had been in and out of hospitals with high fevers and abdominal pain. At Hampton's trial Dr. Baynard Carter of the Duke University Hospital provided additional medical testimony. He told the court that the victim was presently under his care for a hematoma on the left side of her pelvis caused by penetration of the vagina or rectum. His prognosis for her recovery was "at least a good six to nine months."[41]

The impressive array of witnesses assembled by the prosecution at each trial made it virtually impossible for the defendants to deny their part in the crime. When the time came for the defense to present its case, the court-appointed attorneys used different tactics and displayed varying courtroom styles, but they adopted similar approaches to defending their clients, emphasizing mitigating factors such as youth and intoxication. Will Joyce painted DeSales Grayson, the only defendant who was married or had children, as a loyal family man. In three of the trials the attorneys introduced the eyewitness testimony of Josephine Grayson and Leola Millner, Booker Millner's fourteen-year-old sister. Leola testified that she, Mrs. Grayson, and John Redd had been walking along the railroad tracks when Ruby Floyd leaped at the trio out of the darkness and cried for help. Leola had seen Joe Henry Hampton grab Mrs. Floyd and pull her into the woods. Frank Hairston was near Hampton but had not touched the victim, while Howard Hairston and Booker T. Millner were loitering around the bend of the railroad track. Josephine Grayson likewise testified that she had seen only Joe Henry Hampton grabbing the victim. When the women were asked why they had not assisted the victim, Leola explained that she "wasn't nothing but a child" and that "Josephine was sick herself," while Mrs. Grayson replied that Mrs. Floyd had startled and upset her. That was why she had shouted at the victim, she explained.[42]

Both women provided damaging testimony at Joe Henry Hampton's trial. The prosecution called Leola to the stand because she could positively identify Hampton as the man who had pulled the victim into the woods. Hampton's attorney, Joseph Whitehead, made the error of calling Mrs. Grayson for the defense to testify that "there wasn't any commotion" on the railroad tracks nor was a group of men "fussing or fighting over" Ruby Floyd. On cross-examination by Irvin Cubine, however, she revealed that Hampton had grabbed Mrs. Floyd, who "was trying to get away," and had taken her down the track "for a wrong purpose."[43]

Four of the defendants—Joe Henry Hampton, Booker T. Millner, James Hairston, and Frank Hairston, Jr.—testified in their own behalf. Their testimony corresponded roughly to the chronology that Ruby Floyd had provided, but a few important differences emerged. The most legally significant variations were their claims that none of the men had assisted another in raping Mrs. Floyd and that the victim had made no effort to resist. If the jury believed the first claim, it could not convict the defendants of abetting a rape; if it believed the second claim, it could not convict them of rape, because lack of consent was a necessary element of that offense.[44]

According to their testimony Millner, Hampton, Frank Hairston, and Howard Hairston spent most of the afternoon and evening of January 8 drinking with each other. Most of the alcohol had been consumed by the time Ruby Floyd and Charlie Martin passed them on the railroad tracks. She asked for directions to Ruth Pettie's house, which Millner provided. As she proceeded Hampton remarked to the others, according to Frank Hairston, that the woman "looked good enough to hug, or something." The others advised him to leave her alone, but when she and Charlie returned about ten minutes later, Hampton remarked upon her "pretty legs" and put his arm around her waist. She pulled away from him and started to run, but he followed her out of sight, around a bend in the track, as the others yelled for him to stop.[45]

When they caught up to Hampton, they found him lying on top of the woman, apparently having intercourse. According to Frank Hairston she was not protesting, struggling, or resisting in any way. Hairston claimed that he remained behind to persuade Hampton to release the woman while the other two men continued up the track about seventy feet. Hampton told him that he had paid the woman five dollars and did not plan to leave until he was finished. While they continued to argue, Millner spotted Charlie Martin, offered him a quarter, gave him a knife, and secured a promise that he would not tell anyone what he had seen. After Charlie left, Josephine Grayson, John Redd, and Leola Millner walked by. Josephine warned Millner not to return to the others, but after she left he headed back toward Hampton.[46]

Contrary to Ruby Floyd's testimony, Millner indicated that Hampton had moved her into the woods by himself and that no one held her down while he raped her. By the time Millner returned to the scene, Grayson, Taylor, and James Hairston had arrived. Hampton told everyone present, "All you all are in it. You might as well go on and have you some too with the lady." He added presciently, "If they lock one of us up they'll lock us all up." Millner testified that he went to her and exposed his genitals, but as he leaned over her she pleaded, "Please let me go. I want to go home to my children." (The victim had no children). Millner claimed that he lost any urge to rape the woman and returned to the group after only a short time. This was corroborated by Frank Hairston's testimony that Millner "went up and turned and came straight back. He didn't stay no time." The defendants agreed that Frank Hairston was the third man to go to her, not the second as Mrs. Floyd claimed, and Hairston claimed that she had not resisted his advances. "It was just like any other woman," he testified. "She didn't say don't go, push me or anything."[47]

James Luther Hairston provided the most complete account of the events after he, DeSales Grayson, and John Taylor arrived. According to his testimony Hampton went to the woman a second time. He had removed his shirt, and he "stayed on her a little bit longer than the rest." Howard Hairston followed, remaining with her "about ten or fifteen seconds," then Grayson went to her. James admitted that he next approached the woman, unfastened his pants, penetrated her "private parts," and completed sexual intercourse. When asked if she consented, Hairston replied, "She didn't push me away." When he finished she asked him to gather some clothes that she had been carrying. He hunted around the area for the clothing and returned to find John Taylor "getting off the lady." He had not, however, seen Taylor having intercourse with her. Hairston gave the woman her clothes and departed with Taylor, leaving Ruby Floyd alone with Grayson. Throughout the incident, Hairston testified, the woman had not resisted, and only one man was with her at any one time. The others stood watching, but they did not strike her or hold her down.[48]

Each defendant provided either an excuse or a defense for his actions, all of them based on the explanation that a group of young men, their reason dulled by intoxication, had become caught up in the frenzied activity of the moment. Hampton testified that he had been so drunk from the wine and brandy that he could not remember what he had done that night. Millner also blamed alcohol for his part in the assault, claiming, "I know I did wrong about going down there fooling with the lady. I should have went and called help. By me drinking though I don't reckon my mind let me do it and so I ask the Court to have mercy on me." He also denied actually having intercourse with the victim because she had pleaded for the sake of her children. Frank and James Hairston admitted that they had relations with the woman, but they invoked consent as a defense. Like Millner, Frank Hairston threw himself on the mercy of the court, pleading, "I know I was wrong to have gone with the woman. Maybe if I hadn't been drinking I wouldn't have done what I did do. I know I had no reason to have intercourse with the woman. . . . If you give me another chance I promise to be a better boy, never to get into nothing else as long as I live."[49]

The most controversial testimony concerned the validity of the signed confessions. In each case Sergeant Barnes read the confession of the particular defendant on trial. He also related the circumstances under which each statement had been made. Each man had admitted that he had taken part in the assault and had implicated the others as well. Every statement, he reported, had been given "without threat or promise of reward."[50]

Each defendant who took the stand, however, repudiated his confession to some degree. The attorneys for those who exercised their right not to testify also raised questions about the validity of the confessions. When W. R. Broaddus read Frank Hairston's confession back to him, Hairston could not remember making most of the statements and concluded that most of the document was incorrect. When Broaddus asked him why he had signed it, Hairston replied, "I just wasn't thinking at the time." Stephen Martin challenged Howard Hairston's confession on the grounds that Hairston was illiterate and had a speech impediment. He called Irene Hodge, Hairston's aunt, to testify that her nephew could not speak clearly. Barnes remained firm under cross-

examination, however, recalling that he "didn't have any trouble understanding him" and did not have to ask Hairston to repeat anything.
Hampton testified that he had signed the statement because "they
asked me to sign," but he denied ever having read the document to
see what he was signing.[51]

Two of the attorneys raised more serious objections to their clients'
written statements. During Booker Millner's trial Barnes testified that
Millner initially claimed that he "didn't know a thing in the world
about" the crime. After being informed that Frank Hairston had confessed, Millner changed his mind, saying, "If Frank told the truth
about it I reckon I just as well tell the truth." On the stand Millner
countered that the police had badgered him, unrelentingly accusing
him of having intercourse with the woman, until he signed a statement. When Millner read the typed version of his statement, he informed Barnes of an error. "Wait a minute Sergeant Barnes," he said.
"You got that wrong. I didn't say *we* took her up, Joe Henry took her
up on the ridge." According to Millner, Barnes had replied, "That don't
make much difference." Barnes forcefully defended his actions on the
witness stand, however. He indicated to Claude Taylor that on his copy
of the confession he had stricken the word "we" and replaced it with
"he," meaning Hampton. He assured the court, "I didn't want anything
but just exactly what he said. If it was wrong I wanted to change it."[52]

Will Joyce also questioned Barnes about inconsistencies between
Barnes's handwritten copy of DeSales Grayson's confession, which he
transcribed in the interrogation room of the Martinsville police station
as Grayson spoke, and the typewritten copy that Grayson had signed
three days later. The prosecution entered both documents into evidence, and Barnes's recital of their contents revealed a discrepancy.
The handwritten version read, ". . . I saw a man on a woman" while
the typed copy read, ". . . I saw a man and a woman." Joyce seized
upon this difference to impeach Barnes's motives and to question the
thoroughness of his investigation. In the most vigorous cross-
examination of the trials, Joyce forced Barnes to admit he had not carefully proofread a crucial piece of evidence. Joyce then queried, "Do
you mean to tell the jury that with a man's life at stake you thought so
little about the accuracy of a statement you were having him make that
you didn't even read it?" No, Barnes replied, he had simply made a
typewritten copy so that it could be read by the court more easily than
his handwriting. "In other words," Joyce challenged, "you wanted the

one you were keeping yourself to be accurate and it made little difference what was read to the Court and jury." Barnes responded that he thought the contents of the two documents were identical. He was well aware of the severity of the offense, he stated. "That was the reason I was so particular in warning him of his rights and all so the statement could be used." "But you weren't particular," Joyce countered, "about what was in the statement that might incriminate him and send him to the chair?" Barnes protested that Grayson himself had read the typed statement and verified that it was a true copy, but he finally admitted, "I should have read it." Joyce's cross-examination of Barnes was the most effective challenge to any prosecution witness in any of the proceedings.[53]

To round out their defense, the attorneys called several character witnesses, including clergymen, former employers, and relatives. This tactic was designed to convince the juries, which had the final sentencing authority, to decide upon a sentence short of the prosecution's recommendation of death. Scott Hampton testified on behalf of his son, Joe Henry Hampton, and Irene Hodge spoke for her nephews, Howard and James Hairston. Frank Hairston's mother, Bessie Hairston, turned to the jury at the end of her cross-examination and pleaded, "I ask you all jurors to please have mercy on my child and spare his life. I feel he was persuaded by some means in this crime." Ida Millner blamed herself for her son's plight. She had warned him not to go out that night because he had been drinking, but she had not been stern enough when he insisted on going anyway. "I feel sorry in my heart," she continued, "that I am to blame for letting him go out." She begged the court, "I do ask you gentlemen of the court and I do ask the Judge and the jury to have mercy on my son please. Will you please just have mercy. Judge, with a grieving heart I ask you to please help me." As she made this appeal, reported the local newspaper, Booker Millner "broke into loud sobs with his head bowed on a table."[54]

Just as they had done during the questioning of witnesses, the defense attorneys adopted a variety of strategies in their summations to the juries. Some of the attorneys attempted to establish reasonable doubt that their clients had committed the crime. Clarence Kearfott pointed out some minor mistakes in Ruby Floyd's testimony and suggested that her memory of specific details of the crime might be in error. Because of the strength of the prosecution's evidence, however, most of the lawyers implicitly conceded the guilt of their clients and sought to avoid the death penalty by concentrating on mitigating factors such as youth, drunkenness, and remorse. John Taylor confirmed this strategy when he whispered during jury deliberations, "I have never wanted ninety-nine years so much in my life as I do now." Certainly the attorneys in the later trials realized that the pattern of convictions made acquittal for any of the men unlikely.[55]

These attorneys also warned jury members not to allow their knowledge of the sentences in the earlier cases to affect their judgments. Claude Taylor, the young attorney who represented Booker Millner in the third trial, was the first lawyer to advance this argument. Taylor told the jury that the prosecution had tried its two strongest cases first "in order to establish a precedent of punishment," and he urged the jurors to consider only the specific evidence in Millner's case. The effect of this argument was muted, however, by his ambiguous plea that "the only mercy we are seeking is the mercy of an honest verdict." Kearfott and Frank Burton, who represented the defendants in the last trial, argued more forcefully that their clients were less culpable than the earlier defendants. Only one lawyer intimated that the prosecution's strategy had been racially motivated. Stephen Martin, counsel for Howard Hairston, asked the jury to demonstrate that "a man who deserves mercy is given it regardless of his color."[56]

During their closing statements the prosecutors emphasized the severity of the crime and the strong performance of the complaining witness, Ruby Floyd, under difficult conditions. The confession evidence alone, they asserted, proved that the defendants were guilty of attempted rape at least. They also denied the existence of any mitigating circumstances. The crime was "so crude and cruel," Hannibal Joyce argued at Grayson's trial, that the state sought the supreme penalty. "This crime deserves the highest degree of punishment under law, which is death," Irvin Cubine thundered at Howard Hairston's trial. The mention of the death penalty so upset Janet Taylor during her son's trial that she fainted and had to be driven home in an ambulance.[57]

At the end of closing arguments, Judge Whittle instructed the jury on the elements of the crime of rape. The prosecution had to prove each element, he explained, in order for the jury to find a defendant guilty. In Virginia rape was defined as the carnal knowledge of any woman over sixteen years of age against her will by force. The victim need not have resisted physically if "the mind and will of the female were overpowered by fear." Penetration was a necessary element of the crime, but the penetration could be "ever so slight." The jury also could find the defendant guilty of attempted rape if it believed all elements but penetration had occurred; of aiding and abetting a rape; or of assault and battery. He informed the jurors that the law presumed a defendant innocent until the commonwealth proved beyond a reasonable doubt, not a mere suspicion or probability, that he was guilty. In weighing confession evidence the jury was the sole arbiter of credibility and could consider the circumstances in which the statement was given to weigh its reliability. It was solely the power of the jury, he reminded them, to assess a penalty for the crime. Rape was punishable by five years to life in prison, attempted rape or abetting a rape by three years to life, and assault and battery by no more than twelve years in prison. All but assault and battery were also punishable by death. Except in the first two trials, Whittle also informed the jury that Virginia law prohibited any racial distinctions when determining punishment. He refused a defense request to instruct the jury to "scrutinize [the victim's] testimony with great care and caution."[58]

In six day-long trials held over the course of eleven days, six separate juries found the defendants guilty of rape and sentenced them to death. The jury in Millner's trial took the longest time to reach a decision, one hour and forty-seven minutes, while Hampton was convicted in half an hour. All of the juries voted to convict on the first ballot, but some of the later panels showed some hesitancy about the sentences. The juries in the Millner and Howard Hairston cases voted three times before agreeing on the death penalty, and the jury in the last trial, of Taylor and James Hairston, took two ballots.[59]

Although the guilty verdicts surprised no one, the death sentences shocked Martinsville's black community. Most local black leaders were convinced of the guilt of the defendants, but they believed that at least some of them would escape the death penalty because of mitigating circumstances such as youth, intoxication, remorse, and lack of serious criminal records. The defendants' families had eschewed outside legal aid because they believed that local, court-appointed attorneys would save the men from the electric chair. Clyde L. Williams, a local high school teacher at the time, later recalled that the verdicts awakened many in the black community to the depth of racial discrimination in Martinsville and that he and several other black leaders had to quell a protest for fear that it would further undermine race relations in the city.[60]

On May 3, 1949, Judge Whittle officially pronounced sentence upon the defendants. Before he passed judgment he asked the defendants whether they had anything to say. Four of them declined, but Grayson, Taylor, and Millner expressed dissatisfaction with the verdicts. Grayson protested, "I didn't do any harm. I have told the truth. I have always worked hard and have a family and five kids." Taylor continued to argue that he had been forced into the crime by the other men. Hairston informed the court, "I don't feel like I should be punished for rape." Whittle replied tersely to these complaints, "That was a matter for the jury to decide." He scheduled the first four defendants to be executed on July 15 and the remaining three men on July 22. "It is my prayer that God have mercy on your soul," he added. He noted that he had allowed more than sixty days to give them an opportunity to exhaust their legal appeals, commenting, "If errors have been made I pray God they may be corrected."[61]

The following morning, for the first time in the course of the proceedings, large crowds exhibited an interest in the case. Several hundred people crowded into the courthouse square and leaned out of office windows to catch a glimpse of the prisoners as they were transported from the Henry County jail to the Virginia State Penitentiary in Richmond. The outcome of the cases had received a great amount of publicity around the state because the seven death sentences set the stage for an execution record in Virginia. Around 11:30 A.M. prison guards led Taylor and Grayson, both handcuffed with their legs shackled together, from the basement of the jail into a transport van with barred windows parked in the driveway. Joe Henry Hampton, manacled by himself, followed, then the shackled pairs of Frank and James Hairston and Booker T. Millner and Howard Hairston were led to the van. Sheriff's deputies cleared a path through the crowd as five armed state guards drove the men to await their fates in Richmond.[62]

At the conclusion of the trials, Judge Whittle told the lawyers for the prosecution and defense, "You gentlemen . . . have held high the great traditions of the legal profession. You have fairly, fearlessly and ably represented your respective sides, for which I am deeply grateful." Harold Woodruff, the chief probation officer from Danville who had observed the proceedings, believed that the defense attorneys had "contested every inch of legal ground." Another observer, reporter Mel Fiske from the *Daily Worker*, treated defense counsel less charitably. Their performance, he claimed, had been "scandalous." They "stood idly by while the prosecution, the judge and the all-white jury with unbelievable [speed] railroaded the seven to a death sentence." In any other city, he asserted, "they would be confronted with charges to disbar them."[63]

In truth, the quality of the defense varied widely from one attorney to another. Joseph Whitehead, who had the most difficult client to represent, provided a weak defense of Hampton. He only cursorily cross-examined the state's key witnesses, and his closing arguments merely emphasized Hampton's intoxication, lack of education, and poor upbringing. Clarence Kearfott and Frank Burton failed to challenge minor discrepancies in the handwritten and typed copies of the confessions of James Hairston and John Taylor. However, they subjected Ruby Floyd to vigorous cross-examination and produced evidence from another witness that she had lied on the stand when she claimed she had not been warned to stay out of the black neighborhoods of Martinsville after dark. William Carter also challenged the victim's credibility by demonstrating that her testimony had changed from the preliminary hearing to Frank Hairston's trial. Claude Taylor, fresh out of law school, appeared to be overwhelmed by the duty of representing Booker T. Millner in a capital case. He was the first attorney, however, to alert a jury to the prosecution's implicit strategy of building on earlier verdicts to establish a precedent of death sentences for all of the defendants involved in the crime. The defense strategy of avoiding the death penalty rather than seeking acquittals exacerbated the difficulties of representation because, unlike a finding of guilt, which required evidence beyond a reasonable doubt, the jury had virtually unlimited discretion in sentencing. Nonetheless, the attorneys recognized that their clients' best hope lay in some higher court, and with the possibility of appeal in mind each attorney made timely and appropriate motions and objections.[64]

Will Joyce presented a particularly spirited defense of DeSales Grayson, prompting the *Martinsville Bulletin* to characterize the proceeding as "marked with more legal fencing than the previous trials." Both he and Stephen Martin renewed the request for a change of venue, but Judge Whittle denied both motions. Joyce successfully excluded from evidence any testimony about the attack on Ruby Floyd before his client allegedly arrived on the scene. Throughout Hannibal Joyce's opening statement, he objected five times when the prosecutor mentioned the initial attack. Kearfott and Burton employed the same objection during Ruby Floyd's testimony in the subsequent trial. Will Joyce also portrayed the victim in a more unfavorable light than had the other attorneys. In his opening statement Joyce told the jury that a witness would testify that he had told the woman to wait until morning to see Ruth Pettie, advice that she had ignored. "My wife would not have gone down there," he told the jurors. "Your wife would not have gone down there." Her lack of discretion was not a defense to rape, he admitted, but it could provide the jurors with "a picture of the type of mentality that Mrs. Floyd has." He also informed them that out of kindness he might not cross-examine her because she had a tendency to break down on the stand. He urged the jury to remember, however, that "a person in a hysterical state of mind could not be absolutely accurate about everything that she told." [65]

Ruby Floyd's ordeal on the witness stand revealed several patterns of racial and gender control that characterized the mid-twentieth-century South. Traditionally, white southern males had invoked a paternalistic concern for white female chastity as a justification for the summary execution of suspected black rapists. Lynching, they explained, not only punished blacks for violating racial and sexual mores, it also spared fragile women from the trauma of testifying in a public courtroom. By the 1940s antilynching reformers had exposed this rationalization as an oppressive means of controlling blacks and women, and the legal system had assumed many of the coercive functions formerly exercised by family patriarchs. [66]

Under this new arrangement Mrs. Floyd's testimony, in addition to implicating the accused black men, served to warn white women about the presumed dangers of stepping outside prescribed gender roles. Many townspeople did not view Ruby Floyd as a sympathetic figure because her association with the Jehovah's Witnesses, an unpopular religious sect, and her frequent missionary work in Martinsville's black neighborhoods had already raised questions about her judgment. Some observers concluded from her testimony that had she conformed more closely to the ideals of "southern womanhood," which included not straying beyond certain physical and social boundaries, she might have avoided the assault. Following the trials several women wrote to the governor's office asking that the death sentences of the defendants be commuted because the victim had "asked for trouble" and "violat[ed] a strict southern code." Subsequent rumors of her confinement in a mental institution and her husband's desertion also vividly dramatized the purported consequences for women who asserted their independence or flaunted the rules of propriety. Thus the Martinsville trials not only punished unruly blacks who violated criminal statutes and racial and sexual taboos; they also reminded local women of the imagined costs of violating established codes of behavior for white females.[67]

The racial values embodied in the trials also manifested themselves in a different fashion than in earlier cases of interracial rape. Just as the prosecutors did not openly espouse the preservation of white southern womanly virtue, they did not appeal to overt racism. Racial epithets and a mob mentality, clearly evident in cases such as the Scottsboro trial, were noticeably absent from the Martinsville proceedings. Local observers praised the court for maintaining the status quo, but not in explicitly racial terms. Instead, they commended the judge and jury for preserving the general order and stability of the community. E. A. Sale, president of one of Martinsville's largest textile companies, assured Governor William Tuck that "during the trial, anyone walking by the Courthouse would not have realized the trial was going on." The proceedings were "handled in a most orderly manner which is certainly a credit to the Courts of Virginia and to the citizens of Martinsville, including all colors." John P. Smith, an acquaintance of former congressman Thomas G. Burch of Martinsville, told the governor that although "we had a most outrageous crime committed here, . . . the community remained calm and their trial was supervised by a just judge and every right the law affords was thrown around" the defendants. An editorial in the Danville *Bee* addressed the tendency of northerners to question the South's ability to try its black citizens fairly. The Martinsville cases, the editorial retorted, were "a fine example of orderly justice in which the common law has been applied with no greater force to the Negro than it would have been to the white man." It emphasized the court's attention to due process and the "resourceful and courageous" efforts of the defense attorneys. "The Martinsville trials," it concluded, "should stand out in a bright light as typical of southern justice which has been deliberate, fair and well ordained even if frightful in its last analysis."[68]

Nevertheless, seven black men had been sentenced to die for the rape of a white woman. The trials emphasized the restoration of community stability rather than racial retribution, but no one denied that the crime had upset the racial equilibrium of the local community. Six juries agreed that the most effective way to restore the balance was to punish the violators harshly. Whether that punishment translated into a legal claim of racial discrimination, however, remained an issue for the appellate courts.

3

Arrangement in
Red and Black

Despite the efforts of the Martinsville legal establishment to characterize the prosecutions and convictions as strictly a local concern, the large number of defendants, the rapid pace of the trials, and the specter of multiple executions ensured the case widespread outside attention. Publicity from the African-American and radical press and direct appeals from family members attracted the attention of several of the nation's most prominent civil rights organizations. As rival groups vied for control of the case of the "Martinsville Seven," as the men came to be known, they also renewed a decades-old debate over the appropriate methods of combating racial discrimination in the United States.

African-American journalists almost unanimously criticized the guilty verdicts. The Pittsburgh *Courier,* one of the nation's leading black newspapers, likened the "sentence-a-day" case to the Scottsboro affair and characterized the evidence presented at the trials as "a series of contradictions and perjury."[1] The *Louisiana Weekly* decried the "shocking contrast of justice" afforded to blacks in small communities such as Martinsville when compared to the treatment of white defendants. Even Nazi war criminals, an editorial asserted, had received greater due process protections than had blacks in the South. While the *Weekly* professed no desire "to minimize crime or to defend criminals who had no defense," it could not help but observe that "in the South the seriousness of a crime depends not upon the act itself but the color of the person who perpetrates the act." The failure to extend procedural safeguards to African Americans, the *Weekly* concluded, undermined the "respect and faith in our democratic way of life both at home and abroad."[2]

The most strident criticism of the verdicts, however, issued from the American radical press, particularly the *Daily Worker.* The *Worker's* editors adhered more closely to Communist party orthodoxy than any other American newspaper of the Left, but since the end of World War II they had attempted to broaden the paper's appeal to readers with liberal or "progressive" leanings. Reporter Mel Fiske covered the trials for the *Worker* and regularly dispatched reports that criticized the tactics of the police, the quality of the defense, and the "ruthless assembly line legal machine" that "ground out death sentences for seven Negro men." After the final jury announced its verdict, an editorial in the *Worker* decried the "belt-line death verdicts" of seven black men who had "been railroaded to die on the usual frame-up 'rape' charge." Alarmed by the specter of mass executions, the writer called on "public-spirited organizations and citizens" to act immediately to halt "a particularly brutal legal mass murder."[3]

The *Daily Worker's* interest in the Martinsville case grew out of a long history of Communist interest in the affairs of African Americans. The Communist International had courted African-American participation in radical politics since the Russian Revolution, but it had also been accused of placing party objectives over the actual needs of blacks. For example, when the Sixth World Congress in 1928 decided, over the objections of American delegates, to advocate the establishment of an independent Negro republic in the southern United States, few people believed that the Communists held any serious interest in the problems of blacks. The day-to-day operations of the party in the United States differed significantly from these established party principles. During the Great Depression, American Communists became increasingly sensitive to the immediate needs of blacks. Efforts on the behalf of blacks accelerated after 1935, when the party adopted a less militant Popular Front strategy to appeal to non-Communist liberals and other opponents of fascism. Most significant, African Americans in areas as diverse as the streets of New York and the cotton fields of Alabama began to identify the party as one of the few organizations genuinely responsive to their plight.[4]

Throughout the 1930s Communists helped African Americans to combat housing and employment discrimination, organize rent strikes, and curb the abuses of sharecropping, peonage, and convict labor.[5] They found their most striking success, however, in the defense of African Americans accused of crimes. In 1925 a group of Communist party leaders organized the International Labor Defense (ILD), dedicated to providing legal aid to any persons who were "persecuted for their activity in the labor movement." Although the ILD lent assistance to workers, aliens, and other minorities, its efforts on behalf of black defendants, supervised by the ILD's national secretary, William L. Patterson, attracted the most attention. In a series of cases radiating from the Deep South to Maryland and Oklahoma, the ILD earned a reputation among African Americans as a reliable ally in the struggle for racial justice.[6]

Two cases in particular—the Scottsboro rape case in Alabama and the Angelo Herndon conspiracy trial in Atlanta—demonstrated the potential of legal efforts on behalf of African Americans to bring the party to prominence. In June 1932 Herndon, a nineteen-year-old black Communist, was arrested in front of the Fulton County Courthouse for organizing an interracial protest against the suspension of relief payments. A month later a grand jury indicted Herndon for violating Georgia's insurrection statute. The ILD represented Herndon at trial and used the case to link issues of interest to African Americans, civil libertarians, and radicals. Thus Herndon's attorneys challenged the exclusion of blacks from Atlanta juries, argued that the insurrection law violated the rights of free speech and assembly, and emphasized the importance of mass political protest to combat poverty and racism. In 1937 the United States Supreme Court overturned the conviction because Herndon's distribution of literature supporting unemployment insurance, equal rights for blacks, and self-determination for the Black Belt did not pose a "clear and present danger" of insurrection. The Herndon case marked a significant step in the development of free speech doctrine, but more important for the ILD, it publicized the injustices of the southern legal system and linked the Communist agenda to those of civil rights activists, civil libertarians, legal reformers, and Popular Front liberals.[7]

The Scottsboro case proved even more valuable to the ILD. The organization's defense of nine black teenagers falsely accused of rape permitted radical attorneys to dramatize the social and economic injustices of American society. At trial, eight of the nine defendants received the death penalty. On two separate appeals, however, the ILD persuaded the United States Supreme Court that customary practices in southern courtrooms—the exclusion of blacks from juries and the denial of counsel in capital cases—violated defendants' rights under the due process clause of the Fourteenth Amendment. The ILD convinced the prosecution to drop the charges against four of the men, and the remaining defendants received prison terms rather than death sentences. Cases such as these served the dual purpose of challenging the traditional status of African Americans and broadening the base of support for communism as party members entered churches, lodges, and other organizations to raise funds for their clients' defenses. Moreover, the ILD's success in overturning Herndon's conviction and saving the Scottsboro boys from execution convinced many blacks that Communist legal strategy would not necessarily sacrifice black defendants for the sake of party objectives.[8]

The Popular Front dissolved in 1939 after Stalin signed the Nazi-Soviet nonaggression pact, and radical interest in African-American affairs lagged during World War II as the Communist party turned its attention to supporting the wartime needs of the Soviet Union. In the late 1940s, however, as cold war politics forced the Communists into ever-narrowing fields of activity, many party members looked to the burgeoning civil rights movement as a possible source of political influence. In April 1946 the ILD, the National Negro Congress, the National Federation for Constitutional Liberties, the Southern Negro Youth Congress, and several smaller organizations merged to form the Civil Rights Congress. At a meeting in Detroit, over four hundred representatives from the organizations agreed to combat discrimination against racial, ethnic, and political minorities by establishing legal aid societies, raising bail funds, attacking police brutality, and supporting civil rights issues in political campaigns. Fiscal concerns that could be solved by reducing the replication of services led to the merger of these groups, but the delegates also concluded that a large united organization could best weather the impending storm of intensive federal and state investigations of groups suspected of Communist affiliation. The CRC was not associated officially with the Communist party, but Communists held most of the top administrative and policy-making positions, and the organization rarely veered from the increasingly militant party line. Until 1949, in fact, the CRC lent its support primarily to Communists, including Eugene Dennis and ten other high-ranking party officials accused of violating the Smith Act. Nevertheless, local membership spanned the political spectrum, and the large African-American membership ultimately focused the organization on issues of civil rights and racial discrimination rather than problems associated with labor or political dissent.[9]

One historian of the Civil Rights Congress has observed that the National Negro Congress was "the heart of CRC," but the ILD "served as the limbs."[10] Former leaders of the ILD, especially attorneys, infused the CRC with professionals who had a talent for organization, rhetoric, and publicity. The most important figure to carry over from the ILD was William L. Patterson. A dark, heavyset man of medium height, Patterson had grown up in the San Francisco Bay area, and in 1919 he received a law degree from the Hastings College of Law of the University of California. After graduation he moved to New York, and in 1923 he founded the Dyett, Hall, and Patterson law firm in Harlem. The firm's reputation grew quickly, especially in the field of commercial law, and it became the first black law office in the country to represent a white banking establishment. Patterson's friendship with Richard Moore and Paul Robeson, two prominent black Communists, and his participation in the campaign to free Nicola Sacco and Bartolomeo Vanzetti, Italian anarchists who had been sentenced to death, heightened his interest in radical politics. He joined the Communist party in 1926 and in 1932 became the national secretary of the ILD. In 1948 he assumed the job of executive secretary of the CRC, a position he held until that organization's demise in 1956.[11]

Although the CRC continued to work toward legal redress of segregation and discrimination, it relied on mass public protest against political and judicial institutions to a much greater extent than had the ILD. As a CRC pamphlet documenting its successes in the civil rights field explained, "The key to the success of the fight for civil rights has been the mass pressure of the people," not courtroom victories.[12] More traditional civil rights organizations, however, feared that the militance of the CRC would engender a reactionary fear of radicalism and lead to the increased repression of minorities. Because of differences in philosophy, the CRC frequently collided with other civil rights organizations, particularly the National Association for the Advancement of Colored People.[13]

The NAACP was founded in 1909 when a coalition of black and white intellectuals met to consider the torpid progress of race relations since the end of Reconstruction. Most African Americans at the time were denied access to the ballot box, the courthouse, and the schoolyard. Opportunities for economic advancement were nil; violence against blacks was on the rise. Racial segregation was entrenched by law in the South and by custom almost everywhere else. In short, since the end of slavery African Americans had been denied their most basic civil, political, and economic rights.[14]

For the first two decades of its existence the NAACP relied chiefly on lobbying, education, and publicity, particularly through its monthly magazine, the *Crisis,* edited by W. E. B. Du Bois. It also made some initial strides toward seeking redress in the courts. Local attorneys associated with the NAACP volunteered their talents to represent black defendants at trial, including William Patterson, who was arrested in 1917 for protesting American involvement in World War I. The NAACP also began raising constitutional challenges to discrimination in the appellate courts. In 1915 it submitted an amicus brief in *Guinn v. United States,* which overturned the use of the grandfather clause to disfranchise black voters. The NAACP's president, Moorfield Storey, a white attorney, argued before the United States Supreme Court in *Buchanan v. Warley* (1917), which declared residential segregation ordinances to be unconstitutional. In *Moore v. Dempsey* (1923), the Court ratified Storey's arguments that federal courts could intervene to protect the procedural rights of defendants who were tried in state proceedings that labored under the threat of mob action. In his final argument before the Court, at age eighty-two, Storey convinced the tribunal that the all-white primary in Texas violated the equal protection clause of the Fourteenth Amendment.[15]

Impressive as these victories were, they were more a product of Moorfield Storey's personal diligence than any organized effort by the NAACP. As of 1930 the NAACP had no full-time legal staff nor any comprehensive litigation strategy. Indeed, many of the organization's leaders, including Du Bois, opposed placing a primary emphasis on legal issues because doing so drew resources away from the association's efforts to eradicate poverty and promote economic advancement for African Americans. Several events at the turn of the decade, however, convinced the group's leadership to strengthen its legal efforts. Storey died in 1929, leaving responsibility for litigation in the hands of Arthur Spingarn, chairman of the NAACP's Legal Committee. Spingarn was a prominent New York attorney with an impeccable record on civil rights and liberties, but he did not possess Storey's legal imagination nor his talent for oral argument. The following year the NAACP received a grant of $100,000 from the American Fund for Public Service, commonly known as the Garland Fund after its founder, Charles Garland. The money was earmarked to fund taxpayer suits against school districts that failed to maintain equal facilities for black and white students. Thus the NAACP began to search for attorneys skilled in civil rights litigation. Finally, the NAACP's failure to wrest control of the Scottsboro cases from the ILD in 1931 revealed the importance of centralized supervision of its legal efforts. The ILD's success in linking support for the Scottsboro defendants to its economic and political agenda also indicated that litigation efforts could attract new members and complement, rather than compete with, the other components of the NAACP's mission.[16]

In 1934 the NAACP appointed Charles Hamilton Houston, dean of Howard University School of Law, as the association's first full-time counsel. Houston had transformed the university's weakest college into the leading training ground for practitioners of civil rights law. He closed the night school, tightened admissions standards, upgraded the library's holdings, and modernized the curriculum. Students were exposed to many of the brightest civil rights lawyers, who often rehearsed jury summations or oral arguments in front of Howard students and faculty before going into court. Many students gained practical experience by assisting attorneys in the preparation of briefs and arguments. Most important, Houston emphasized the use of historical, sociological, and statistical methods of argument and encouraged students to define the practice of civil rights law broadly. He carried this philosophy to the NAACP, where he advocated a unified approach to resolving the disparate problems associated with discrimination, segregation, and racial violence. By the time one of Houston's former students, Thurgood Marshall, assumed Houston's position in 1938, the NAACP had become irrevocably wedded to the legalistic method of combating racism in America. The creation of the NAACP Legal De-

fense and Educational Fund in 1939, which gave the association's litigation activities tax-exempt status, further enhanced the organization's
ability to fashion a viable constitutional litigation strategy.[17]

Because NAACP leaders believed in gradually eroding segregation
and discrimination through legalistic means, they frequently collided
with the Communists' insistence on mass protest and direct action.
Unlike the Communist party, the NAACP did not seek to restructure
the American social and economic order, only to include African
Americans within that order. Criminal cases often evoked the most
pronounced antagonism between the groups because of the publicity
and notoriety that surrounded the trials of alleged murderers and rapists. The NAACP leaders opposed Communist defense of black defendants on the grounds that the Communists placed party objectives
above the interests of the defendants, but in reality both groups pursued cases that advanced their respective institutional goals. Leftist
organizations competed with the NAACP for potential members, and
the successful defense of an African American could attract widespread support, as the ILD discovered after its initial victory in the
Scottsboro case. Consequently, when NAACP attorneys defended Jess
Hollins in Oklahoma for rape and represented George Crawford in his
Virginia murder trial, they devised their strategy in part to disprove
the ILD's contention that strictly legalistic methods could not avail in
southern courtrooms.[18]

The rabid anticommunism of the cold war era intensified the conflict between the NAACP and the Communist party. During the late
1930s and early 1940s the NAACP had secured its position as the preeminent civil rights organization in the United States. The creation of
the CRC, however, awakened fears that the NAACP would again be
subjected to leftist propaganda and invective. Like the ILD, the CRC
highlighted the prosecutions of blacks to dramatize the racial injustices
of American society and gain support for the radical movement. Representatives of the CRC personally handled some cases, such as the
Willie McGee rape case in Mississippi (1945–51), but it usually sought
to cooperate with moderate organizations such as the NAACP and
the American Civil Liberties Union (ACLU). Cold war imperatives
prompted both groups to reject these overtures, however, as southern
politicians attributed the growth of the civil rights movement to Communist inspiration. As Roy Wilkins, a prominent NAACP administrator, argued in his autobiography, "We were having enough trouble get-

ting Congress to consider even the most elementary civil rights legislation; the last thing we needed was to give ammunition to red-baiting southern congressmen and senators, who would have loved nothing better than to paint us pink." The most dramatic showdown between the NAACP and the Civil Rights Congress occurred in the winter of 1949–50 when the NAACP refused the CRC's request to participate in the National Civil Rights Mobilization, a planned congressional lobbying alliance of racial, religious, and labor organizations. The NAACP's swift apprehension and dismissal of CRC "delegates" who infiltrated the mobilization provided a clear public demonstration of the NAACP's abhorrence of civil rights activists who associated with radical political movements.[19]

Against this background leaders of the Virginia State Conference of the NAACP considered in early May 1949 whether to represent the Martinsville Seven on appeal. Immediately after the trials, relatives of the defendants asked the NAACP to intervene in the cases. On May 6, four days after the trials ended, Martin A. Martin, vice-chairman of the conference legal staff, interviewed each of the condemned men at the Virginia State Penitentiary in Richmond. Meanwhile Jerry L. Williams, a Danville attorney who also served on the legal staff, drove to Martinsville to discuss the case with William Muse, president of the local NAACP branch, and William Alexander, a Martinsville lawyer. Following this investigation, the Virginia State Conference announced on May 12 that it would "actively enter" the posttrial proceedings.[20]

The NAACP had not represented the men at trial because NAACP policy discouraged its attorneys from representing criminal defendants unless they were clearly innocent. As Thurgood Marshall explained to his legal staff, the NAACP was "not a legal aid society"; its limited resources had to be expended where they would do the most good. Marshall believed that at the trial level defending innocent African Americans would be the most effective way to battle the racial injustices of the southern legal system. Upon appeal, however, the standard for representation became whether the case could establish any important legal precedents "for the benefit of due process and equal protection in general and the protection of Negroes' rights in particular." As W. Lester Banks, executive secretary of the Virginia State Conference, explained, the issue was not the guilt or innocence of the Martinsville defendants but whether they had received a fair trial. The NAACP, he said, had a "solemn duty and obligation to expose and focus attention on a society that by its customs, practices, policies, and traditions [made] possible the whole unfortunate Martinsville affair."[21]

In addition, the NAACP frequently entered cases late in the process because it relied on its local branches and the African-American press to inform it of potentially significant cases. Often these cases did not receive any publicity until after the penalties, usually death sentences, were announced. According to the Richmond *Afro-American,* one of Virginia's leading black newspapers, attorneys from the Danville branch of the Virginia State Conference had investigated the possibility of representing the men at trial, but after the families of the defendants spurned their initial inquiries, reportedly on the advice of Martinsville civic leaders, the branch did not pursue the matter further. The *Afro-American* and its leading competitor, the Norfolk *Journal and Guide,* did not give the case extensive coverage until the death sentences began to mount. Once the trials concluded, the prospect of seven black men being executed at once alarmed Virginia's African-American community, especially since the state had never sent more than three convicts to the electric chair in one day. Thus the Virginia State Conference viewed the case as an opportunity to advance the cause of due process and equal protection and to demonstrate its commitment to assisting black Virginians, especially poor blacks in the rural areas of the state.[22]

More radical groups also began planning campaigns to save the Martinsville Seven. Progressive party members in Virginia and North Carolina solicited letters and petitions asking Virginia's political and judicial leaders to halt the executions. The Progressive party, established in 1948, was not a Communist organization, but its support for civil rights and its attack on Harry Truman's anti-Soviet foreign policy attracted many Communists who wanted to participate in mainstream politics. Although the party's presidential candidate, Henry A. Wallace, polled less than 3 percent of the vote in the 1948 election, the party persisted through the support of Popular Front liberals and traditional New Dealers who believed that Truman had perverted Franklin Roosevelt's original vision of social and economic justice. In North Carolina the People's Legislative Conference, a Progressive party undertaking, sponsored a tour of the state by relatives of the defendants and urged concerned citizens to send letters of protest to Judge Kennon Whittle. In Virginia, Wilbert Reavis, chairman of Richmond's Progressive party organization, asked the justices of the Virginia Supreme

Court of Appeals to grant an appeal "so that these men might be afforded justice." Taking his cue from the radical press, Reavis cited the pace of the trials, the racial composition of the juries, the unreliability of the complaining witness, and "the threat of lynch mobs" as reasons why "a just trial was impossible." The people of Richmond, he asserted, were "shocked by the conviction and death sentence of the seven men."[23]

Although the Progressive party attracted some initial publicity to the case, widespread radical interest did not begin until the Civil Rights Congress entered the case. Soon after the trials Josephine Grayson, the wife of DeSales Grayson, visited William Patterson at his New York office. As Mrs. Grayson recounted her husband's ordeal and the hardships that she and her family had endured, Patterson experienced, he later recalled, "a new level of hatred for my country's rulers." The reasons for Patterson's reaction to her story were both personal and political. The grandson of a slave, Patterson maintained throughout his life that his mother had been conceived when a white master raped his grandmother. More important, he believed that one of the white establishment's primary weapons of oppression was to brand black men as criminals, particularly as rapists of white women. Patterson convinced the CRC executive board that the case raised issues of central concern to the organization, and the board authorized Patterson to offer the CRC's assistance to the men. One day in early June, Patterson accompanied Mrs. Grayson to the Virginia State Penitentiary to meet with DeSales Grayson. Patterson outlined the CRC's legal strategy and convinced Grayson that it would be "a fatal mistake to depend alone upon the justice of the courts—that they had none," and that a mass campaign for popular support would be necessary. Grayson agreed and signed a retainer for the legal services of the CRC.[24]

On June 12 a group of forty men and women, about thirty of whom were black, met at the A. D. Price Funeral Home to form a Richmond branch of the Civil Rights Congress. Among those attending were Communists, labor union members, and representatives of the NAACP. After Josephine Grayson addressed the meeting, William Patterson formally announced that his organization would undertake Grayson's appeal and that he would try to secure the assistance of O. John Rogge, a former United States assistant attorney general who had represented the "Trenton Six," a group of New Jersey blacks convicted of murder.[25] Although only Grayson had signed a retainer, Patterson promised that the appeal would "be so phrased as to be of maximum benefit to the other six defendants." Many of the charges that Patterson leveled at state and local authorities paralleled the fair trial issues raised by the NAACP, including the presence of an all-white jury and the rapid succession of the trials. However, Patterson also drew explicit comparisons to the Scottsboro case and asserted, "I am convinced that Grayson is innocent." The meeting concluded with a pledge to collect fifteen thousand signatures by July 4 demanding a new trial.[26]

The entry of outside groups into the case upset many Martinsville citizens, who steadfastly maintained that the case was strictly a local matter. Irvin Cubine, the commonwealth's attorney who had prosecuted the case, professed to have "no quarrel with the basic principles of the NAACP," but he objected to civil rights attorneys who believed "that there cannot be a fair trial if it involves the prosecution of a member of the Negro race." In his opinion the NAACP's entry into the case would "prove to be a greater handicap than an advantage to the Negro race." Kay Thompson, editor of the *Martinsville Bulletin,* objected to the efforts of the Communists, who were trying to upset "the fine, friendly relations [between the races] that have always existed in our community." Moreover, Thompson believed that the CRC did not genuinely care about the fate of the defendants. By arousing prejudice and distorting the truth, the Communists hoped "for a few more recruits among the ignorant and uninformed, and that . . . is just about the extent of their interest in the welfare of any one of the seven men doomed to die." Both Cubine and Thompson resented the interference of outside groups in an affair which they believed local authorities had already resolved fairly and judiciously.[27]

Although Cubine and Thompson considered the NAACP and the CRC as part of a uniform threat to local values, NAACP leaders wanted nothing more than to distance themselves from William Patterson's organization. On June 13, the day after the CRC entered the case, Martin Martin announced that neither the NAACP nor his law firm would be associated "with any organization which has been declared subversive by the United States Attorney General." He stated that the defendants had agreed "several weeks ago" to allow the NAACP to represent them and that Grayson had not informed him of any change in that arrangement. If the CRC entered the Grayson case, he warned, the NAACP would withdraw from his appeal, reject any cooperation with the CRC, and represent the remaining six men only if the CRC did not enter their cases.[28]

Martin's antipathy toward Patterson's organization stemmed largely from personal experience and belief. For one thing, Martin adhered to a conservative philosophy on the sanctity of property rights, a principle threatened by organizations that espoused a restructuring of the capitalist order. He also had a long association with the NAACP and was committed to its strategies and principles. In the early years of his law career, he had served as president of the NAACP branch in Danville. After moving to Richmond he joined the legal staff of the state NAACP as vice-chairman. This association with the NAACP undoubtedly acquainted him with the history of animosity between the NAACP and radical groups. Finally, Martin had personally experienced the conflict that Communists could generate when they entered a case. In 1941 the Workers' Defense League (WDL), a "militant, politically nonpartisan organization" associated with the Socialist party, asked Martin to collect evidence of jury discrimination in Pittsylvania County. This information would be used to appeal the conviction of Odell Waller, a black sharecropper accused of murdering his white landlord. Waller had been represented at trial by the Revolutionary Workers' League (RWL), a group of Trotskyists dedicated to spreading the principles of revolutionary Marxism, and Martin had observed the manner in which the RWL had disrupted the WDL's efforts on appeal. The ILD had not asserted itself in the Waller case, but the WDL also considered that organization a political rival. Like most Americans, Martin probably did not perceive any practical distinctions between the RWL, the ILD, and the CRC.[29]

On June 14 Martin met with George Elwood, temporary chairman of the Richmond Committee of the CRC, to discuss the CRC's participation. Elwood submitted that "the only important question is to save the seven lives at stake." The CRC did not seek publicity for its own aggrandizement, he explained, but rather "to place defense of these seven men before the bar of public opinion in Virginia and throughout the nation." Martin agreed that "our sole concern . . . is to do everything possible for these men," but because of the CRC's refusal to emphasize legal redress, the NAACP would be "unable to cooperate with them in this matter." Martin did agree, however, to allow the defendants to select their own legal representatives.[30]

Disagreement soon emerged, however, about the meaning of this compromise. William Patterson understood that the meeting had re-sulted in a proposal for a joint defense of the seven men, subject to the approval of the NAACP national office. Martin, on the other hand, maintained that he only agreed to allow the prisoners to select their own attorneys, not to associate with any clients represented by the CRC. In order to resolve this disagreement, Patterson and Emanuel Bloch, another CRC attorney, met with Thurgood Marshall, Marian Wynn Perry, and two other NAACP lawyers in the national office. By that time, however, Grayson had repudiated his retainer with the CRC after his brother met with Mel Fiske in Washington and expressed fears "about what kind of an organization CRC might be." The other men also informed Martin that they would continue to rely on the NAACP to represent them. The CRC learned of this decision sometime during the week of June 19 but waited about two weeks before George Elwood publicly announced that the CRC would withdraw from the case. At the same time, Patterson privately alerted CRC branch leaders to "be ready to move in for the appeal to the United States Supreme Court."[31]

Martin Martin and Thurgood Marshall warned Patterson that if the CRC "developed a mass campaign they would publicly declare that it was detrimental to the struggle for these men's lives." Patterson per-sisted in his belief, however, that "only the movement of the people as a whole guarantees a victory." Other CRC officials shared Patterson's views. George Elwood urged the NAACP to wage "an aggressive cam-paign to mobilize the people of America behind a new trial." Alice Burke, state chairman of the Communist party of Virginia, sent an open letter to J. M. Tinsley, president of the Virginia State Conference of the NAACP, in which she promised the NAACP "the wholehearted support of all freedom-loving people" and urged "all Virginians who believe in real justice" to launch a "militant campaign" to halt the exe-cutions. Thus while the CRC relinquished responsibility for the legal appeals, it continued to participate in publicity campaigns for the seven.[32]

Although the CRC actively fought for control of the Martinsville cases, the resolution of the incident probably served the CRC's inter-ests even better than a joint defense effort by the two organizations. CRC finances frequently ran at a deficit so that it could not always afford the court costs and fees associated with legal proceedings. Allowing the NAACP to undertake the burden of litigation freed the

CRC to devote its resources to garner mass public support for the defendants. The CRC had already generated enough publicity that if the
legal appeals were successful, the CRC could share credit for the victory, yet it could distance itself from any responsibility if the cases were
lost. A failed appeal would also bolster Patterson's arguments that the
legalistic efforts of the NAACP were insufficient to save the men.[33]

To the NAACP the CRC's constant efforts "to horn in on the cases,"
in the words of Lester Banks, represented a lack of concern for the
fates of the condemned men and a desire to discredit moderate civil
rights organizations. William Patterson's misinterpretation of the compromise on DeSales Grayson's defense represented, at least to NAACP
leaders, the typical tactics of the Communists, who offered to form
alliances with liberal organizations on the one hand while publicly
branding them as uncooperative with the other. In the fall of 1949,
when William Patterson sought permission for the CRC to participate
in the National Civil Rights Mobilization, Thurgood Marshall reminded Roy Wilkins that the "conduct of the Civil Rights Congress in
attempting to disrupt the defense of the Martinsville men was dis-
gusting to say the least." Marshall believed that the CRC used offers
of cooperation "for the sole purpose of making untruthful statements
concerning the program and policy of the NAACP" and that Patterson
was "more interested in playing politics than in cooperating" with
the NAACP.[34]

The NAACP also remained extremely skeptical about the CRC's interest in the fates of the condemned men. Ever since their experience
with the ILD during the Scottsboro cases, many black leaders maintained that Communists defended African Americans only in those
cases that served party interests. Marshall echoed these sentiments
when he explained to William Patterson: "We have never been convinced that the Civil Rights Congress is primarily interested in the
protection of the rights of Negroes. We have never been convinced that
their primary interest is in the particular Negroes involved." Therefore,
Marshall concluded, the NAACP would not cooperate in any action
that did "not have as its primary importance the protection of the
rights of the individuals involved."[35]

Marshall's cynical assessment of Patterson's interest in the Martinsville case overstated the extent to which Communist ideology
guided the CRC's conduct of African-American affairs. Radical groups
often continued to lend moral and financial support to prisoners in

southern jails long after the propaganda value of their cases had been exhausted. The CRC maintained a Prisoners' Relief Committee which wrote to inmates regularly and provided financial assistance to their families.[36] In the Martinsville case Patterson claimed that he relinquished the CRC's claim to represent Grayson "in the interests of all seven men" because the NAACP convinced him that the CRC's presence in the courtroom would jeopardize the appeals. Nevertheless, ideological interests clearly guided Patterson and other CRC leaders. The CRC executive board approved the Grayson retainer because the case raised the issues of discrimination and racial violence that the CRC wished to publicize, and CRC press releases linked the Martinsville Seven to similar cases in an effort to reveal the capitalist conspiracy of racial and economic oppression in America. While Patterson and his organization remained sensitive to the problems that their participation could cause for the defendants, they refused to forgo the publicity that a case as sensational as the Martinsville affair could provide.[37]

By the same token, however, NAACP leaders resented the CRC's participation not only because it adversely affected their clients but because it undermined their efforts to link black civil rights to the cold war liberal agenda. Many American political leaders were beginning to pay heed to the nascent civil rights movement as a means to quell Soviet criticisms of segregation and racial violence that compromised the United States' democratic ideology. At the same time, however, southern politicians asserted that Communist agents had inspired growing demands for black equality. Thus the NAACP had to distance itself from any organization considered subversive in order to remain a viable force in American politics. Cold war politics, coupled with the historical animosity between the NAACP and more radical groups, led NAACP leaders to reject out of hand any offer of cooperation from leftist organizations because it threatened their efforts to join the liberal consensus.[38]

The NAACP had many reasons for rejecting an alliance with the Communists, but those reasons were aimed primarily at preserving the reputation and integrity of the national office. Thus it made little sense to fight the battle for control of the cases at the local level. Although Thurgood Marshall and Roy Wilkins met briefly with William Patterson and stayed in contact with the Virginia State Conference, Martin Martin and J. M. Tinsley conducted the bulk of the negotiations. These efforts afforded them no opportunity to begin preparing the appeals or to start raising funds. The delay was especially costly because the state conference had yet to receive any legal or financial assistance from the national office. The policy also confused the leaders of local branches elsewhere, who recognized the common interests of the two organizations and wanted to help nearby CRC chapters publicize the case, but who felt hamstrung by the dictates of national NAACP leaders.[39]

The struggle for control of the Martinsville appeals exacerbated tensions between the NAACP and the Civil Rights Congress that had existed since the CRC's predecessor, the International Labor Defense, began operating in 1925. The divergent manner in which each organization proposed to handle the cases highlighted fundamental disagreements over strategy, ingrained suspicions of motive, and fierce competition for membership. For example, the CRC's insistence on direct action and mass protest clashed directly with the NAACP's belief that only carefully planned litigation could advance the cause of civil rights. The negative characterizations that leaders of the groups attributed to their rivals underscored the extent to which historic distrust between the organizations doomed any efforts at cooperation. The NAACP's strident rejection of William Patterson's overtures also indicated that the CRC had emerged as a viable challenger to the NAACP for leadership of the civil rights movement. The Martinsville case intensified the rivalry between the CRC and the NAACP because it starkly raised issues of concern to both groups, attracted national publicity, and lent itself to no easy solution. As the appeals progressed both organizations continued to pursue the cases in a manner consistent with their respective ideological and institutional interests.

4

Appealing the Judgments

Having resolved the dispute with the Civil Rights Congress, at least temporarily, the NAACP began developing a strategy to challenge the seven death sentences. In earlier cases the NAACP had attacked coercive interrogations of suspects, discriminatory methods of jury selection, and prejudicial trial procedures on the grounds that they violated the due process clause of the Fourteenth Amendment. Most of these cases, however, involved innocent black defendants erroneously convicted of crimes. The apparent guilt of the Martinsville Seven presented a special difficulty before state and federal judges who adhered to traditional views on interracial crime and the importance of social order. Moreover, in the wake of the political and social transformations that followed World War II, the courts were modifying earlier decisions safeguarding individual rights to provide greater protection for public safety and community stability. Nevertheless, attorneys for the NAACP elected to pursue traditional routes for challenging the convictions of the Martinsville Seven before launching a more innovative attack on the southern legal system.

The Virginia State Conference of Branches did not maintain a full-time legal staff, relying instead on the volunteer efforts of attorneys around the state with occasional assistance from the NAACP's national office. The Richmond law firm of Hill, Martin, and Robinson, founded in 1943, comprised the heart of the state legal staff. Oliver W. Hill, the chairman of the state staff, and Spottswood W. Robinson III, special counsel for the NAACP's southeast region, spent most of their time supervising desegregation litigation, while Martin A. Martin, vice-chairman of the legal staff, specialized in criminal matters. All three had attended Howard University School of Law in the 1930s where they studied statistical, historical, and sociological methods of legal argument. During the 1940s the firm worked on most of the major civil rights cases in Virginia. It won several suits in the lower federal courts and scored its first Supreme Court victory in 1946 when the Court struck down a Virginia statute requiring racial segregation on inter-state buses that traveled through Virginia.[1] They received almost no financial compensation for their civil rights work, but they supported it by building a lucrative practice representing banking, insurance, and real estate interests in Richmond's African-American community.[2]

The firm's three partners presented contrasting but complementary personalities. Oliver Hill, a tall, balding, physically imposing man of forty-two, possessed the most political acumen. Hill favored a moderate, gradual approach to achieving racial equality, founded upon legal action and increased political participation for blacks, because, he explained, "standing on a corner whooping and hollering never impressed me." Born in Richmond, Hill grew up in Roanoke before moving with his parents to Washington, D. C., where he attended high school. In 1933 he graduated with honors from Howard law school along with his close friend Thurgood Marshall. He then opened a law office in Roanoke, where he began organizing black teachers to demand salaries equal to whites, but he had difficulty building a practice. His steadiest client, the Norfolk and Western Railroad, assigned him the depressing task of garnishing the wages of local workers, so Hill left Roanoke in search of more enlightening work. He spent the next several years supporting himself as a waiter in Washington, where he attempted to unionize the city's restaurant workers. In 1939 Hill moved to Richmond, where an established African-American business community provided a steady flow of clients. In December 1942 Hill agreed to join a partnership with Martin and Robinson once he returned from military service. After the war, in addition to supervising the NAACP's legal work in Virginia, Hill became one of the state's most prominent black politicians. In 1947 he narrowly missed being nominated for a seat in the state General Assembly in the Democratic primary. He also worked with Lewis F. Powell, Jr., one of Richmond's most prominent white attorneys, on the Richmond city charter revision committee that established at-large elections for the city council. In 1948 voters elected Hill the first black city councilman in Richmond since the turn of the century.[3]

Eight years younger than Hill, slender, bespectacled Spottswood Robinson did not strike as imposing a figure as his partner, but he lent impeccable scholarly credentials to the firm. In 1939 Robinson joined the faculty of Howard law school after graduating with the best academic record in the history of the school. In 1943 he relinquished some of his teaching responsibilities so that he could join the partnership with Hill and Martin, specializing in property and real estate law. In 1948 Thurgood Marshall asked Robinson to organize a litigation program to equalize facilities in elementary and secondary schools. While Hill and Marshall earned their reputations as fiery courtroom orators, the methodical Robinson performed the essential fieldwork of investigating school quality, soliciting willing plaintiffs, and petitioning local school boards for relief. After observing firsthand the stark disparities in quality between black and white schools, Robinson became one of the first NAACP attorneys to advocate a direct attack on the doctrine of "separate but equal."[4]

As the firm's specialist in criminal law, thirty-nine-year-old Martin A. Martin assumed primary responsibility for preparing the Martinsville appeals. Martin "didn't have the polished edge" of his partners, according to Roland Ealey, a friend from Howard law school, but his theatrical demeanor and rambunctious personality made the burly attorney an effective force in the criminal courtroom. After completing law school at Howard University in 1938, Martin established a practice in Danville, where he represented the Danville Savings Bank, the state's oldest black-owned financial institution, and several other prominent business interests. He also became president of the local branch of the NAACP, in which capacity he witnessed the administration of justice to blacks in Southside Virginia. During the early 1940s, in addition to representing black teachers in salary equalization suits, he volunteered his services in several criminal cases. One of these, the case of Odell Waller, a black tenant farmer sentenced to death for murdering his white landlord, attracted national publicity. Before joining Hill and

Robinson in late 1943, Martin worked briefly for the Department of Justice prosecuting aliens. He was the first black attorney to be appointed to the Justice Department's criminal division.[5]

Martin was more conservative than his partners, particularly on the question of property rights. While representing a defendant who had participated in a civil rights sit-in, for example, Martin privately told Oliver Hill that he disapproved of such tactics because he believed the demonstrators had trespassed on private property. He also had reservations about the NAACP's campaign to desegregate public schools, preferring to pursue equalization remedies because he was, Hill recalled, "something of a separatist anyway." Nevertheless, he was committed to the fight against racial discrimination and worked especially hard to desegregate public transportation.[6]

Three other attorneys, all members of the Virginia State Conference legal staff, helped Martin examine the trial records, research the law, and prepare the appellate briefs. His chief deputy was Samuel W. Tucker, a lawyer from Emporia, about sixty-five miles south of Richmond. Growing up in Alexandria, Tucker developed a passion for civil rights and the law at an early age. When he turned twelve he began working in a law office, and at the age of fourteen he organized protests against segregation on buses and electric trains that ran between Alexandria and Washington, D.C. He never went to law school, but while attending Howard University as an undergraduate he met Oliver Hill, a first-year law student, and they later studied for the bar together. Because he enjoyed practicing in Emporia, he declined an invitation to join Hill's firm in 1943, but he continued to work closely with the firm on civil rights cases. Roland Ealey, a close friend of Martin's, had graduated from Howard law school a year behind Martin. He taught briefly at Lincoln University in St. Louis and served in the United States Army before settling permanently in Richmond in 1946 to practice law. At that time Ealey was not as experienced as the other attorneys in civil rights work or criminal litigation, but he enthusiastically labored on every aspect of the appeals process. His dedication even caught the attention of the Civil Rights Congress, which asked him to represent some CRC clients in the Richmond area. Finally, Jerry Williams, from his office in Danville, provided the team with access to necessary documents in the Martinsville circuit court and a practitioner's perspective on the customs and procedures of trial courts in that region of the state.[7]

Before Martin Martin could begin preparing the appeals, he had to request stays of execution from the governor of Virginia, William Mumford Tuck. Tuck was not the only official authorized to issue reprieves, but as the only nonjudicial officer with that power, he had greater discretion to grant the requests in the absence of formal legal arguments. Martin had ordered copies of the trial records in May, but he did not receive them until the end of June. Because he would not have time to review thoroughly the one thousand typed pages of transcripts and present a formal request to a state supreme court justice before July 15, the first scheduled execution date, Martin petitioned Tuck for a ninety-day reprieve to prepare the appeals.[8]

After the NAACP announced its intention to petition for a stay, letters and telegrams from clergymen, union members, Communists, Progressive party members, and other citizens flooded the governor's office. Much of the correspondence appeared to have been influenced by the publicity campaign of the Civil Rights Congress. Some obviously radical groups, such as the Communist Club of Buffalo and the South Side Labor Youth League of Pittsburgh, echoed the Communist party dogma that "the phoney charge of rape has been traditionally used in the attack against the Negro youth by big business interests." Less strident correspondents, however, also emphasized arguments that appeared prominently in CRC and Progressive party literature. For example, a law student from Miami, which had one of the more active CRC chapters in the South, criticized the performance of the court-appointed attorneys, the lack of black jurors, and the "frail story of a hysterical woman." Others complained about the rapid pace of the trials, the failure to grant a change of venue, the use of coerced confessions, and the severity of a punishment which "seemed aimed at suppression of the Negro people rather than at achieving justice." The broad geographic range from which these letters arrived also attested to the interest generated by the case and the effectiveness of the various publicity campaigns.[9]

Another group of letter writers admitted that the men deserved to be punished for their crimes but argued that execution was too severe for an offense which had not resulted in the death of the victim. A Michigan minister wrote, "The death penalty for rape under any circumstances short of brutal murder is altogether too severe." A Progressive party member from Ohio acknowledged that the defendants "should be sentenced to the penitentiary for a few years," but he labeled the death sentences for men who "never committed a murder" an example of "white supremacy" and "American fascism." Most of the writers attributed the harsh sentences to the race of the defendants, while others argued that the victim should bear partial responsibility for the attack because she "was violating a strict southern code in going to a Negro district after dark and without proper escort." One writer surmised that a gang of white men accused of raping a black woman would hardly have been arrested, much less sentenced to death, while another noted that a white Virginia man recently convicted of decapitating his wife received only a twenty-year prison term. Neither of these correspondents could be described as progressive in matters of race relations. One described herself as "no advocate of Civil Rights," while the other recommended permanent separation of the races to prevent violence. However, their comments exhibited a concern among many white southerners that the treatment of black defendants reflected poorly on the ability of southern courts to administer justice equitably.[10]

Finally, Governor Tuck received several letters and telegrams from people who supported the convictions and death sentences. All but one of these letters came from within the state of Virginia, suggesting that the immediate threat to personal safety and racial stability posed by the offenders shaped local attitudes toward the crime. All of the correspondence expressed, in varying degrees, a belief in white supremacy, a fear of violent crime, a concern for the plight of the victim, and indignation at interference by Communists and the NAACP. One man asked Tuck why he would "waste time on these savages" whose brutal actions and "syphilitic infection have certainly ruined the victim physically and mentally." A woman complained that "the National Association of Negroes had better use their funds to teach Negroes to be *human* at least," and she begged the governor not to postpone the executions because it would "only encourage more crimes." A Lynchburg resident complained about outsiders who questioned the administration of justice in Virginia and wondered whether the citizens of Martinsville should be "commended or condemned for not having taken the law in their own hands." He concluded, "If the State of Virginia hasn't funds enough . . . to stamp these seven off the face of the earth, let me know and I'll start a campaign to get you so much money, our Federal debt will seem but a pittance."[11]

Others seemed more concerned with the Communists' interest in the appeals. A Michigan resident mailed Tuck several clippings from the *Daily Worker* and warned him that "you may be swamped with protests . . . from the Communists in America. So don't let them mislead you." A seventy-eight-year-old Virginia farmer who had received some "pernicious literature" from the "communist element of our state" complained that he had never seen anything "to rile me as much as this scathing denunciation of our administration of justice." Tuck responded that he was well aware that "a great part of my mail relating to these trials originates with groups apparently identified with the Communist movement," and he assured his correspondents that he would not be influenced by "persons who do not seem to understand legal processes."[12]

Some supporters of the Martinsville Seven worried that public opinion might lead Governor Tuck to deny the petition for a stay of execution. They feared that the corpulent governor, considered by many Virginians to be a buffoon whose only convictions consisted of a love for liquor, cigars, and country music, would be swayed by the popular sentiment against the condemned men. Furthermore, Tuck's record on race relations exhibited no sympathy with the goals of the NAACP. Having resided for most of his life in South Boston, about sixty miles east of Martinsville, and represented Halifax County for eighteen years in the Virginia legislature, Tuck shared the racial sentiments of most white Southside Virginians. As a loyal member of Virginia's conservative Democratic party machine, led by Senator Harry Flood Byrd, Sr., he supported state sovereignty and states' rights so ardently that followers of the Byrd organization jokingly labeled Tuck the Virginia politician "most likely to secede." Tuck rarely resorted to racial invective, but he publicly supported the poll tax and segregated school systems and opposed federal civil rights legislation. In 1945 African Americans had supported Tuck's opponent, Moss Plunkett, in the gubernatorial primary, and Tuck made little attempt during his political career to court black voters.[13]

Martin Martin, however, expressed confidence that Tuck would stay the executions. Martin knew that governors of Virginia had regularly granted stays of execution shortly after sentencing. A request for clemency or commutation might have political ramifications, but a reprieve was merely a temporary measure to allow prisoners to pursue their constitutional right of appeal. Moreover, during his tenure as governor,

Tuck had instituted several significant reforms in the administration of justice in Virginia. Despite the fiscal conservatism of the Byrd organization, he had increased funding for the state's penal institutions. He abolished the practice of flogging and ended the use of chain gangs in prisoner work camps. He also restored to the governor the pardoning power, which had previously been exercised by a Board of Pardons and Reprieves. These reforms reflected Tuck's desire to bring the legal processes of the state in line with modern expectations of due process. Granting temporary stays to the Martinsville Seven, the governor explained to a concerned citizen, would demonstrate "to the country at large" that the state of Virginia was "willing for every individual to have full recourse to his legal rights" and would "be very helpful in overcoming the impression that the South is guilty of racial hatred."[14]

At the same time Tuck's response to the request for a reprieve illustrates the considerable authority that the executive in Virginia exercised over the course of the state's judicial process, at least at the appellate stage. On July 5, 1949, Governor Tuck met with Martin, Hill, and Robinson to discuss the petition for a stay of execution. The attorneys explained that they had only received copies of the trial record the previous week and asked the governor to postpone the executions for ninety days to allow time to examine all six transcripts thoroughly. Tuck, however, would agree only to grant a more customary thirty-day reprieve. The governor assured the attorneys that he was not rejecting their request outright, but he explained that he would have to consult with his attorney general before extending the stay. "I do not intend," he promised, "to do anything that would embarrass in any way a bona fide effort to use every recourse of the law in these cases." In the meantime he urged the lawyers "to use all due diligence" in preparing the appeals, and Martin promised to work as fast as he could. At the end of the ten-minute meeting, Tuck promised to issue a written order that afternoon.[15]

On August 3 Martin visited the governor's office again to request a thirty-day extension of the stays of execution. Martin explained that NAACP attorneys had been working constantly on the cases but that it would take two to three more weeks to complete work on the appeals. He assured the governor that he would file appeals with the Supreme Court of Appeals before the court began its session on September 5. Convinced that Martin had demonstrated "genuine progress" in developing the appeals, Tuck postponed the executions until September 16 and 23 "to afford ample opportunity for [them] to exhaust [their] legal remedies."[16]

While Martin and his colleagues pursued the appeals, the office of the Virginia State Conference of Branches orchestrated a campaign to raise money for legal costs. During its forty years of existence, the NAACP had developed a system for conducting criminal cases which effectively marshaled its limited resources. While volunteer attorneys concentrated on legal strategy, the state and national offices instituted broad public information programs. Speakers sought support from churches, labor unions, and civic organizations; volunteers distributed leaflets outlining the facts of the cases; and media liaisons maintained close contact with the press. These measures were intended primarily to generate interest in the case that would translate into donations of time or money. However, they also permitted the NAACP to monitor the public presentation of the case so that publicity generated by competing organizations, such as the CRC, could be corrected if necessary.[17]

In accordance with this policy, W. Lester Banks, executive secretary of the Virginia State Conference, appointed a Martinsville Seven Defense Fund Committee to raise funds to finance the cost of appealing the death sentences. The conference had been accepting donations on behalf of the seven since the NAACP agreed to accept the case in May. Once Governor Tuck granted the stays, however, the conference needed to raise a large amount of money in a short period of time. Banks explained to Roy Wilkins, for example, that "well over $1000.00" was needed simply to type the trial records. Therefore, the committee, comprised of the Reverend Robert I. Taylor, the Reverend W. B. Ball, and James P. Spencer, a member of the conference's executive board, agreed to lead an aggressive drive for contributions to "this worthy cause in defense of these men now awaiting their doom in the penitentiary."[18]

The committee decided that the most effective way to secure contributions would be to contact the ministers of every church in the state. James Spencer, the secretary of the committee, explained to each congregation the facts of the case and asserted that "the seven men could not have been given a fair trial in eight days." He emphasized the high cost of legal fees, clerical help, and publicity expenditures, which would "run into thousands of dollars." In order to coordinate the conference's program with any defense fund efforts that had already been initiated by local branches, he promised to credit all contributions received by the state office toward the annual quota set for the NAACP branch in its city or county. Finally, Spencer reminded church members that the stays of execution were not indefinite and urged them to act immediately.[19]

The initial response to the fund drive, according to Banks, created "a small trickle of funds, but nothing like enough to meet our current obligations in the cases." By August 22 the conference had received contributions from forty-seven churches, four local branches of the NAACP, twelve individuals, and the Business and Professional Men's Club of Halifax. The sum of these donations, however, barely surpassed $1,000. The First Baptist Church in Manakin provided the largest congregational contribution, at $36.81, but none of the other churches raised more than $20. Individual contributions tended to be higher, but most of these came from the families of the convicted men. Scott Hampton sent $130, and Bessie Hairston and James Millner gave $100 each. Janet Taylor and Irene Hodge contributed $12 and $35, respectively. The Martinsville branch of the NAACP raised $55.54, more than any other branch that contributed to the defense fund.[20]

In an effort to boost contributions, the Defense Fund Committee designated the week of September 4 as "Martinsville Seven Week," with the goal of raising $5,000 on behalf of the men. The committee selected the week to coincide with the opening of the September term of the Virginia Supreme Court of Appeals, when the NAACP expected the court to consider a petition for appeal. The response, Banks hoped, "would be a bit more immediate and generous" than previous efforts. The committee again focused its efforts on churches, but it also targeted social clubs, civic organizations, fraternal lodges, and similar groups. This time the committee not only solicited donations through the mail but also sent attorneys into local communities to explain the case and invited relatives of the men to make personal appeals. On the last day of the drive, for example, Martin, Banks, and Ida Millner, the mother of Booker T. Millner, attended a mass meeting at the Bank Street Baptist Church in Roanoke while Oliver Hill, Roland Ealey, and Bessie Hairston, the mother of Frank Hairston, spoke at Richmond's Moore Street Baptist Church.[21]

A persistent weakness of the NAACP's branch structure was the failure to coordinate the programs of the national office with the activities of its local units. The frequent lack of communication between New York and the outlying branches created two problems: the appearance of renegade branches that operated contrary to national policy and a lack of attention by the national organization to issues of central importance to the local offices. The first problem never emerged seriously in Virginia. One of the earliest branches of the NAACP had been established in Richmond in 1915, and at the time of the Martinsville case sixty branches existed within the state. By 1955 Virginia would boast more members than any other state. J. M. Tinsley's twenty-year tenure as president of the Virginia State Conference supplied the organization with continuity of leadership. Finally, the close friendship between Thurgood Marshall, Oliver Hill, and Spottswood Robinson provided the Virginia NAACP with personal contacts in the national office that many other branches did not possess.[22]

The preoccupation of the national office with other issues, however, directly affected the Martinsville case. Lester Banks repeatedly demanded greater support for the Martinsville Seven from New York. In his report to Roy Wilkins on the fund-raising campaign, Banks reminded Wilkins that the state conference had "entered the cases largely upon the insistence of the National Office," which had assured Banks that the conference "would receive the full backing of the National Office, financial and otherwise." The Martinsville Seven Defense Fund Committee had nearly exhausted the sources of support within Virginia, Banks explained, and "the time [had] come to call upon the National Office to throw its full weight behind this fight." Therefore, he suggested that Wilkins "take immediate steps in assuming the initiative in launching a nation-wide publicity and fund raising campaign, in behalf of the seven Martinsville men." Banks also asked Henry Lee Moon, the NAACP's director of public relations, to come to Virginia during Martinsville Seven Week "to personally conduct the over-all campaign." Such a move would be "psychologically wise," Banks believed, because it would demonstrate that the Martinsville Seven had the full support of the national organization. Banks also emphasized the importance of acting immediately because "the best time to focus nation-wide attention on the cases [is] before the Supreme Court of Appeals has passed on them." Moon could not participate because of prior obligations, but by the end of the year the national office would spend over $4,000 toward legal costs and publicity expenses. The bulk of the responsibility for raising defense funds, however, remained in the hands of overburdened local branches.[23]

Meanwhile, attorneys for the NAACP combed the trial record looking for procedural errors that would provide the grounds for an appeal. On August 26, 1949, they submitted a petition for a writ of error to the Virginia Supreme Court of Appeals which charged the lower court with four significant violations of due process. The strongest argument concerned the failure of the trial court to grant a change of venue or venire despite the gravity of the offense, the large amount of pretrial publicity devoted to the case, and the small population from which to select an impartial jury. Second, they believed that the trials should have been spaced at longer intervals to avoid creating a cumulative effect of guilt on the later defendants. Third, they challenged the admission of the confessions into evidence because the statements had been obtained before their clients could see counsel or even relatives. Finally, because their main concern was the severity of the sentences rather than the convictions, the attorneys objected to Judge Whittle's questioning of jurors regarding their attitudes toward capital punishment.[24]

On September 5, 1949, Martin Martin, Roland Ealey, Jerry Williams, and Samuel Tucker appeared before the Supreme Court of Appeals on the opening day of its annual term in Staunton, Virginia. Unlike criminal defendants in most states, those in Virginia's courts did not have an automatic right of appeal. This idiosyncracy gave the Supreme Court of Appeals, the state's only appellate court, tremendous discretion over the cases it heard. Before arguing the merits of their case, the attorneys had to convince the court that the issues raised by the trials were worthy of further review. Martin came prepared for oral arguments, but because the docket for the brief session was already crowded, the justices informed him that they would take his petitions under advisement. At the opening of court the following day the court announced that it would grant writs of error in each of the cases. Only two days remained in the Staunton term, however, so the court postponed oral arguments until its regular session began in Richmond. The executions, the justices noted, would be "automatically stayed" until the final disposition of the appeals. A month later Martin learned that the cases would be heard at the beginning of the new year.[25]

On January 9, 1950, Martin, Tucker, Ealey, and Williams presented oral arguments before the Supreme Court of Appeals. Ealey began with a brief review of the facts of the case and summarized the allegations of error by the trial court: failure to grant a change of venue, questioning prospective witnesses on their attitudes toward the death penalty, admitting the confessions into evidence, and holding trial on "practically successive days." The lawyers would argue all of the cases together, Ealey explained, although not every point pertained to each case. For instance, the argument concerning the spacing of the trials did not relate to Joe Henry Hampton's prosecution because he had been the first defendant to be tried. To ascertain which arguments applied to a specific case, Ealey referred the court to the separate briefs submitted on behalf of each petitioner.[26]

Next the attorneys addressed the substantive points of their argument. Tucker began by challenging the trial court's refusal to grant a change of venue or venire. In order to meet the legal standard for a change of venue, he argued, the defendants did not have to prove that a fair trial was impossible in Martinsville, only that conditions created "a reasonable apprehension" that an impartial proceeding would be unlikely.[27] The pretrial publicity in the press and the testimony at the venue hearing far exceeded this standard. Articles published in the local newspaper "were calculated to crystallize public sentiment that each of the accused should forfeit his life." Chief Justice Edward Hudgins pressed Tucker on the implications of this argument for the First Amendment, but Tucker insisted that freedom of the press "does not give newspapers the right to pre-try a case." Press coverage in this instance did not emanate from independent investigation by reporters but simply parroted information supplied by officials of the local community who wanted "to pre-try these cases in the newspaper and before the public and to secure a verdict of guilty and the sentence of death."[28]

An examination of the testimony on the motion for a change of venue, Tucker continued, indicated "beyond a doubt that these newspaper articles had been widely read and thoroughly discussed and that there were few, if any, within the entire city who entertained doubt as to the guilt of the accused." Of the twenty-five witnesses who testified on the motion, seventeen of them stated that discussions of the case revealed "strong popular opinion that all were guilty," and three others had heard discussions that reflected a "general opinion of guilt." Most of them also indicated a "popular feeling . . . that the accused should be electrocuted." This testimony demonstrated that "there was practically universal feeling in the community that the accused were guilty and a fairly general feeling that they should be put to death." Tucker conceded that only nineteen prospective jurors were excluded for having already formed an opinion, but that merely indicated that most of the jurors did not have "sufficient regard for their oath to admit that their emotions and mental reactions were those of the normal citizens." In Frank Hairston's trial, for instance, one juror was excluded only because Hairston's attorney happened to overhear the juror discussing the case.[29]

In addition to hostility against the individual defendants because of their crime, the seven men also faced racial prejudice from the jurors. It had long been "the general usage, feeling and sentiment," he argued, that death was the only appropriate punishment for a black man charged with raping a white woman. Newspaper accounts of "the pitiful condition of the victim of the alleged attack," fed to reporters by unscrupulous prosecutors, were designed to "arouse a sense of indignation and resentment on the part of all citizens, particularly the male whites from which the juries were to be drawn." Given that the authorities had taken steps to prevent mob violence, it was not unthinkable that some men, "inspired by a distorted sense of social duty and loyalty to public sentiment . . ., might find it convenient to disavow their feelings to be placed in the best position to assure that the lives of none of the defendants would be spared." Such prejudice could only have been overcome, he contended, by either moving the location of the trial or selecting a jury from outside the region.[30]

The attorneys next argued that the lower court erred by holding trials on "practically successive days." Normally, they conceded, a speedy trial benefited the accused. In this case, however, when six trials were held over the course of eight working days, "mounting public approval of previous verdicts made it increasingly difficult for [subsequent juries] to dissent." The precise point at which this occurred could not be determined, although they believed that the response to "public clamor" influenced even the first trial. Certainly as prospective jurors in the later cases learned of the guilty verdicts and death sentences in the earlier ones, they "came under the increasing influence to go along with the previous juries" until "at some point it became apparent to all talesmen yet to serve that they could not render a verdict [more] lenient than the previous verdicts and keep face in the community."

The proximity "in time and distance" between the proceedings created a cumulative presumption of guilt which differed little from convictions obtained by hurrying defendants to trial under pressure from a mob. In short, the Martinsville court had denied the defendants due process with practices that "railroaded [the defendants] to the electric chair in assembly line procedure."[31]

Counsel for the appellants also questioned the admissibility of the confessions. The evidence that the seven defendants had been coerced or subjected to the third degree was tenuous because they signed written statements so quickly. However, recent United States Supreme Court decisions permitted appellate courts to review the voluntariness of a confession as a question of law.[32] The attorneys argued that the confessions in these cases should have been ruled inadmissible because at the time of their arrest the defendants were so intoxicated they could not even recall the incident. Police investigators took advantage of this condition when they took the men into custody and repeatedly questioned them "either while under the effects or after-effects of this drinking, while without the aid, assistance or advice of any relatives or counsel." These circumstances rendered the confessions inadmissible because the alcohol, coupled with the defendants' youth and their seclusion from friends, relatives, and legal counsel, impaired their ability to make a confession voluntarily.[33]

The most novel charge by the appellants, and ultimately the most significant, concerned Judge Whittle's questioning of prospective jurors regarding their attitudes toward the death penalty. Part of their argument revolved around the intent of the legislature in passing an 1847 statute which prohibited a person "whose opinions are such as to prevent his convicting anyone of an offense punishable with death" from serving as juror in a capital case.[34] This statute, the attorneys argued, applied only to mandatory capital offenses, such as treason, where an aversion to the death penalty might lead a juror to vote for acquittal. Since the passage of that law, the legislature had given juries the discretion to impose or withhold the death penalty in cases of rape, burglary, robbery, and first-degree murder. Accordingly, a juror might have conscientious scruples against capital punishment and still be willing to convict a defendant of a particular crime. Given the "mounting popular opposition to capital punishment," the attorneys concluded, the state "should not require juries for serious felony offenses to be selected only from an element of the population whose callousness might increase as its numbers decrease."[35]

The crux of the appellants' argument, however, did not turn on the intent of the legislation but rather on the custom of Virginia juries to consider the race of defendants during sentencing. The trial judge had questioned prospective jurors about the death penalty, Martin asserted, in order to prejudice the jurors toward a specific penalty for the accused because they were black. Prior to the Civil War, the death penalty for rape had been reserved exclusively for black men who raped white women. In 1866 the legislature eliminated the formal racial distinction, but it continued to be "the policy, practice, custom, and usage of juries in Virginia . . . to sentence Negroes charged with such crime to death, while seldom if ever has a white person, convicted of a similar crime, been given such a sentence." Therefore, the death sentences in the Martinsville cases had not been motivated by the strength of the evidence but rather by the customary treatment of black rapists. The summary discharge of any prospective juror who objected to imposing the death penalty further supported the notion that only one penalty would be appropriate for the offenders. Such questioning by the prosecutor might have been permissible, but when the trial judge, of his own accord, asked the jurors whether they had conscientious scruples against capital punishment, he gave an informal custom of local juries the official imprimatur of the state. The actions of the court, the attorneys concluded, were "well calculated to mislead other members of each jury that the Judge concurred with the prevailing sentiment that all found guilty should be put to death."[36]

J. Lindsay Almond, Virginia's attorney general, responded for the commonwealth with his assistant, Henry T. Wickham. Almond was an accomplished orator and a skilled attorney with over twenty years of experience in the criminal law as a defense lawyer, prosecutor, and judge in Roanoke. Since becoming attorney general in 1948, Almond had shrewdly guided Virginia on a middle course in the field of desegregation, satisfying the letter of recent federal court mandates while preserving the spirit of the state's racial caste system. Attorneys who stood opposite Almond in the courtroom, including Thurgood Marshall, readily acknowledged his legal talent. The stocky, white-haired barrister was a politician, nonetheless, who had exchanged a seat in Congress for the attorney general's position with an eye to one day occupying the governor's office. Almond ordinarily relied on his assistants to argue before the Supreme Court of Appeals, but in cases of political significance, such as the desegregation cases, Almond would speak for the people himself. Oliver Hill later speculated that Almond argued the Martinsville appeals because the notoriety of the case provided an ideal forum for publicizing his views on crime and race relations. Whatever his motives, Almond's vigorous support of the trial court during oral arguments reinforced his reputation as an advocate of the racial status quo and a guardian of law and order.[37]

Almond's arguments challenged the legal standards for reversal set forth by the appellants and emphasized the impeccable conduct of Judge Whittle and the court-appointed attorneys. Regarding the change of venue, Almond asserted a presumption against moving a trial unless the defendant affirmatively proved "that a fair trial could not be obtained." The trial record in these cases, he argued, could not support that contention. Only one witness who testified on the motion for a change of venue "stated unequivocally . . . that the defendant could not get a fair and impartial trial." The newspaper accounts of the crime "were written with restraint" and "were not inflammatory." The *Martinsville Bulletin* never mentioned the word *rape* in its stories and did not publish the name of the victim until nine days after the assault. The Supreme Court of Appeals already had refused to require changes of venue, Almond reminded the justices, in cases that featured newspaper reports much less temperate than those published in the *Bulletin.* Hence, the appellants could not demonstrate that an overwhelming prejudice against the defendants warranted moving the location of the trials.[38]

Almond also denied that the court erred in admitting the confessions into evidence. The credibility of an alleged confession, he maintained, was a question of fact which the jury had to weigh in conjunction with other evidence. He admitted that an appellate court could invalidate even a reliable confession if it had been obtained illegally, but in this instance nothing indicated "that the questioning of these defendants was of long duration and under duress, threat or promise of reward" or that the suspects "were kept *incommunicado* for a period of time." None of the defendants had denied signing the statements voluntarily, and only Joe Henry Hampton claimed that he did not know what he was signing. Furthermore, he reasoned, the defendants' court-appointed attorneys "would never have consented" to any actions of the trial court that might have jeopardized their clients' rights, yet none of the "able and experienced counsel" had voiced any objection to the confessions.[39]

Almond's responses to the remaining assignments of error were less persuasive. With regard to the complaint that the verdicts rendered in the initial trials unduly influenced subsequent jurors, he argued that all of the jurors stated under oath "that the result of the previous trials would not influence their verdict or sentence in the instant case and that they could absolutely give the defendant a fair and impartial trial." Although some of the jurors expressed agreement with the earlier verdicts, they were capable of impartiality because in each case "the defendants' defense is different and all of the witnesses are not the same." Almond addressed the issue only in terms of disqualifying jurors and did not comment on whether prejudice toward the defendants could have been reduced by holding the trials at longer intervals. On Judge Whittle's disqualification of jurors who had conscientious scruples against imposing the death penalty, the attorney general simply asserted that the plain meaning of the statute authorized Whittle to engage in such an inquiry and that the defendants had been treated no differently than any other person charged with a capital crime.[40]

In concluding his arguments Almond asked the court to uphold the convictions and death sentences of the Martinsville Seven. The trial records indicated that each defendant had received a fair trial free from prejudice and judicial error. He reminded the court that the defendants had committed a "serious and hideous" offense in which the victim placed "the finger of guilt on each and every one of the defendants." Each jury, he concluded, had been "fully justified in returning the maximum penalty provided under the statute."[41]

On March 13, the opening day of the following term of the Supreme Court of Appeals, the court announced its decision. The seven men who sat behind the expansive bench at the front of the courtroom— Chief Justice Edward W. Hudgins, Herbert B. Gregory, John W. Eggleston, C. Vernon Spratley, Archibald C. Buchanan, Abram Penn Staples, and Willis D. Miller—epitomized the traditionalism and conservatism that had characterized the Virginia judiciary since the founding of the nation. The average age of the jurists was about sixty-three years old; only Miller was younger than sixty. Four of the justices hailed from rural areas in or near Southside Virginia. Staples was a native of Martinsville, although he grew up in nearby Roanoke. Staples, Eggleston, and Hudgins had served in the General Assembly, and the rest of the justices had ties to either the Byrd machine or their local Democratic party organizations. Miller and Spratley had held office as commonwealth's attorney, one of the traditional means of political advancement within the Byrd organization, and Staples had served as attorney general for thirteen years before joining the court. All of the justices were well-respected scholars of the law, and only Staples and Eggleston had lacked prior judicial experience. Philosophically the court ranged from the "ultraconservatism" of Miller to the more progressive ideals of Gregory, who believed that the law could act as a vehicle for social change. They all shared a belief in the sanctity of property rights, a concern for law and order, a paternalistic attitude toward blacks, and a commitment to judicial restraint.[42]

Chief Justice Hudgins initiated the proceedings, delivering the judgments in the cases for which he had written the opinions. Hudgins had been selected by lot to write the opinion in the Martinsville case, and he opened by announcing the court's unanimous decision to affirm the convictions. Hudgins read only the holding of the case, not the full opinion, then deferred to his colleagues as they announced the results in the cases for which they were responsible. As soon as Justice Miller, the junior member of the court, finished reading his judgments, a number of reporters hurried to the fourth floor of the Supreme Court building, where court employees were distributing the full text of the decisions, to discover the reasoning behind the court's unanimous decision in the Martinsville case.[43]

Chief Justice Hudgins was recognized more as an administrative innovator who had modernized the procedures of the court than as a creative jurist, and his opinion in *Hampton v. Commonwealth* exhibited his lack of judicial craftsmanship. He relied heavily on the arguments of the attorney general, quoting extensively from the trial records and the commonwealth's brief. He cited numerous cases in a conclusory fashion, rarely attempting to justify the application of precedent cases to the Martinsville proceedings. Nevertheless, the opinion clearly emphasized that the court would allow local judges and juries broad discretion to deal with violent criminal behavior.[44]

In accordance with the tradition of the court, Hudgins briefly summarized the facts of the case, then addressed the issues raised by the appellants point by point. The trial court was "in a better position to pass on the question" of a change of venue because of its familiarity with local circumstances, Hudgins stated, and the Court of Appeals would not reverse the ruling unless the appellants demonstrated a clear "abuse of discretion." No change of venue had been warranted in these cases because the "fairly accurate accounts" of the press had been published "in as mild and temperate language as could be expected from the nature of the crimes." In ruling on the confessions, the court expressed support for strong law enforcement. "It is the duty of police officers," Hudgins wrote, "to obtain all available information . . . to assist them in ascertaining the criminal agent." This included questioning persons suspected of committing the crime. "Cruel, unjust, or coercive methods" of interrogation would not be tolerated, but the experience of the defendants, Hudgins concluded without explanation, did not fall within that prohibition. As for Judge Whittle's questioning of the jurors, Hudgins conceded that the "defendants' argument perhaps would be appropriate if made to the legislature, but it is not appropriate in a judicial forum."[45]

The court also found no evidence that the rapid succession of the trials had impaired the jurors' abilities to render impartial verdicts. Hudgins reached this conclusion on the evidence that the last defendants to be tried, James Hairston and John Taylor, based their defense on the consent of the accuser, while the first defendant, Joe Henry Hampton, had blamed intoxication for his part in the assault. Hudgins ignored evidence, however, that both of these arguments had been invoked in the other trials. Hudgins also noted that "some of the witnesses who were summoned and testified did not testify in the other cases." Yet Ruby Floyd, Sergeant Barnes, and Dr. Ravenel, the witnesses who provided the most damaging testimony, had appeared at each trial. Finally, Hudgins placed great faith in the jurors' abilities to recognize and admit their own biases. All of the jurors, he remarked, after being thoroughly examined by both sides, stated under oath "that they had no prejudice for or against the defendants, and that they would go into the jury box and give them a fair and impartial trial."[46]

Hudgins struck particularly harshly at the charge that racial prejudice had influenced the jury to sentence the defendants to death. The court could not find "a scintilla of evidence" to support the allegation that Virginia juries reserved the death penalty for blacks. Hudgins cited with approval Judge Whittle's pretrial statement to the attorneys that warned of the problems presented by the interracial character of the crime. The jury had rendered the harsh sentences only because of the brutality of the crime and the overwhelming evidence against the defendants. "One can hardly conceive of a more atrocious, a more beastly crime," Hudgins wrote. "Each defendant's participation in the criminal acts charged was established beyond the shadow of a doubt." This argument by the attorneys, he concluded, was "an abortive attempt to inject into the proceedings racial prejudice, which the trial court was extremely careful to avoid."[47]

Immediately following the court's announcement, Martin intimated that his next step would probably be an appeal to the United States Supreme Court but that he wanted to explore other options. On March 23 he met with his colleagues to plan their next action. Although they had not been surprised by the decision of the court, they believed they had raised some legitimate issues, particularly regarding the change of venue, that merited further consideration. Three avenues appeared open. First, they could seek a rehearing in the Supreme Court of Appeals. Martin ruled out this course of action because the decision of the court had been unanimous. Second, they could ask the governor to commute the sentences to life imprisonment. The attorneys shied away from this route, however, because it involved political variables over which they had no control. The governor would be subject to the climate of public opinion, and, Roland Ealey later recalled, "the wind certainly wasn't blowing in our favor in a case like this." They also suspected that the governor would be influenced by the unanimity of the court. On April 4 Martin expressed his preference for legalistic action at a conference of the NAACP's national legal staff in Washington. The committee elected to apply to the United States Supreme Court for a writ of certiorari.[48]

On April 12 Judge Whittle set the new execution dates for May 26 and June 2. Because the Supreme Court was not scheduled to meet again until May 29, Martin asked the new governor of Virginia, John S. Battle, to stay the executions until after the Court could hear the petition. Battle waited until Martin filed the petitions for review with the Court on May 19. Three days later, after consulting with Attorney General Almond, Battle ordered reprieves of sixty days. Some constituents accused Battle of granting the stays to cultivate the black vote, a charge which he found "unmerited and ... very near to being insulting." He had only issued the reprieves, he explained, because Almond needed additional time to prepare the commonwealth's response opposing the new petitions.[49]

In addition to planning the new appeals, Martin had to contend with a resurgence of radical interest in the case. With a few scattered exceptions, the Civil Rights Congress had adhered to its promise not to undermine the NAACP's legal efforts with an independent publicity campaign.[50] After the decision of the Supreme Court of Appeals, however, the organization could no longer maintain its silence. The day after the court's announcement, William Patterson declared that "the Negro people of America" could not afford to "sit by any longer, while NAACP counsel risk the lives of seven men on their false theory that reliance can be placed on a Supreme Court which includes Poll-Tax Tom Clark," referring to the conservative Texan who had joined the Court in 1949. The only way to save the Martinsville Seven from the electric chair, he exhorted, was to engage in "mass meetings, open air demonstrations before court-houses, and protest campaigns to governors, judges, and all concerned."[51]

Accordingly, the Richmond branch of the CRC organized a Citizens' Committee to Save the Martinsville Seven to coordinate a protest and publicity campaign. At a March 23 meeting at the Leigh Street A.M.E. Church in Richmond, the committee mobilized participants to "take the Martinsville Seven case to the United States Supreme Court" and to demand a rehearing in the state court from Chief Justice Hudgins. It also appealed to local churches to "pray for justice for the Martinsville Seven . . . every Sunday until the men have been saved from the electric chair." At the same time the Progressive party of Virginia at its annual convention criticized the NAACP for the slow progress of the case. The Civil Rights Congress also began applying pressure on federal officials. On May 19 six representatives of the citizens' committee delivered a petition signed by 3,000 Virginians to Charles E. Cropley, the clerk of the Supreme Court, that asked the Court to grant certiorari in the Martinsville cases. They also presented a similar petition to the Department of Justice asking Attorney General Howard McGrath to intervene as a friend of the court to argue for a new trial and request a reduction in the sentences. Neither McGrath nor Cropley would comment on the petitions. In Richmond, Martin Martin "made it crystal clear" that he wanted no interference from radical organizations, and he tried to dissuade concerned citizens from joining the protest efforts.[52]

On June 3 the United States Supreme Court met to consider the petition for certiorari. Like the Virginia Supreme Court of Appeals, the

Supreme Court possessed broad discretion over which cases would appear on its final docket. Most of the cases reviewed by the Court each year arrive via petitions for writs of certiorari, documents that attempt to convince the Court that there are "special and important reasons" why it should hear the case. Because of the Court's role as a policy-making body, justice to the individual litigant is a less important factor in selection than the presence of issues of broad constitutional significance. If four members of the Court vote in conference to hear the case, the Court grants certiorari and schedules the case for oral argument. Very few petitions survive this screening process. In the 1949–50 term, when the Martinsville Seven sought review, the Court granted certiorari in only 94 out of 1,033 petitions.[53]

The petition submitted by Martin argued only that the trial court erred in failing to grant a change of venue. The "undue attention from the public press," Martin asserted, created an "atmosphere of prejudice and hostility" against the accused which demanded the movement of the trials. The petition did not mention the confessions or the screening of the jury because the petitioners wanted to focus the Court's attention on what they considered their strongest argument. Martin noted, however, that the interracial character of the crime was "not without significance. Such circumstances tend to arouse the most violent emotional reactions."[54]

On June 5 the Court announced that it would not review the Martinsville case. Judicial conferences are held in secret, and the Court does not publish its reasons for denying certiorari. However, a memorandum circulated to all the justices may shed some light on the Court's reasoning. The memorandum was prepared by one of the law clerks for the justices to distill the main arguments of Martin's brief. It noted that Martin had not challenged the conduct of the defense attorneys or the trial judge as unfair, only the atmosphere of the community. "While there is indication that popular sentiment [against the defendants] was crystallizing as the trials progressed," the writer explained, "petitioners fall somewhat short of demonstrating that a fair trial, under minimum 14th Amendment standards, was impossible." Because "it seems clear that any jury would have found petitioners guilty," the memorandum concluded that the failure to grant a change of venue did not violate the constitutional rights of the defendants.[55]

To many white Virginians the Supreme Court's action vindicated the commonwealth's judicial process. "From the moment of their arrest," the Danville *Register* boasted, "the seven condemned Negro rapists of Martinsville have been given the full protection of rights every human is guaranteed under the Constitutions of Virginia and of the United States." The citizens of the state welcomed the Supreme Court review because no one wanted "Virginia's reputation for justice to all its people to be . . . placed under a cloud." The Supreme Court had spoken, and although the justices had provided no reasons for their action, the meaning of the case was "quite clear." All seven men had "enjoyed their full rights," and the state was free to administer their just fate: "death in expiation of their crime against society." The purpose of judicial review, therefore, was to ratify the state's methods of preserving public order, not, as their attorneys suggested, to invalidate the social and racial assumptions that contributed to the operation of Virginia's legal system.[56]

The appellate courts that reviewed the Martinsville cases possessed a similar view of the role of the judiciary. Throughout its history the Virginia Supreme Court of Appeals had adhered to a philosophy of judicial restraint characterized by traditional methods of legal analysis, adherence to precedent, and deference to the legislature.[57] This jurisprudential approach, coupled with the court's discretionary power over its docket, enabled the justices to support the prevailing social order, particularly with regard to racial issues. In the first half of the twentieth century, the court handed down only one decision generally favorable to blacks, invalidating educational and understanding tests for voters.[58] The court's treatment of blacks accused of crimes was even more striking. For example, between 1900 and 1949 the court upheld the death sentences of seven men convicted of rape or attempted rape, reversed the death penalty in one case, and denied petitions for writs of error in five other cases involving capital punishment for rape. All of the cases involved African-American defendants. Nearly 83 percent of the forty-six black men executed for rape during that period did not appeal their convictions, indicating that black defendants had difficulty even gaining access to the appellate courts. In each case that reached the court, the justices refused to acknowledge the presence of discrimination or unfair procedure even though the evidence was strong enough that four of the defendants later had their sentences commuted to life imprisonment by the governor. As Roland Ealey later explained, the justices "knew the wishes and desires of the community and . . . the policies of the state, so they performed them."[59]

Because of the limitations of the state judiciary, the attorneys for the NAACP turned to the federal courts for relief. Martin, Hill, and the other lawyers believed that the United States Supreme Court at least would grant certiorari in the case because under Chief Justice Fred M. Vinson the Court had evidenced some sensitivity to the rights of African Americans in cases involving restrictive covenants and the segregation of graduate and professional schools. During the 1940s the Court had also issued several favorable decisions in the area of criminal procedure.[60] However, following the deaths in 1949 of justices Frank Murphy and Wiley Rutledge, two of the Court's more liberal members, the Court began to deliver opinions that placed social stability over individual rights. In criminal proceedings particularly the Court rarely intervened unless evidence clearly suggested that the defendants might "have been unjustly convicted rather than unfairly tried." It had returned most of the discretion in matters of jury selection to state and local agencies. In cases involving coerced confessions, the justices tended to overlook all but the most egregious abuses, perceiving the widespread incidence of crime to be a greater threat than strong-arm police tactics. The Court's refusal to hear the Martinsville appeal was consonant with its policy during a period of rapid social and political change of avoiding cases that involved problematic constitutional issues.[61]

The appeals of the Martinsville Seven failed because the prevailing attitude at all levels of the state and federal judiciary at midcentury emphasized the preservation of social order over the values of due process. From the beginning of his involvement with the case, Martin never claimed that his clients were wrongfully convicted, only that the hostility and prejudice against the defendants produced excessively harsh sentences. In dealing with tradition-bound courts that were steadfastly avoiding controversy and consciously promoting public safety over individual rights, however, this approach did not promise easy success because the ability to punish criminals swiftly went to the heart of preserving local order. As a result Martin began to consider a direct challenge to the constitutionality of the death penalty as the only means to save the seven young black men from imminent death.

The Martinsville Seven in the Henry County jail shortly after their arrest. *Left to right:* Booker T. Millner, Frank Hairston, Jr., Howard Lee Hairston, Joe Henry Hampton, John Clabon Taylor, Francis DeSales Grayson, and James Luther Hairston. (Reprinted, by permission, from *Martinsville Bulletin*, Sept. 6, 1949)

Martin A. Martin, *center,* principal attorney for the Martinsville Seven on appeal, discusses the case with journalists Oscar Haynes and Alice Dunigan, shortly after seeking clemency for the seven from Governor John S. Battle in July 1950. (Copyright, Afro-American Newspapers Archives and Research Center, Inc., 1991. Reprinted with permission)

On January 31, 1951, after Judge Sterling Hutcheson denied a writ of habeas corpus for the Martinsville Seven, nearly 500 delegates in the "Crusade to Richmond" sponsored by the Civil Rights Congress met in an integrated meeting at the Leigh Street Methodist Church in Richmond. (Copyright, Afro-American Newspapers Archives and Research Center, Inc., 1991. Reprinted with permission)

For three days before the executions, members of the New York Council of Arts, Sciences, and Professions braved sleet and freezing temperatures to picket the White House in an around-the-clock "death watch." (Copyright, Afro-American Newspapers Archives and Research Center, Inc., 1991. Reprinted with permission)

From the evening of January 31, 1951, until the last executions on February 5, demonstrators took turns praying for the Martinsville Seven on the lawn of Capitol Square in Richmond. Participating in the first shift were, *left to right*, Constance Mortfort of Greenville, S.C.; the Reverend L. Cicero Weddington of Gary, Ind.; Aubrey Grossman, organizational secretary of the Civil Rights Congress; and Senora B. Lawson of Richmond. (Reprinted by permission of Richmond Newspapers, Inc.)

Demonstrators gather in Richmond's Capitol Square following the first executions on February 2, 1951. (Reprinted by permission of Richmond Newspapers, Inc.)

To many radicals and civil rights activists, the Martinsville Seven case symbolized the treatment of African Americans by southern courts. (Reprinted from *Daily Worker*, Feb. 1, 1951)

5

"A More Novel,

Innovative Strategy"

Challenging the

Death Penalty

During the first round of appeals, the NAACP attorneys relied on traditional due process arguments rather than broad attacks on the prevailing legal order. Even when challenging the disproportionate sentencing of African Americans, Martin A. Martin narrowly framed the issue in terms of the trial judge's authority to question prospective jurors about their views on capital punishment. The failure of these arguments, however, spurred Martin to abandon narrow procedural challenges in favor of a frontal attack on the discriminatory application of the death penalty. As a result, the attorneys introduced historical, sociological, and statistical evidence to prove systematic discrimination against blacks in capital cases. In fact, this was the earliest instance in which lawyers marshaled statistical evidence to prove systematic discrimination against African Americans in capital cases, rather than focusing on procedural errors within a particular case.

Because this new strategy directly challenged the operation of the criminal justice system in Virginia, it also attracted the attention of the Civil Rights Congress. Around the middle of 1950, several cases in which the CRC and the NAACP maintained an interest had reached a head. Attorneys from the NAACP were busy preparing to appeal to the United States Supreme Court the convictions of three black citrus workers accused of raping a teen-aged housewife in Groveland, Florida, while NAACP lawyers in Georgia worked to gain the parole of Rosa Lee Ingram, a black mother of twelve children convicted of murdering a white sharecropper. Meanwhile, in Mississippi CRC attorneys labored to save Willie McGee, a black truck driver convicted of raping a white woman, from dying in the electric chair a day before the Martinsville Seven were scheduled to be executed. The obvious parallels between these cases, coupled with the NAACP's identification of a historical pattern of discrimination in capital sentencing, led the CRC to renew its efforts to join forces with the NAACP.[1]

On June 7, 1950, two days after the United States Supreme Court denied certiorari in the Martinsville Seven case, William Patterson wrote to Roy Wilkins, administrator of the NAACP, to request that NAACP and CRC leaders meet "to discuss the steps that are necessary to mobilize the progressive sentiment of America in opposition to this dastardly conspiracy to railroad these men to their death." Patterson's letter asserted the innocence of the seven and emphasized the futility of legal action, the efficacy of mass public protest, and the necessity of linking the Martinsville case to similar cases in other states. The actions of the Supreme Court, Patterson asserted, demonstrated the futility of relying on legal redress because "the nine powerful men on that bench are following the example of Pontius Pilate." He reminded Wilkins that "the legal lynchers are united," as evidenced by the pattern of injustice in the death sentences against "the innocent Negro youth in Groveland, Florida" and "the travesty of justice that is the case of Willie McGee." The way to counteract their power was a joint effort on the part of civil rights organizations because "concerted mass action alone can reverse that decision of death and win life for these men." By joining forces the NAACP and CRC could "raise such a tempest against this hellish Dixiecrat justice as can force open the cells of the death house and restore life to these men."[2]

In Wilkins's absence Thurgood Marshall responded to Patterson's request for joint action. Citing "several deliberate misstatements of fact" in the letter, Marshall defended the NAACP's reliance on the courts and reiterated the traditional objections of the NAACP to Communist involvement in its affairs, particularly the belief that party interests, not the lives of the individual men, were the principal concerns of the CRC. He deplored Patterson's criticism of the Supreme Court and commented that "if all lawyers would spend more time on preparing their cases than in finding characterizations for the courts, we would make more progress." The Martinsville appeals, the Groveland cases, "and any other cases under the jurisdiction of" the NAACP would be "carried forward in a lawfullike manner within the lawful machinery of our government." In short, Marshall concluded, "we have never been convinced that the Civil Rights Congress is primarily interested in the protection of the rights of Negroes. . . . We therefore have no intention whatsoever of permitting you to interfere in any of these cases."[3]

Patterson complained to Anne Shore, executive secretary of the Detroit CRC, that Marshall's response to his call for unity was "as rotten a statement as I have ever seen in all my life." In a lengthy letter to Marshall, copies of which were distributed to the press, Patterson accused Marshall of missing the point that the Martinsville case was "symptomatic of the oppression of Negro Americans throughout our great land." "This act of terror—this crime of government," he argued, "is not inconsistent with the American way of life as it is reflected in the relations of the officials of federal, state, and city governments to the Negro people." The "hush-hush policy" of the NAACP had failed to save the men because it neglected to harness "the overwhelming strength which derives from the support of the people." A direct appeal to the citizens of the country was "not only lawful, but [had] been regarded as such by presidents and leading men in government," including Thomas Jefferson, Andrew Jackson, Abraham Lincoln, and Franklin Roosevelt. "This is no time for petty bickering or name-calling," Patterson concluded. "Whatever our differences may be on other questions, surely we can work together to save the Martinsville Seven. Surely the men whose lives are at stake would want to see us united to save them."[4]

Despite the eloquence of Patterson's plea, Marshall and Wilkins had to wonder about his sincerity because at the same time that the CRC sought cooperation, it publicly criticized the NAACP for refusing to participate in a joint campaign. This tactic was designed to inform citizens concerned with civil rights about the opposing positions of the organizations so that they would pressure the NAACP to reverse its position. For example, a CRC member from New York City, alarmed by the sentences of the Martinsville Seven and Willie McGee, wrote to Marshall, "The issue at stake . . . is not Communism but the lives of eight innocent negroes, who have been framed by the lynchcrats of the South with the collusion of this administration." Criticisms such as these, however, reinforced the belief of NAACP leaders that the CRC simply was using the case to impugn the NAACP and its efforts publicly. As a result, they steadfastly opposed any effort to involve the CRC in the Martinsville affair.[5]

Meanwhile, Martin A. Martin and his colleagues began drafting a legal brief arguing that Virginia juries had engaged in discriminatory sentencing practices. During the 1940s several researchers had undertaken systematic studies of racial disparities in capital sentencing. Guy Johnson, an ethnographer at the University of North Carolina's Institute for Research in Social Sciences, concluded in a study of homicide sentencing in Virginia, North Carolina, and Georgia that blacks convicted of the murder of whites were more likely to be sentenced to death and to have that sentence carried out than blacks who killed other blacks or whites who murdered members of either race. Harold Garfinkel, a criminologist at the institute, confirmed Johnson's findings in his own study of North Carolina murder prosecutions. The Southern Conference Educational Fund (SCEF), a social welfare organization based in New Orleans, used data from the United States Census Bureau to determine that 93 percent of the men executed for rape in thirteen southern states between 1938 and 1948 were black.[6]

The lawyers for the Martinsville Seven most likely knew of these findings because in their first appeal to the Supreme Court of Appeals they had alluded to the custom of Virginia juries to reserve the death penalty for rape for blacks. They had not, however, provided any concrete evidence of this practice. Perhaps a systematic survey of rape convictions in Virginia might yield some evidence upon which a new argument could be built. Samuel Tucker and Roland Ealey asked the superintendent of the Virginia State Penitentiary to supply them with a complete list of all death row prisoners who had been convicted of rape, including information about their race, the race of their victims, and whether their sentence had been carried out. As the attorneys analyzed this information, Ealey later recalled, it struck them "like a bolt of lightning" that since at least 1908, when the state took over executions from local jurisdictions, forty-five black men had been executed for rape in Virginia while no white man had ever suffered a similar penalty for that crime.[7]

Striking as this evidence was, Martin hesitated to present it in a judicial forum after the courts had already rejected his more traditional due process claims. On the other hand, the revelations might be persuasive enough to convince the governor to commute the sentences to life imprisonment. Therefore, the attorneys decided to seek executive clemency for the seven from Governor John S. Battle. In the meantime, Tucker and Ealey could tabulate and analyze the data from the penitentiary so that they could make a more sophisticated legal argument should the clemency plea fail.

On June 23 Martin filed a petition with the governor asking him to commute the sentences of the seven because the death penalties were "unduly harsh and extreme." As in the legal appeals, Martin brought Battle's attention to the "unusual incidents of the trial which petitioners feel prejudiced them in the minds of the jury," including the method of obtaining the confessions and the rapid succession of the trials. Unfettered by the procedural and evidentiary constraints of the courtroom, however, Martin also confronted directly the social and economic factors that had led to the death sentences. Prior to the assault, he noted, the petitioners had been "hard working young men" of "good moral character," who had been accorded "little or no social or economic advantage." In support Martin appended brief biographies of each man that emphasized their youth, lack of education, underprivileged circumstances, and lack of serious criminal records. More significant, Martin directly challenged the discriminatory application of the death penalty. "The prime reason [his clients] were sentenced to the electric chair," he asserted, "was because all of them are colored and the prosecutrix was a white woman and the juries were composed of all white men." After he received the petition, Governor Battle agreed to meet with Martin and any other interested parties once Martin returned to Richmond after Independence Day.[8]

Martin's petition to the governor delighted William Patterson and other leaders of the CRC. The NAACP's commutation strategy appealed to Patterson's organization because the specific emphasis on the race of the defendants meshed closely with the CRC's contention that racial discrimination motivated all interracial rape convictions. Moreover, an elected official such as the governor provided a more susceptible target for the type of mass action favored by the CRC. Since Marshall and Wilkins had rejected any cooperative effort, the CRC launched an independent campaign to convince Governor Battle to grant clemency to the Martinsville Seven. Several other organizations organized similar parallel campaigns, including the Capital Press Club, an organization of black Washington journalists, and the Virginia Council of Churches.[9]

The primary strategy of the CRC was to conduct public meetings that would convince large numbers of people to put pressure on Governor Battle to grant clemency. Josephine Grayson, the wife of Francis DeSales Grayson, toured the state at the CRC's expense to appeal for funds and to urge listeners to send letters and telegrams to Battle. On Father's Day she visited the Hood Temple A.M.E. Church in Richmond to ask the congregation "in the name of my five small children . . . to help save their father." On July 1 the Committee to Save the Martinsville Seven staged a demonstration at Richmond's Byrd Airport to arouse awareness of the case among some Virginia Union University students preparing to embark on a global "Crusade against Communism." At a mass rally at Madison Square Garden, Patterson linked the Martinsville cases to those of Willie McGee, the Hollywood Ten, the Foley Square Eleven, and other jailed Communists. Leaders of the Communist party praised the CRC for "carrying on the proud tradition of the International Labor Defense" and urged party members to demand that President Harry Truman "take moral responsibility for the lives" of the Martinsville Seven.[10]

In addition to generating support for the men, the CRC also sought to discredit the testimony that had convicted them. Several months earlier the CRC had hired private investigators to track down some of the witnesses who had testified at the trial. On June 15 the *Daily Worker* reported that Ruby Floyd had "disappeared immediately" after the trials and that the investigators had been unable to locate her. The *Worker* suggested that "Martinsville authorities" had asked her to go into hiding so that she could not be questioned about her "apparently well rehearsed, . . . trumped up story." Subsequent press releases from the CRC characterized Mrs. Floyd as a mentally unstable woman whose testimony could not be trusted. These efforts to cast doubt upon the veracity of the victim were ironic in light of the CRC's claims to oppose male supremacy and support the rights of women. They also left the organization open to criticism because NAACP attorneys had already admitted publicly that their clients' guilt was not in question, only the severity of the punishment.[11]

The publicity given to the Martinsville Seven by the CRC, the

NAACP, and other organizations brought a flood of correspondence into the governor's office. About two-thirds of the letters appeared to have been influenced by the information distributed by the CRC or similar organizations, although most of the writers did not express any overt radicalism. The remainder of the letters came from people who opposed the death penalty, belonged to religious organizations, or feared that the executions might interfere with the United States' efforts to export democracy. Another measure of the CRC's influence was the origin of the correspondence. Letters and telegrams arrived from at least a dozen different states, but more than half of them were postmarked in New York, the city with the strongest branch of the CRC and the easiest access to radical publications like the *Daily Worker*. Battle also received petitions from CRC chapters in Seattle, Chicago, and Mobile, Alabama.[12]

In keeping with the arguments raised by Martin in his petition to the governor, most of the correspondents emphasized the race of the defendants as the deciding factor in the death sentences. A form letter circulated by the Virginia Council of Churches admitted that the crime of rape "deserves the just condemnation and the vigorous restraining action of the state" and that the seven men should "pay for the crime they have perpetrated against an individual and against society." The letter noted, however, that "no white man in Virginia has ever been condemned to death for rape alone, even when the victim was white." The state's "judicial record in the field of rape lends unmistakable support to [the] belief," the letter concluded, that "Negroes guilty of rape are judged not solely on the basis of their crime but on the ground of their race as well." Several letters referred to a recent incident in which two white Richmond police officers who had raped a black woman only received seven-year prison sentences. Such examples aptly supported Arthur Hirshfield's observation in another letter that "their 'skin' is their crime."[13]

Other letters agreed that racial factors had influenced the sentences, but they refused to concede the guilt of the defendants. Drawing explicit parallels to the Scottsboro case, these writers asserted the innocence of the seven and urged commutation or, at least, a new trial. According to Morris Schappes of New York, "the prima facie case of their innocence is patent to many." Gerda Lerner of Astoria, New York, noting that the last of the Scottsboro defendants had been released from prison in early June, argued that "in the case of the 'Martinsville Seven' the innocence of the men can be similarly proven, given time and another trial."[14]

Another argument for clemency, closely related to the racial arguments, emphasized America's reputation for promoting equality throughout the world, a reputation which could be damaged by unfair treatment of blacks at home. The letter prepared by the Council of Churches emphasized that disproportionate sentencing of blacks was neither "good Christianity or good democracy." While such practices were indefensible at any time, the executions of the Martinsville Seven might "cost us far more dearly in these critical days when a Communist adversary makes ready capital of all our failures in the practice of democracy." A couple from Philadelphia recommended that "since we seem to be in the midst for a drive for democracy abroad, it seems more timely that we try some in the South." As long as "atrocities" like the "'frame-up' of the 7 Negroes in Martinsville" continued, another writer asserted, "no one in the world will be willing to accept any kind of leadership from America." Commuting the sentences therefore would not only demonstrate the impartiality of Virginia's criminal justice system, it would also aid the United States in its efforts to wage a cold war against communism.[15]

The remaining letters focused on issues other than race in arguing for clemency. Some based their pleas on principled opposition to the death penalty. Bernard Dabney, a member of an interdenominational organization which performed religious work in state institutions, asked Battle to commute the sentences because "only God has the authority to take a man's life." Until the commonwealth decided to "take its place among those forward-looking states which have abolished capital punishment," he noted, "the only alternative . . . is a commutation of their sentences." Others, like a self-described "old grandmother" from Roxbury, Virginia, just east of Richmond, decided that the death penalty was not warranted in this case because of the behavior of the victim. She asserted that "when girls and women travel alone in lonesome places they are not much afraid of men" and suggested that "the surest way [to stop rapes] is to operate on the men who do it. . . . Locking them up only makes them worse." Finally, a former resident of Martinsville who had lived there during the trials questioned the paternalistic assumptions that underlay the death sentences. "I am an unmarried, white woman who travels alone and need[s] protection as much as any one," she wrote. "But I do not feel that this man's execution will benefit me."[16]

Battle also received letters from four of the convicted men. The letters, which were all written on the same day and used similar language, were probably inspired by the ministers who were keeping them abreast of commutation efforts on their behalf. Each letter was written in its author's own hand, however, and all of them focused on different aspects of their cases. Joe Henry Hampton emphasized his newly discovered religious faith and asked Battle to commute the sentences because although he was not yet a Christian, "I do want to be a worker for the Lord, and saviour, Jesus Christ." He prayed "day and night that God will bless [Battle]. And all those who are taking an interest in the cases." Booker T. Millner had also studied scripture during his year in the penitentiary, having read "the New Testament through three times" in addition to "a lot of books on the Bible." If his life was spared, he promised to "help someone to find God before it's to late." Like the others, Frank Hairston asked the governor for "a chance to help someone that's traveling the same path I was traveling" but he placed more emphasis on Battle's temporal power. "I know my life is in your hand," he pleaded, "and I know that you are the only one to go to here on earth." DeSales Grayson made a plea on behalf of his wife and five children and asked the governor to forgive him for a momentary indiscretion, since he had "been a working man all my life and has been honest."[17]

Battle answered all of the prisoners' letters promptly, but his replies offered little hope to the condemned men. He promised to give their cases "the most serious attention" and assured them that "my only thought will be to decide on the basis of right and justice." However, he noted that he and Governor Tuck had granted several reprieves in order that their lawyers "might have every opportunity to carry your appeals to the Supreme Court." Judges at the highest levels of the state and federal judiciary, he reminded them, had already decided that they had received fair trials.[18]

The Reverend Robert Anderson, acting as John Taylor's spiritual advisor, also sent Battle a cryptic letter alleging that "from certain statements from [Taylor] which I have carefully weighed, there are alleviating circumstances in favor of these men." Battle invited Anderson to attend the clemency hearing, but after Anderson missed the meeting because he was out of town, Battle did not pursue the matter further.

Anderson later revealed that the allegations involved the validity of the confessions.[19]

On July 7 Governor Battle conducted a clemency hearing on behalf of the Martinsville Seven. Unlike his predecessor, John Stewart Battle fit the image of a distinguished governor with his handsome features and gentlemanly manner, although he lacked William Tuck's oratorical ability. A loyal Democrat, Battle had cultivated the friendship of Harry Byrd during his twenty-year service in the General Assembly, and he weathered the first serious challenge to the rule of the Byrd organization during the 1949 gubernatorial primary. Like Tuck, Battle supported some progressive initiatives, especially with regard to school construction, but his innate conservatism held little promise that he would support the clemency petition. The grandson of an ardent secessionist and Confederate war hero, Battle adhered strongly to the official policy of segregation and the informal practice of white paternalism toward blacks. He was astute enough to recognize that race relations would not remain static, but he firmly believed that the course of change should be determined gradually by white Virginians, and he resisted efforts by the NAACP to hurry the process in the federal courts. These attitudes blinded the governor to the significance of racially disparate punishments. In addition, Battle abhorred controversy and avoided making decisions that might upset the stability that characterized his administration. In fact, the controversy over the Martinsville case, according to the governor's biographer, "produce[d] Battle's first crisis as Governor." Finally, although Virginia law granted the governor sole discretion to grant clemency, regardless of legal precedents or rules of evidence, Battle was inclined to defer to the judgment of the courts, which had found no error in the trial proceedings.[20]

Twenty-one men and women of both races assembled in the Senate chamber of the state Capitol to speak on behalf of the seven men. The group consisted mostly of clergymen, but the audience also included Lester Banks, executive secretary of the Virginia State Conference, and several civic club members. Martin Martin began by reviewing the case and advanced the principal points raised by the clemency petition: the defendants' lack of serious prior criminal records, their lack of educational and economic opportunities, and the influence of racial factors on their sentencing. Nine other speakers elaborated on these points. John H. Marion, the white pastor of Bon Air Presbyterian Church in Richmond, remarked that the sentences hardly seemed "in accord with principles of equal justice," given that no white man in Virginia had ever been sentenced to die for rape. When Battle countered that state records of executions only dated back to 1908, Marion responded that, in any event, "it is hard to escape the feeling that race figured in the severe sentences." Citing Lewis Lawes, the New York prison warden who opposed the death penalty, Marion also denied that capital punishment had any deterrent effect on crime.[21] W. L. Ransome, the black minister of the First Baptist Church in South Richmond, compared the case to the two policemen who had received seven-year sentences for the rape of a black woman. "When two well-trained men get sentences like that," he wondered, "it seems strange that we should convict seven ignorant men for the same crime." Father T. E. O'Connell of St. Paul's Catholic Church emphasized the finality of the sentences and argued that since some of the men might not be guilty, the governor could not err in commuting the sentences to life imprisonment. Roberta Wellford, a white woman who identified herself only as a "civic leader," added that "the administration of law should be so scrupulous there could never be any doubt that justice is done." Finally, Joseph T. Hill, the black president of the Virginia General Baptist Association, placed partial responsibility on the commonwealth for the incident because state-run liquor stores allowed people "to drink all they can buy." Since the defendants had been drinking all afternoon before the crime, he noted, "I'd think of our own guilt" in placing liquor at their disposal.[22]

Ida Millner, mother of Booker T. Millner, spoke on behalf of the families of the men. Janet Taylor, mother of John Taylor, and Scott Hampton, father of Joe Henry Hampton, attended the meeting but did not speak. Mrs. Millner apologized for their failure to control their children, noting that "we tried to teach our children the best we could but somehow they strayed from our teachings." She acknowledged that "our children should have punishment" for their crime but nothing as severe as the death penalty. "We would be the gladdest and happiest mothers in the world," she told the governor, "to know that they had life in prison."[23]

Still wary of external interference that might damage his clients' case, Martin concluded the meeting by emphasizing to Battle that all of the day's speakers were loyal Virginians, not outside agitators. Although "some quasi-liberal and quasi-Communist groups have tried to get into this, to make it another Scottsboro case," he assured the governor that "we have used every effort to keep them out." In return,

Martin pleaded, "we feel that justice will be granted in Virginia." At the end of the hour, Battle commended the participants for their "dignity and restraint" and promised to give the "intensely serious matter . . . all the thought and study of which I am capable."[24]

As Battle pondered his decision, supporters of the Martinsville Seven continued to put pressure on the governor to grant clemency. The Citizens' Committee to Save the Martinsville Seven scheduled a rally for July 21 at the Leigh Street Methodist Church in Richmond "to provide an opportunity for the people to express their demands that the Governor let these men live." The Harlem Civil Rights Congress called for "a week of prayer for the lives of Willie McGee, the Martinsville, Va. Seven, the Trenton Six and the other victims of Jim-crow terror in our country." The CRC's national office reported that publicity on the McGee and Martinsville cases "is now appearing throughout Europe and Latin America." The *Daily Worker* published stories about the families of the men that depicted gloomy Independence Day celebrations in Martinsville's black community and touching scenes of mothers reading and rereading letters from their imprisoned sons.[25]

The state's major African-American newspapers also ran editorials in support of the seven. The Norfolk *Journal and Guide,* read by more people than any other black newspaper in the South, had publicized the case since the convictions and had helped to raise funds for their legal appeals. The *Journal and Guide* harbored much more conservative views than most other African-American periodicals of the time, however, and many blacks criticized its editor, P. B. Young, for his restrained criticisms of the Martinsville controversy. Young portrayed the evidence of sentencing disparity as an unfortunate blot on the state's otherwise exemplary reputation for "equality of treatment under the law." In light of world events, he noted, "Virginia cannot afford to subject itself to the charge of partiality and injustice by inflicting upon its Negro citizens, simply because they are Negroes, more severe punishment for a given crime, than it imposes on its white citizens." Although Young did not "condone crime under any circumstances," he concluded that "the best ends of justice will be served if the men's lives are spared."[26]

By contrast, the Richmond *Afro-American* issued a scathing indictment of the state's social and economic order, which had produced "this putrid carcass of racism that has all but reduced to utter social corruption the body politics of Virginia." By using race as a criteria in criminal sentencing, the citizens of Virginia had "permitted a system of fascism to be superimposed upon the democratic framework of our government." Although commutation "would not meet the ends of justice in light of the facts," it would, "at least, spare their relatives from the horror and disgrace resulting from death in the electric chair."[27]

On the evening of July 24, Battle denied the petition for clemency. Throughout his statement the governor, a skilled attorney, adopted a legalistic tone, characterizing the participants' comments as "oral arguments" and consistently referring to the trial records, "all of which I have studied with care." Battle declined to recite "the revolting details of this crime," but the facts of the case, he asserted, demonstrated that each man raped Ruby Floyd while the others "held, threatened, beat, scratched and in other ways abused their victim." The confessions of the defendants and their testimony at trial described the crime "in all of its gruesome details." Several witnesses, including the victim, corroborated these details, despite being "subjected to searching cross examination" by "seven able and competent lawyers." Seventy-two jurors heard the testimony and "without a dissenting vote, . . . condemned them to death." Procedurally, the trial judge had been "scrupulously careful to see that every precaution was taken to insure fair and impartial trials," and two separate appellate tribunals had decided that no grounds existed to reverse the verdicts.[28]

While the heinous nature of the crime and the overwhelming evidence against the defendants especially convinced the governor to reject the clemency plea, he also addressed two other issues that had affected his decision. Commenting on "the unwarranted attempt to attack these convictions by injecting a racial issue," he indicated that "some of the most damning evidence against the accused Negroes came from the lips of members of their own race." Battle also clearly resented the pressure being applied by radical groups. Most pleas for clemency, he recognized, had come from "reputable and sincere Virginians," but the executive office had also "been flooded with communications of a different type 'requesting' and 'demanding' the release of 'these innocent men.'" "No fair minded person," he complained, "can read the evidence in these cases without being convinced, beyond the shadow of a doubt, of the guilt of all the defendants." Cognizant of "the grave responsibility placed upon me," Battle concluded, "I have searched the records and my own conscience" without finding any grounds to set aside the findings of the courts. "I have no course, therefore, other than to deny the prayer of the petition."[29]

Reaction to the governor's decision from supporters of the Martinsville Seven was swift and harsh. At an emergency meeting of the Citizens' Committee to Save the Martinsville Seven held the morning after Battle's announcement, the group denounced "the governor's callous indifference to colored lives" and called on President Truman to use "his high office to keep the Martinsville seven alive." The Richmond *Afro-American* proclaimed Battle's conscience to be "as bare as Mother Hubbard's cupboard" and accused him of missing the point of the meeting because "he was asked for tender, Christian compassion, not stern justice, and he let Christianity down."[30]

From Battle's point of view, such criticisms were entirely unfair. Like other state executives he believed that clemency should be granted only in extraordinary circumstances, such as when new evidence arose or when knowledgeable officials such as the prosecutor, trial judge, or attorney general recommended commutation. A governor might occasionally infer from a dissenting opinion or a lukewarm affirmation of a guilty verdict that leniency was merited, but the solid unanimity of the Supreme Court of Appeals in the Martinsville case left no doubt in Battle's mind that the jury had acted fairly and reasonably. Sometimes in cases involving multiple offenders a governor might weigh the relative guilt of the defendants, but that usually occurred when the defendants were tried together, not when separate juries recommended the death penalty, as in this case. Furthermore, many of the demands for the prisoners' release appeared to have been inspired by Communist publicity. Battle, cautious by nature anyway, probably deemed it politically unwise to appear to be bowing to radical influence, especially in what he perceived to be a case of obvious guilt.[31]

With the first executions scheduled for July 28, only four days remained after Battle's announcement to act on behalf of the seven. The CRC, assuming that any further legal action would be futile, decided to concentrate its efforts on persuading President Truman to intervene. On July 25 William Patterson escorted Josephine Grayson and Rosalee McGee, wife of Willie McGee, to the front gate of the White House. After a guard refused to admit them because they did not have an appointment, the women waited outside the gate, speaking to reporters and passersby, while Patterson and a small delegation telephoned

White House secretaries, Justice Department officials, and representatives of the national Democratic party organization. After about five hours George Triedman, the chief of the Justice Department's civil rights section, agreed to see Herbert Aptheker and three other representatives of the CRC. After hearing their statements, however, Triedman concluded that federal intervention was not merited in either case.[32]

At the same time the CRC and the Citizens' Committee to Save the Martinsville Seven urged their members to put pressure on President Truman to act. Telegrams to the White House reminded the president that he "had been elected on a program of civil rights" and that a grant of "presidential clemency" would be "an expression of good faith." The committee asserted that executive intervention was "a long-established practice," citing President Woodrow Wilson's efforts to save Tom Mooney, a Socialist labor leader, and Truman's own pardon of the former mayor of Boston, James M. Curley, on a mail fraud conviction. These examples, however, ignored the limited power of the president in a federal system to interfere with the judicial processes of the states. The Curley case was irrelevant because he had been convicted of a federal crime, over which Truman had a pardoning power. Wilson had taken an active interest in the Mooney case, in which the California Socialist was convicted of murder, but his influence was limited to urging California governor William D. Stephens to grant Mooney a new trial. Stephens later commuted Mooney's sentence to life imprisonment, but the extent of Wilson's influence is unknown. In practical terms, then, the appeal to Truman was designed more to attract public attention to the plight of the Martinsville Seven than to persuade Truman to intercede.[33]

While the CRC emphasized political action, the NAACP elected to try one more appeal to the legal system. Recognizing that they needed a "more novel, innovative" strategy "to get any relief," the attorneys for the seven rejected oblique procedural challenges in favor of a direct attack on the discriminatory application of the death penalty. Armed with the statistical evidence of racial discrimination in the application of the death penalty, Martin petitioned the Hustings Court of the City of Richmond for a writ of habeas corpus, arguing that the defendants had been denied equal protection under the Fourteenth Amendment to the United States Constitution. On July 26, 1950, the day before four of the prisoners were scheduled to die in the electric chair, Judge

M. Ray Doubles stayed the executions until the court could hear arguments in September.[34]

The reprieves breathed new life into the efforts to save the Martinsville Seven. The Virginia State Conference designated the week of August 27 as "Martinsville Seven Week," with the goal of soliciting funds to pay the prisoners' legal costs. J. M. Tinsley, the president of the conference, appealed urgently to Virginia churches and charitable organizations for their "moral, spiritual, and financial support" and reminded them that the NAACP had already spent thousands of dollars on the cases, "a considerable sum of which still is due." On August 22 the Richmond Citizens' Committee to Save the Martinsville Seven transformed itself into the Virginia Committee to Save the Martinsville Seven at a conference attended by representatives from Norfolk, Suffolk, Powhatan, Alexandria, Roanoke, and Richmond. Josephine Grayson addressed the gathering and provided her husband with an alibi that she had been unable to supply a year earlier at his trial. "I am more firmly convinced than ever that the whole conviction was a frame-up," she informed Grayson's supporters, because her husband "was home when the alleged crime was supposed to have occurred." Those in attendance pledged to redouble their efforts to halt the executions, beginning with a petition campaign to Judge Doubles.[35]

At the same time William Patterson renewed his efforts to join the NAACP in a joint defense effort. Only hours before Doubles had issued his order, attorneys for the CRC had obtained a reprieve for Willie McGee. Patterson congratulated the NAACP on winning a stay of execution for the Martinsville Seven "immediately after our worldwide appeal that won [a] stay for innocent Mississippian Willie McGee." In the wake of these successes, Patterson believed that "united action [between] our two organizations can secure release of [the] other twenty Negroes facing electrocution frameup charges [in] nine states." Walter White, executive secretary of the NAACP, referred Patterson to Thurgood Marshall's earlier rejection of a proposal for joint action, adding curtly, "We can see no reason to change this position."[36]

Participation by the CRC worried NAACP leaders not only because of the historical animosity between the two groups but also because of misrepresentations that were circulating about the CRC's role in the case. A message from the Harlem Civil Rights Congress credited the CRC with winning "partial victories in the Willie McGee and Martinsville 7 cases." John Pittman, a columnist for the *Daily Worker*, attributed the reprieves for the Martinsville Seven to the CRC's success in staying the McGee execution. "For how could the lyncher class give ground on a case fought by the Civil Rights Congress, an organization it has branded as 'subversive,'" Pittman queried, "without also retreating on a case handled by the NAACP, an organization whose leaders it dearly prizes as willing reformist tools for circumventing the Negro people's militance and detouring it into the innocuous channels of legalistic controversy?" He also asserted, incorrectly, that both stays had been granted at the behest of the Truman administration in response to the outpouring of protest from all corners of the globe. Although William Patterson had graciously credited the NAACP for its success, Pittman reminded readers that "the mass protest movement for the Martinsville Seven was organized primarily by the CRC and its supporting organizations," so that "whatever role the NAACP played in this case was the product not of its lackey leadership, but of the many thousands of its rank and file Negro members who worked and fought for both McGee and the Martinsville youths." Once again NAACP leaders had to wonder why offers of cooperation were accompanied by attempts to denigrate moderate civil rights organizations.[37]

The Virginia State Conference also resisted cooperation with other groups because it could not separate those with genuine concern for the seven from those with suspect political motives. At the beginning of September, J. M. Tinsley received several complaints from contributors who had donated money to groups misrepresenting themselves as agents of the NAACP. He and Lester Banks promptly notified James F. Smith, chairman of the Committee to Save the Martinsville Seven, that "the NAACP has consistently since its original connection with the case . . . refused to become associated with any other group or organization in the raising of funds." Tinsley and Banks did not discourage the committee from continuing its campaign independently and wished Smith "godspeed" in his efforts. They could not, however, authorize him to solicit funds on behalf of the NAACP. This was due partly to official NAACP policy but also to local uncertainty as to the precise status of the committee. The Richmond *Afro-American* identified the committee vaguely as "a part of or affiliated with" the CRC and reported that many Richmonders believed that it was "being influenced by a Communist master mind." In light of the desperate situation of the seven, state and national NAACP leaders determined that they could not afford any association with groups of questionable background.[38]

Meanwhile Martin, Tucker, and Ealey prepared their arguments for the habeas corpus proceeding, relying on the contention that the death penalty for rape in Virginia was reserved for African Americans. That the attorneys waited so long to advance the racial disparity argument in the courts should not be surprising. The purpose of the initial appeals had been to correct any procedural errors that the trial court had made. Therefore, the lawyers had been limited to raising issues that appeared in the formal record of the trial. Since Judge Whittle never had an opportunity to rule on the equal protection issue, the attorneys could not have legitimately raised the issue on direct appeal. A habeas proceeding, by contrast, is not a direct appeal of a trial court's judgment but rather a separate civil action challenging the legality of a prisoner's detention. Like most jurisdictions, Virginia required criminal defendants to exhaust their direct appeals before they undertook a collateral attack on their conviction. Once they brought the habeas action, however, Martin, Tucker, and Ealey could broaden the basis of their arguments to allege racial discrimination in capital sentencing.[39]

The attorneys probably also hesitated to challenge the death penalty directly because of the vigorous support for capital punishment at the middle of the twentieth century. After a brief flurry of activity during the Progressive era, when nine states abolished the death penalty and others modernized the punishment by removing the authority to perform executions from local jurisdictions and adopting "humane" methods of execution, efforts to reform capital punishment faded. Support for the death penalty, as measured by public opinion polls, rose steadily between the mid-1930s and mid-1950s while opposition to capital punishment declined. By the 1940s and early 1950s, the death penalty reform movement was moribund as concerns of crime control and domestic security led to calls for harsher treatment of felony offenders. In such an environment, arguments that emphasized procedural errors in a particular case enjoyed more success than broad attacks on a form of punishment supported by most of the population.[40]

Finally, midcentury conventions of constitutional argument discouraged Martin and the other lawyers from adopting a strategy based on equal protection. Hailed as a bulwark of liberty for African Americans upon the passage of the Fourteenth Amendment, equal protection arguments had fared poorly since the end of Reconstruction. Cases such as *Plessy v. Ferguson* (1896) rendered the equal protection clause impotent because they gave states tremendous authority to regulate the conduct of black citizens. As late as 1927 Oliver Wendell Holmes, one of the preeminent jurists of the twentieth century, derided the clause as the "usual last resort of constitutional arguments." Almost all of the NAACP's successes in the field of criminal procedure had been achieved by invoking the constitutional guarantees of due process, not equal protection. Only since the end of World War II had state and federal courts begun tentatively to consider arguments grounded in equal protection analysis.[41]

Nevertheless, Martin decided to pursue the racial disparity argument for a couple of reasons. On the practical side Martin knew that an adverse ruling of the hustings court could be appealed to the supreme courts of Virginia and the United States. If either of those tribunals agreed to review the cases, a final ruling might be delayed for as long as two years. In the meantime the attorneys could amass further evidence to convince others of the validity of their new argument and at the same time would be prolonging the lives of their clients.[42]

Furthermore, the new approach provided an opportunity to link the NAACP's criminal litigation efforts to the equal protection strategy of the organization's desegregation campaign. In July 1950, after winning a number of suits equalizing teacher salaries and physical plants at black schools, Thurgood Marshall announced that the NAACP would abandon its fifteen-year-old strategy of pursuing equalization suits in favor of a direct assault on the "separate but equal" doctrine. While the equalization campaign had publicized the gross disparities in quality between schools for blacks and whites and had achieved some improvement in the education of black children, it had never adequately addressed the causes and consequences of legally enforced segregation. Meanwhile, NAACP attorneys had successfully challenged racially restrictive covenants in the United States Supreme Court by introducing sociological and economic evidence about the effects of housing discrimination. Thus the new school desegregation strategy relied on extralegal evidence, particularly the testimony of social psychologists, to establish that segregation perpetuated racial discrimination and subordination, regardless of the material equality of educational institutions.[43]

The members of the Hill, Martin, and Robinson law firm not only were familiar with Marshall's new litigation strategy, they assumed a vital role in implementing it. Martin Martin had already achieved some success in desegregating public transportation in Virginia. Spottswood Robinson and Oliver Hill had begun laying the groundwork for litigation to desegregate the state's school systems, and their work would ultimately be joined with cases from four other states in *Brown v. Board of Education* (1954). At the same time, Martin and Samuel Tucker started developing their broad attack on the death penalty. All of these efforts represented the beginning of a campaign to use equal protection arguments, founded upon statistical and sociological data, to challenge systemic racism and discrimination in American society.[44]

Although the NAACP had shunned cooperative efforts with other organizations, it now invited the American Civil Liberties Union to explore the legal implications of the statistical findings on death penalty sentencing in Virginia. On July 28 Thurgood Marshall spoke to Herbert M. Levy, ACLU staff counsel, about the sentencing disparity arguments that Martin, Tucker, and Ealey had developed. Marshall asked Levy whether the ACLU would be willing to submit an amicus curiae brief once the case reached the Virginia Supreme Court of Appeals. A brief to the hustings court, Marshall feared, "would do more harm than good."[45]

The NAACP sought the assistance of the ACLU even as it rejected the advances of other groups because the two organizations shared similar philosophies and objectives. Although the NAACP had never placed a high priority on civil liberties cases unless blacks were specifically involved, the ACLU considered racial equality an essential ingredient for individual liberty. During the 1940s it had filed amicus briefs in almost all of the NAACP's desegregation suits before the United States Supreme Court. Both groups also believed that litigation was the most effective way to achieve social change. Finally, the ACLU and the NAACP had both purged Communists from their memberships and viewed the CRC's involvement in the Martinsville case with suspicion. Like Marshall, Levy chided the CRC for attempting "to hop on the band wagon and get what publicity it could for the Communists."[46]

For various reasons, however, the ACLU never assumed an active role in the Martinsville appeals. During the first week of August, Levy presented Marshall's proposal to the ACLU's policy committee. Although no one on the committee doubted that racial discrimination in the administration of justice existed in the South, some members questioned whether a case involving gang rape was the appropriate vehicle to challenge the Virginia law because "it was not clear that these defendants had been subjected to capital punishment because of their color rather than because of the callousness of the crime." Only under special circumstances did the ACLU permit its lawyers to join cases before the United States Supreme Court had agreed to review them, so the committee deferred its decision and asked Levy to examine the record of the case for evidence of actual discrimination. Since the Supreme Court never granted certiorari, the ACLU never got another opportunity to consider entering the case. Recognizing that the issue was likely to arise again, however, the committee engaged a New York attorney, David Sive, to continue researching the sentencing disparity question.[47]

At 9:30 in the morning on the last day of September, Martin, Tucker, and Attorney General J. Lindsay Almond presented two hours of oral argument before Judge Doubles. Habeas corpus proceedings are technically suits to challenge unlawful imprisonment, and Doubles's court, the Hustings Court, Part II, of the City of Richmond, had jurisdiction to hear the petition as the first court of record in the city in which the prisoners were held. The attorneys respected the fifty-year-old jurist for his integrity and scholarly reputation. A graduate of the University of Chicago law school, M. Ray Doubles had served as dean of the University of Richmond law school for seventeen years before donning his robe in 1947. He subscribed to the philosophy of judicial restraint, however, and believed that courts should defer to the legislature on matters of public policy. That jurisprudential approach did not bode well for Martin's attack on a long-standing custom of the state. Martin probably would have preferred to bring suit in federal court, but in 1948 Congress had passed an act which required defendants to exhaust all state remedies before seeking relief in a federal forum. Therefore, he had to petition the hustings court and, if necessary, appeal its ruling before he could avail himself of federal remedies.[48]

Before arguments commenced, Judge Doubles expressed his displeasure at the political turn that the case had taken. Ever since he had granted the hearing, he complained, some people, "either because of their ignorance of a sense of ethics such as that which restrains a lawyer, or because of willful design, have mailed communications to the court . . . tending to influence a court as to what its decision should be." The correspondence, which Doubles turned over to the clerk of the court, included twenty-six postcards asking him to "use the influence of his office" to order a new trial, seventeen letters from residents of various states, a signed petition from Suffolk, Virginia, a telegram, and a copy of an editorial from the Richmond *News Leader* which complained "that 'due process' has more than run its course." Doubles assured the attorneys that the statements would "in no wise influence the court in its decision."[49]

Martin began his argument by summarizing the statutory history of rape in Virginia. Prior to the Civil War, white men convicted of assaulting white women could receive no more than twenty years in prison, while free blacks could receive up to twenty years or the death penalty. Following the adoption of the Fourteenth Amendment, the legislature eliminated the racial distinctions, but the prescribed punishment for rape remained either a maximum of twenty years in prison or the death penalty. Martin contended that this provision "either required, or authorized and permitted, the courts to make distinctions in the punishment between white and Negro persons convicted of rape." Although the legislature increased the permissible prison term to life imprisonment in 1924, Martin charged that by that time the courts and juries in Virginia had "without exception continued in force the immunity of white men" from the death penalty.[50]

To bolster these arguments Tucker produced statistics gathered from state penitentiary records to demonstrate that fifty-three blacks had been sentenced to death and forty-five blacks had been electrocuted for rape, while no white Virginian had ever been executed for the crime. Although the state records only dated back to 1908, this pattern had existed, Tucker asserted, "since the beginning of time." An examination of the reported cases of the Virginia Supreme Court of Appeals indicated that of the rape cases appealed to the court before 1908, three had involved white men who received sentences between ten and twenty years, while three involved black defendants, all of whom received the death penalty. One white rapist had been sentenced to death in 1939, but his subsequent commutation and pardon supported the theory that capital punishment was reserved exclusively for African Americans. The fact that almost twice as many blacks as whites were sentenced to life imprisonment further indicated that heavier punishments were reserved for black defendants. African Americans were entitled to the same protection of the law as whites,

Tucker concluded, and "if you can't equalize upward [by executing more whites], we must equalize downward."[51]

Martin admitted that this particular charge had "never been presented to a court anywhere." To support his novel argument, he referred the court to a line of United States Supreme Court decisions involving the exclusion of African Americans from jury service. Martin had particular expertise in this area of the law because, while still practicing in Danville, he had supervised the collection of evidence of jury discrimination in the Odell Waller case.[52] In *Strauder v. West Virginia* (1880) the Supreme Court held that laws barring blacks from jury service violated the equal protection clause. This ruling ended official exclusion of black jurors, but many states turned to the discretionary authority of public officials such as jury commissioners to circumvent the Court's antidiscriminatory goal. *Neal v. Delaware* (1881) held that the absence of blacks from juries over a number of years constituted prima facie evidence of discrimination, but the courts rarely outlawed the practice unless specific proof of purposeful discrimination could be produced. However, in *Norris v. Alabama* (1935), another landmark case to emerge from the Scottsboro trials, the Court ruled that when the defendants introduced evidence that no black had sat on a jury in over twenty years, the Court would presume systematic exclusion unless the state could prove, beyond mere assertions of good faith by court officials, that it did not intend to discriminate on a racial basis. These cases, Martin argued, demonstrated an emerging judicial consensus that long-term patterns of racial discrimination at any stage of the criminal process, supported by historical and statistical evidence, were sufficient to prove that a defendant's rights had been violated, even in the absence of specific proof of discrimination in his individual case.[53]

The difficulty with this argument, Martin recognized, was to overcome the state action requirement of the Fourteenth Amendment. Since the *Civil Rights Cases* (1883) the Supreme Court had held that the Fourteenth Amendment only prohibited discriminatory state legislation or discriminatory actions taken by state agencies or officials acting "under the color of state laws," not discrimination by private citizens. Obviously statutes that specifically prohibited blacks from jury service or jury commissioners who purposely excluded African Americans from the jury pool satisfied the state action requirement. It was unclear, however, whether the decisions of individual jurors, who were generally regarded as reflecting the conscience of the community rather than the official policies of the state, constituted state action. Martin contended that because Virginia law gave juries sole discretion in sentencing, they performed an essentially judicial function and had, as arms of the courts, systematically discriminated against blacks convicted of rape. Recalling the language of *Yick Wo v. Hopkins* (1886), one of the Supreme Court's earliest interpretations of the equal protection clause, Martin concluded that although the Virginia rape statute might be fair on its face, it had "been applied and administered with an evil eye and an unequal hand."[54]

Although the nominal respondent in the suit was the superintendent of the penitentiary, W. Frank Smyth, Jr., a thirty-five-year veteran of the Virginia corrections system, the real target of the case was the judicial system of Virginia. According to the Richmond *Afro-American,* Attorney General Almond "made an impassioned oratorical plea" on behalf of the commonwealth's most august institution. There was only one answer to opposing counsel's "unnecessary contumacious charges" that blacks in Virginia were routinely put to death without due process, he argued. "There's not a word of truth in it and they know it." To introduce a record of disproportionate rape convictions for blacks was "tantamount to saying more Negroes have committed the crime of rape in Virginia." The only relevant issue in this case was the severity of the crime, and nowhere "in all the annals of Anglo-Saxon jurisprudence" did there exist a comparable record of "such unspeakable and bestial horror." He challenged the defense to recall any similar incident that involved seven white men "brutally ravishing a defenseless woman of any color." These cases "represent the maximum of guilt," and that was why, "irrespective of race or color, maximum punishment was applied." Almond accused opposing counsel of abusing the writ of habeas corpus, "trifling with the court," and delaying the cause of justice by introducing the issue of racial discrimination into the case even though the trial judge "was determined to keep it out." Playing to Judge Doubles's concerns about external pressures on the court, Almond complained that the attorneys had turned the case into "a propaganda football, distorting not only law but fact before this court."[55]

Samuel Tucker briefly rebutted Almond's arguments. The attorney general's emphasis on the severity of the offense proved the argument of the defendants because it implied that "when Negroes commit the crime of rape upon white women it is more heinous and dastardly than when white persons commit the same crime upon either white or colored women." This attitude had produced a dual system of justice which required "that Negroes should be punished by one standard and white persons punished by another where the crime of rape is committed." Citing the case of the Richmond police officers, Tucker argued that the dual system discriminated not only against black defendants but also against black women who were the victims of white rapists. He asked Judge Doubles not to be blinded by the specific facts of the Martinsville case because the issue was "not so much the life or death of the seven" as it was the absence of "equal and exact justice."[56]

On October 5 Judge Doubles denied the petition. He emphasized that he was not concerned with the facts of the case and remarked that "no one can read the records and come to any other conclusion than that a jury would have been amiss in its duty if it had failed to fix the maximum lawful penalty." His only concern was whether the sentence of death could be lawfully assigned. Turning first to the performance of the juries in the Martinsville cases, he found "no evidence of any discrimination in fact." The records revealed a careful effort by the trial court to examine and exclude any juror who harbored prejudicial attitudes against the defendants. Doubles commended Judge Whittle for the "exemplary manner in which [he] presided over and supervised the conduct of the cases," adding that his behavior "could well serve as a model for trial judges throughout the Commonwealth."[57]

Because the trial juries had not engaged in discriminatory conduct, Doubles had to address the petitioners' "abstract" notion that "because of alleged discriminations in the past, no Negro can be lawfully sentenced to death in Virginia for rape at the present time." Reviewing the NAACP's statistics on rape convictions and death sentences, he noted that "the decrease in the percentage of death penalties given by juries in recent years is revealing."[58] The key issue, however, was whether this historical pattern of jury conduct constituted state action. The jury exclusion cases cited by the defendants were inapposite, Doubles reasoned, because in those cases the agency or official "responsible for the selection of jury lists [was] directly under and subject to the control of the court." By contrast, a jury, "while an arm of the court in a very necessary sense, nevertheless is not an agency of the government in the sense that a jury commissioner is." A jury was "as much a representative of the defendant as it is of the state, or to state it more accurately it is not a representative of either party but is an independent arbiter of the guilt or innocence of the accused." Even assuming that the juries that had issued death sentences for rape had been motivated by racial factors, the petitioners could not demonstrate that an official policy of discrimination, rather than the independent actions of separate juries, resulted in the death verdicts. "Certainly 54 different juries sitting over a period of 42 years in localities from all over the state," he asserted, "cannot be said to be acting under any concerted action, policy or system for which the state is responsible."[59]

Doubles also questioned whether a judicial forum was the proper arena in which to raise the issues argued by the defendants. To establish the principle that patterns of past discrimination barred the state from sentencing blacks to death, every judge presiding over the trial of a black defendant for rape would, when instructing the jury, either have to omit any reference to the death penalty or overturn any verdict that fixed the penalty at death. "This would result, of course, in partial repeal of a statute admittedly fair on its face." In addition, to ensure equal protection, trials of white defendants would be subject to the same restrictions. This would be tantamount to repealing the death penalty clause of the rape statute, a function which properly belonged to the legislature. Therefore, the only remedy for the situation described by the defendants was to seek modification of the statute through the legislative process because Doubles was not aware of "any judicial device whereby the courts could lawfully achieve such results."[60]

Following Doubles's pronouncement the attorneys immediately made plans to appeal the ruling to the Virginia Supreme Court of Appeals. On October 19 Martin filed a petition for a writ of error, charging that Doubles "apparently did not grasp the legal issues involved and did not give due weight to the petitioners' constitutional rights." Between the hustings court ruling and the filing of the petition, Judge Whittle had rescheduled the executions for November 17 and November 20. The court was not scheduled to convene until the twentieth, so Chief Justice Hudgins took the unusual step of calling a special session for November 3.[61]

At the hearing Martin and Tucker continued their argument that white men "have always enjoyed an immunity from the death penalty for rape in Virginia" while capital punishment "has been imposed solely upon Negro men convicted of rape upon white women." Martin took issue with Doubles's contention that the lower court could not lawfully alter the term of punishment set by a jury, countering that any finding of the jury may be overturned if it violates the constitutional and legal rights of the accused, regardless of the weight of the evidence. Lindsay Almond filed an opposing brief and attended the one-hour hearing, but he did not speak because court rules permitted only the party that applied for a writ of error to make oral arguments.[62]

After recess for lunch the court returned and announced that it had rejected the petition. The justices did not provide any reasons for denying the writ, but their questions during oral argument exhibited several concerns. Hudgins emphasized the facts of the case and suggested that no other crime in memory evidenced the brutality of the "mass rape at Martinsville." Justice Miller echoed Doubles's concern that abolishing the death penalty for blacks would open the door for equal protection claims by white defendants, effectively abolishing the death penalty. Justice Eggleston worried that if defense counsel's statistical evidence was accepted, "no Negroes could be executed unless a certain number of white people" were killed as well. Upon leaving the courthouse Martin informed reporters that he would appeal immediately to the United States Supreme Court for a writ of certiorari and that he would not ask Governor Battle for a stay of execution "unless it is absolutely necessary."[63]

Because only two weeks separated the Martinsville Seven from their scheduled encounter with the electric chair, the CRC and the Committee to Save the Martinsville Seven announced plans to send a national delegation to Richmond on November 15 to demand a pardon from the governor. The joint announcement by William Patterson and James F. Smith, chairman of the committee, confirmed many Virginians' suspicions that the committee shared the radical political beliefs of the CRC. Again the organizations emphasized the necessity of mass popular protest to save the lives of the Seven. "The lesson that the people of Virginia must learn," Smith admonished, "is that they cannot rely on the judges appointed by the Byrd-dominated state legislature." The action of the Supreme Court of Appeals "once again proves that even the most logical arguments by the most able lawyers cannot convince judges who are themselves steeped in the white supremacy system of Virginia's rulers." Patterson commended the NAACP for its efforts and encouraged it to continue its legal strategy, but he noted that "the decision is really in the hands of the people. We believe that these monstrous attacks upon the Constitutional liberties and human dignity of Negroes will not stop until an outraged public calls a halt."[64]

Despite its criticism of the NAACP's strategy, the CRC began incorporating the sentencing disparity argument into its publicity. An announcement advertising the delegation to Richmond cited the statistics that the attorneys had collected, and an editorial in the *Daily Worker* quoted extensively from Martin's brief. The Southern Conference Educational Fund sent Governor Battle similar statistics for thirteen southern states that revealed that 187 blacks and 15 whites had been executed for rape between 1938 and 1948. The influence of the NAACP's statistics was not limited to leftist organizations, however. After the hustings court ruling, P. B. Young, the conservative editor of the Norfolk *Journal and Guide*, wrote several editorials that reflected his frustration over the state's double standard of punishment.[65]

The sentencing disparity arguments also sensitized people to the treatment that white suspects and defendants involved in interracial crimes received. For example, in the second week of November, Martinsville authorities released a white service station owner on bail after he was charged with criminally assaulting a black woman. Two weeks later an all-white jury in Isle of Wight County acquitted a white mill worker of sexually assaulting a sixteen-year-old black girl. These cases alarmed many black and white Virginians and lent added credence to the argument that Virginia maintained a double standard for blacks accused of rape. Ironically, the *Daily Worker* remained unaware of its own double standard. It accused the Martinsville garage owner of attempting "to smear the character of" his alleged victim, but it simultaneously asserted that Ruby Floyd had "told a story full of discrepancies, then disappeared and has not been found since."[66]

In addition to the Richmond delegation, many branches of the CRC organized local rallies. The most ambitious program was undertaken by the Civil Rights Congress of Michigan, which invited Josephine Grayson on her "first trip North" to speak at a rally with the author Howard Fast. According to Anne Shore, leader of the Detroit chapter, "Mrs. Grayson really took the town by storm." After she spoke to the mass meeting, she stayed in Detroit for a week to be interviewed by newspaper reporters, speak to the weekly meeting of the Baptist Ministers' Conference, and address several trade union meetings. According to Shore, Mrs. Grayson was "able to break through several 'right-wing' unions," all of which contributed money to the CRC, the NAACP, or

Mrs. Grayson personally. As a result of this success, Mrs. Grayson made trips to Chicago and other midwestern cities as well.[67]

The activities of the CRC drew a caustic response from the NAACP. At the annual membership meeting of the NAACP Legal Defense Fund, Thurgood Marshall informed the members of the CRC's plans and promised to oppose the organization vigorously. Marshall, Martin, and Tucker took great pains to distance themselves from the protest effort for fear that it would damage their clients' chances of success. "We want to make it clear to the general public, and particularly to those whose primary interest is equal justice for the Martinsville Seven," they announced, "that neither the NAACP nor the lawyers representing the defendants . . . knew anything about this move." The interest of the CRC, they continued, "lies only in espousing their political philosophy."[68]

Although Patterson and other CRC leaders undoubtedly linked the success of the Martinsville campaign to the continued vitality of the organization and the Communist party, the NAACP's suspicion of their motives was not entirely merited. A list of rules distributed to each participant in the delegation admonished: "Do not give in to any provocation. Avoid arguments with anyone; such arguments will not help save the life of the Seven." Other rules emphasized the need for harmony to accomplish the purpose of the delegation: a full pardon for the condemned men. However, the historical animosity between the organizations, the CRC's frequent criticisms of the NAACP, and fundamental disagreements about strategy convinced Marshall and the other lawyers that cooperation was impossible.[69]

On November 10, one week before the executions were to begin, Governor Battle received a message from the CRC informing him of the delegation and requesting an audience with him. Later that day Martin Martin met with the governor to inform him that he would not be able to petition the Supreme Court before the executions because of delays by the attorney general's office in producing the records needed to prepare his case. That evening Battle announced that he would grant a final stay of approximately seventy-five days "to allow defendants full opportunity to assert any legal right they may have." He also noted that a reprieve was justified because the rules of the Supreme Court allowed the state thirty days to answer an appeal. Martin promised to have the petitions ready within a week.[70]

Because of the stay the CRC prudently canceled the Richmond delegation, substituting for it a "victory parade" through Harlem which featured uniformed black veterans of World War II and William Patterson's first public address since returning from a European tour. News of the reprieve also convinced the CRC to keep its promise not to interfere in the legal efforts of the NAACP. On November 18 John Clabon Taylor wrote to Patterson from prison to ask for the CRC's assistance. Patterson informed Taylor that "the NAACP is handling the legal aspects of the case" and that the CRC "could play no part in that phase of the fight unless specifically authorized by you to do so." He promised Taylor that he would persist in "waging a fight along all possible lines outside of the courts."[71]

Patterson continued to make contradictory public statements that confounded NAACP officials. In his speech in Harlem, he praised the NAACP "for the magnificent manner in which this case was handled by its legal staff." At other times, however, he implied that the mass protest efforts of his organization, especially the threat of a march on the state capital, had secured the reprieves. "The Governor, aware of the nationwide delegation" organized by the CRC, "responded to the demands of the people that these men should not be the victims of a monstrous act of discrimination." To Martin and his colleagues, this was yet another example of the CRC's manipulation of the accomplishments of the NAACP to justify its tactics of political protest. Martin reacted so bitterly to Patterson's statements that Thurgood Marshall was forced to make a statement crediting Martin, "who has borne the brunt of the appeals of this case," with securing the stays. The reprieves "had nothing whatsoever to do with this proposed march on Richmond, which could only have done more harm for the seven men involved and for the cause of justice."[72]

During the last week of November, Martin, Tucker, and Roland Ealey, aided by Marshall, submitted their petition to the United States Supreme Court. They continued the argument originally developed in the hustings court that in cases of rape involving white women, Virginia courts and juries had always reserved the death penalty for blacks while "white men have always had an immunity from such penalty." The attorneys urged the court to "once and for all reemphasize the proposition that no state shall make or enforce any law requiring, authorizing or permitting different and greater punishment upon some of its citizens than upon others by reason of race or color." Although the Virginia statute was not unconstitutional on its face, they argued that "it should also be made clear that customs, practices and usages having the same prohibited result are likewise contrary to the supreme law of the land." Reviewing the execution statistics of the commonwealth, they warned the Court that the pattern of executions "constitutes a serious challenge to an essential principle of our democratic government: Equal and exact justice to all men of whatever race, creed or persuasion." Both Thurgood Marshall and Supreme Court officials believed that this case marked the first time that the Court had been asked to review racial disparity in criminal sentencing.[73]

A month later Lindsay Almond submitted a reply brief which asked the Court to dismiss the petition because "it is completely hostile to the jury system to argue that persons convicted of the same offense should receive the same punishment without considering the heinousness of the offense and the extenuating circumstances." Each case is to be evaluated on its specific facts, he argued, and none of the reported cases cited by the petitioners demonstrated that any white person had been guilty "of offenses of equal atrociousness." Furthermore, those cases invalidated their argument that a "double standard" of punishment had been applied because each jury had been properly apprised of the full range of penalties, including death, regardless of the defendant's race. In any event, he concluded, the only pertinent issue was whether the seven prisoners had been denied due process at their particular trials. No evidence existed in the record that any of the six juries had discriminated against the defendants or that their race or that of the victim influenced the jurors in any way.[74]

On December 29, 1950, the justices met in conference to consider the petition for a writ of certiorari. Four days later, on the second day of the new year, the Court denied the writ. Once again the Court did not comment upon its reasons, but a memorandum circulated among the justices revealed some concerns that might have been raised in conference. One difficulty, the memorandum noted, "lies in making a finding of discriminatory punishment upon the basis of action taken by widely separated juries over a long period of years," especially when "no contention is made that the statute itself is discriminatory (it plainly is not) or that the trial judges have discriminated in their charges to the jury." Based on the NAACP's statistics and "common knowledge," the writer admitted that "Virginia juries might well be more prone to give the death penalty to Negroes convicted of raping white women." But even if the action of those juries constituted state action, "the principal difficulty lies in the unavailability of a practical remedy." If the petitioners were to have any relief, then "all negroes given the death penalty in Virginia for rape of a white woman will be entitled to a reversal until enough white men are executed to bring the figures into balance." In a handwritten notation Justice Harold Burton added that requiring African-American representation on juries, a practice which was already being enforced by the Court, was "the only effective way to get at this type of discrimination."[75]

The strategy adopted by Martin and Tucker during the collateral appeals stage meshed well with the NAACP's belief that social and cultural factors influenced legal development as much as, if not more than, prescribed doctrines of legal behavior. Much as Thurgood Marshall, Spottswood Robinson, and Oliver Hill began to challenge the formalist doctrine of separate but equal by demonstrating the actual inequality of schools, Martin and Tucker were convinced that the fairness of capital punishment could be contested if they could demonstrate that unequal sentences resulted from racial factors rather than other considerations like the magnitude of the crime. This approach grew naturally from their training at Howard law school, where Charles Houston had admonished them that lawyers were either "social engineers or parasites."[76]

The NAACP's efforts failed, however, because its new strategy did not conform to the judiciary's conception of the proper method of legal argument or the proper scope of judicial review. Martin and Tucker had amassed compelling evidence of sentencing disparity based on race in rape cases, but to transform that evidence into a legal remedy required courts willing to consider empirical, historical, and other extralegal methods of proof. The type of evidence that the attorneys produced to support their allegations appealed mainly to jurists who wanted to accomplish social reform through legal means, a mantle which neither the Virginia courts nor the Supreme Court under Chief Justice Vinson wanted to assume. Throughout the twentieth century, and especially in the postwar period, the Virginia Supreme Court of Appeals was rarely persuaded by the sociological and empirical arguments employed by the NAACP in its brief. The Supreme Court was more amenable to sociological proof, but usually as evidence of the "reasonableness" of state legislation, not as a justification for striking it down. The Vinson Court especially preferred arguments based on legal precedent to more innovative approaches to legal change.[77]

The NAACP's strategy also required a willingness on the part of the courts to second-guess the judgments of juries and legislatures and to place the values of due process and equal protection above the punitive function of the criminal law. Every judge who considered the habeas corpus proceedings emphasized the heinous nature of the crime and the evidence linking the defendants to the attack. Given the brutality of the offense and the obvious guilt of the defendants, the courts were reluctant to invade the sanctity of the jury room and impute racially discriminatory motives for the death sentences. This concern was compounded when the attorneys argued that a historic pattern of discrimination existed. The large number of possible circumstances that any given jury in any locality might consider in assessing punishment made the task of proving a statewide policy against blacks almost insurmountable, especially given the conservatism of the courts.[78]

The difficulty of implementing a remedy for the constitutional violations alleged by the NAACP also daunted the courts. Assuming that discrimination existed, the courts had two options. First, they could strike down Virginia's death penalty statute as unconstitutional per se. This would have been difficult because the statute itself did not specifically prescribe punishments based on race. Furthermore, the courts of Virginia very rarely exercised judicial review in that fashion. The United States Supreme Court was more willing to scrutinize state criminal regulations, particularly with regard to guarantees of fairness during arrest and trial, but it rarely interfered with the states' prerogative to affix appropriate penalties for convicted felons.[79] Since the courts viewed the abolition of the death penalty as an exclusively legislative domain, the only remedy for the disparity appeared to be a suspension of executions of African Americans until a proportionate number of whites had been executed. Such an approach would not only upset a system of social control based upon racial difference, it would also violate accepted standards of judicial power and equity to individual defendants.[80]

Lastly, the change in strategy by the NAACP gave the involvement of the Civil Rights Congress added significance. As long as the attorneys adhered to traditional due process arguments, they could distance themselves from organizations that espoused more fundamental criticisms of the prevailing legal system. By initiating a broad challenge to discrimination in the administration of justice, however, they fueled radical complaints about the American social, legal, and economic order. The tactical and strategic techniques that differentiated the CRC from the NAACP grew less significant to public officials as the goals of the two organizations grew more similar. Governor Battle, for example, explicitly denied Martin's request for clemency in part for fear of appearing to be swayed by Communist propaganda. The judges involved in the case were more circumspect, but they were equally aware of the CRC's involvement, as evidenced by Judge Doubles's denunciation of outside interference in the judicial process. Martin, Tucker, and Ealey thus faced the dual challenge of convincing a skeptical judiciary to accept their novel equal protection arguments while simultaneously distancing themselves from left-wing organizations that championed similar criticisms of Virginia's structure of punishment.

6

The Eleventh Hour

The Supreme Court's denial of certiorari on January 2, 1951, left exactly one month until the first scheduled executions. The NAACP had not convinced any judges of the efficacy of its sentencing disparity arguments, nor had the CRC succeeded in persuading the governor or the president to intervene in the case. "The slim thread of American jurisprudence," wrote a reporter for the Richmond *Afro-American*, "was fast unravelling over the heads of the seven condemned men."[1] Nevertheless, as the executions approached, the two civil rights organizations adhered to their respective philosophies—the CRC by continuing its mass protests and the NAACP by appealing to the legal system.

Following the Supreme Court's decision, William Patterson warned that the Court would prove to "be a weapon of terror against the Negro people in the country in the coming year." Because the Martinsville Seven could not rely on the courts for justice, he announced that "the first fight of '51" would be a "crusade to Virginia" cosponsored by the CRC and the Virginia Committee to Save the Martinsville Seven. Patterson invoked the CRC lore that the threat of a similar delegation in the previous November had persuaded Governor Battle to grant a stay of execution. On January 30, he predicted, between 250 and 500 "democracy-loving whites and Negroes" would enter the governor's office bearing fifty thousand signatures demanding that John Battle "revoke this infamous sentence."[2]

While Patterson exhorted the public, Aubrey Grossman, the national organizational secretary of the CRC, worked behind the scenes to ensure an orderly and effective delegation. An attorney with Marxist sympathies, Grossman had polished his organizational skills in the labor movement during the 1930s and 1940s. He urged the leaders of the local chapters to "go ahead under full speed" to raise money, circulate petitions, and secure statements from prominent citizens on behalf of the seven. He recommended that they not organize work stoppages or student strikes "unless the community feeling has reached such a point that this is a natural result." He asked all chapters east of the Mississippi River to send delegates to Richmond and established modest quotas for each branch. In order to keep the plans for the delegation operating smoothly, he insisted that the chapter secretaries "report twice a week on everything which has been or is planned on the campaign," and he asked for reports by telegram after January 20. As the date for the delegation drew nearer, Grossman pleaded with "the many chapters that have not yet reported to us" to let him know what actions they were taking.[3]

In order to publicize the delegation, Grossman arranged to have Josephine Grayson speak at several church and trade union meetings around the country. Grossman had suggested this project to her in December after her impressive showing in Detroit. At the time he estimated that she would have to spend about two weeks away from her home in Portsmouth, Virginia, mostly in the New York area. Once the CRC laid plans for the delegation, however, she spent most of the month speaking at rallies in Virginia, the Northeast, and the Midwest. Mrs. Grayson began her tour with meetings in Richmond and Norfolk, then headed north to New York City, Hartford, New Haven, and Boston. In Chicago she appeared at a protest rally with Mahalia Jackson, the well-known gospel singer, before continuing on to Wisconsin and Ohio. In making the case for saving the life of her husband and the other men, Mrs. Grayson stressed the inconsistencies in Ruby Floyd's testimony and questioned her disappearance. DeSales Grayson wrote to the CRC that he was proud of his wife and "would like to get back with her and my five children. . . . So all you good people keep up the good work."[4]

The efforts of Aubrey Grossman and Josephine Grayson inspired a number of CRC chapters to join the delegation. Chapters in Chicago and Detroit promised fifty delegates apiece. Branches from New York and Pennsylvania also guaranteed large contingents. Chapters that could not afford to send delegates scheduled local rallies. Even the Arizona CRC promised one delegate, the seventy-three-year-old chairman of the Phoenix chapter, Dorothy Murphy.[5] The delegation also attracted participants from outside the CRC. Grossman's publicity efforts succeeded in obtaining the participation of the People's Defense League, a biracial civil liberties organization based in North Carolina, and several ministerial alliances from Florida, Chicago, and Philadelphia. The Martinsville Seven also received tremendous labor support. The executive board of the United Auto Workers' Ford Rouge local in Detroit voted to send a delegate to Richmond. The UAW Plymouth local, the United Packinghouse Workers Union in Chicago, and the Furriers Joint Council in New York City followed suit. Officers of the United Electrical, Radio, and Machine Workers and the Louisiana Progressive Trade Union Council sent letters to Governor Battle and President Truman demanding clemency for the seven. Grossman also authorized trade unionists to organize "a short work stoppage of, say, ten minutes" to publicize the plight of the seven.[6]

The participation of labor, clergy, and civil libertarians reflected the success of Grossman's efforts to "establish somewhat broader auspices for this Crusade than we had last time." Another indication was the number of letters, telegrams, and petitions that reached the governor's office. D. V. Jemison, a Selma, Alabama, clergyman who presided over the National Baptist Convention, appealed to the governor to commute the sentences of the prisoners in order to promote "good-will in and among the races." He admitted that "if these Negroes are guilty they should be punished," but "that punishment should not be death." Other correspondents were more strident in their comments, labeling the trials "frame-ups" and "legal lynchings." Many of the writers illustrated their points with inaccurate examples drawn from CRC publicity, stating that the confessions had been "obtained by police brutality" and that the defendants had been "denied their own lawyers and forced to accept white southern lawyers appointed by the State of Virginia." A petition from a UAW local in Dearborn, Michigan, incorrectly stated that "a lynch atmosphere surrounded the trials." Some of the letters cast doubt on the veracity of the victim, characterizing her as "the woman who cried 'rape.'" All of the correspondents emphasized the pattern of discriminatory sentencing that characterized the treatment of rape cases in Virginia.[7]

In an effort to demonstrate the CRC's broad appeal, the organization's supporters staged smaller demonstrations in Richmond in the weeks just before the delegation was scheduled to arrive. On January 16 the Virginia Committee to Save the Martinsville Seven picketed the city's public auditorium to protest the segregation of the audience attending a concert by Marian Anderson, the black contralto who in 1939 had given a much-publicized concert on the steps of the Lincoln Memorial after the Daughters of the American Revolution refused to let her sing at Constitution Hall in Washington. The local NAACP also boycotted the Richmond concert. Anderson continued with the recital but nearly 80 percent of the seats were vacant, "a strict financial flop," according to Roy Wilkins. During the performance demonstrators outside the auditorium passed out leaflets that read, "Seats reserved for Negroes—Death Penalty reserved for Negroes." This effort to link discrimination in the criminal justice system to broader issues of segregation and civil rights had become a common element of mass protests against the executions since the NAACP uncovered the statistical evidence regarding sentencing disparity. When the CRC delegates arrived at the end of January, they continued to protest the segregated transportation, lodging, and dining establishments that they encountered during their stay in Virginia.[8]

While the CRC planned its delegation, NAACP attorneys launched a final legal assault on the death sentences. After a meeting with Oliver Hill, Spottswood Robinson, and Thurgood Marshall, Martin A. Martin decided to petition the federal district court in Richmond for a writ of habeas corpus. On January 22 he filed a petition which attacked the constitutionality of Virginia's rape statute. The statute had been designed to immunize white men from the death penalty, the petition contended, and Virginia courts had consistently administered the law in a fashion which exacted "a different and greater punishment" for blacks accused of rape. Martin included the death penalty statistics for rape that he had presented to the hustings court, but he bolstered them with additional evidence that the state of Virginia had never executed a white man for assault or attempted assault, while several black men had been executed when the victims of the assaults were white females. This pattern of punishment, the petition argued, violated the equal protection clause by denying to African-American defendants "the benefit of that immunity from the death penalty ... which to white citizens was secured by Virginia statutes in force prior to adoption of the 14th Amendment."[9]

On January 25, five days before the delegation was scheduled to appear, William Patterson wrote to Governor Battle to inform him of the impending visit and to request an appointment. Although the event was organized by the CRC and the Committee to Save the Martinsville Seven, Patterson took pains to emphasize the diverse nature of the delegation. Somewhere between two hundred and five hundred delegates would visit Richmond, he estimated, "some Negro, some white, some representing unions, some representing churches, some representing other types of organizations." Patterson preferred that Battle meet with the entire delegation, but if that was impracticable, he asked that the governor meet with at least one representative from each state and organization participating. "Almost every delegate will represent some different organization, some different social grouping," he explained, "and may have something special to say as to the thinking and action of his group on this question."[10]

Patterson's attempts to demonstrate the broad popular appeal of the delegation did not convince many observers, who remained skeptical of any movement sponsored by a leftist organization. An editorial in the Danville *Register* remarked, "Just how many of the scum who have changed their loyalty from Uncle Sam to Uncle Joe the CRC can bring into Virginia's capital city remains to be seen." The Norfolk *Journal and Guide* reported that the delegation "was believed to have been Communist inspired, with purely political motives." The national office of the NAACP advised its local branches not to join the delegation or sign any petitions. If they sent communications to the governor, they should do so as individuals, not in the name of any group. The NAACP also asked J. M. Tinsley, president of the Virginia State Conference, to organize an independent delegation from Virginia localities. The governor's office, as if preparing for an enemy assault, doubled the guard around the state Capitol and alerted the state militia to be prepared should trouble arise.[11]

On Tuesday, January 30, approximately four hundred demonstrators from more than fifteen states arrived in town. Most of the delegates were white. Governor Battle agreed to meet three representatives of the group. At noon Aubrey Grossman, James L. O'Rourke, a member of the Ford Rouge local, and Alfred M. Waller, a spokesperson for the Baptist Ministers Conference of Pittsburgh, met Battle in his conference room in the Capitol. At the beginning of the meeting, Grossman argued that "there must have been some vital moral reason" why so many people would have traveled so far on behalf of the seven, and he asked the governor to enlarge the meeting "to give a better cross section of the point of views represented." Battle agreed to hear four additional persons: Anne Shore, executive secretary of the Detroit CRC; Amos Murphy, a white minister from Lawrence, Massachusetts; L. Cicero Weddington, a black minister from Gary, Indiana; and Mary Bilbo, who represented a "young people's group" from New York. Two members of the delegation explicitly distanced themselves from the CRC. Waller emphasized that his presence was a result of Josephine Grayson's influence, not that of the CRC, while O'Rourke reminded Battle that his union "certainly couldn't be considered left wing." [12]

The spokespersons concentrated on the same issue that the NAACP had raised in court, the discriminatory application of the death penalty. In view of the fact that no white man had ever been executed for rape in Virginia, Murphy argued, "it seems to us the Martinsville seven would be dying solely because of the color of their skin. We feel that this would certainly be unchristian and undemocratic." Battle allowed each delegate to speak freely, but his curt responses to their pleas indicated that he had grown weary of this troubling controversy and was eager to bring it to an end. He asked Grossman, "Do you think they can tell me anything I don't know about this case?" When O'Rourke criticized the speed of the trials, Battle retorted, "We don't fool around in Virginia." He became visibly angry when one of the delegates questioned the victim's morals. Waving above his head a pair of leaflets prepared by the CRC, he complained that "things of this kind . . . which have dastardly things in them" had distorted the facts and unfairly provoked racial antagonism. [13]

At the close of their appeals, Battle refused to intervene in the case. The guilt of the prisoners, he told them, was beyond doubt. The "false propaganda" and "dastardly lies" that accused the jurors of racial discrimination ignored the horrible brutality of the rape, which "may well have been the most atrocious crime ever committed in America." The prisoners, he concluded, "had not been convicted because they are Negroes and should not be released because they are Negroes." Exhibiting his characteristic deference to the judiciary, he told the group that a stay of execution was "up to the courts." If the demonstrators expected a pardon, he added, "they were wasting their breath."[14]

At 2:30 that afternoon Martin Martin and Samuel Tucker entered the courtroom of Judge Sterling Hutcheson to argue their clients' case. A native of Mecklenburg County in Southside Virginia, the fifty-six-year-old judge had served for eleven years as United States attorney for the eastern district of Virginia before Franklin Roosevelt appointed him to the bench in 1944. Hutcheson knew the attorneys from the Hill, Martin, and Robinson firm's efforts to equalize school facilities in his jurisdiction, and he had ruled in their favor many times. The benches of his courtroom were filled to capacity, and several hundred delegates who had been denied an audience with the governor crowded the hallways of the Post Office building that housed the federal district court.[15]

Martin argued that federal intervention was justified because the "variation in punishment," established by penitentiary records, violated the defendants' rights of due process and equal protection. Attorney General Almond denied the existence of a state conspiracy to execute blacks and argued that to mandate uniform standards of punishment without regard to individual cases would turn Virginia's judges and juries into "statutory robots." At the close of arguments, around 5:45, Hutcheson refused to issue the writ. Technically his ruling ended there because he decided that the issues raised by the attorneys had been "fully answered by the highest courts of the state and nation," leaving him without jurisdiction over the matter. Even so, after "a careful study of all the pertinent papers," he also addressed the merits of the case. The Virginia statute, he noted, made no distinctions based on race and was therefore valid on its face. The application of the statute, which had resulted in the sentencing patterns revealed by the petitioners' evidence, fell within the scope of the discretion of the trial courts. Degrees of punishment, he asserted, "are to be determined by judges and juries based on the degree of aggravation of the offense." The defendants had exhausted their legal remedies in the appellate courts, Hutcheson concluded, and "there the case should end."[16]

Around five o'clock that afternoon, a group of about thirty people representing the New York Council of Arts, Sciences, and Professions stepped out of a bus into the freezing Washington winter to begin a vigil in front of the White House. The group, led by Shirley Graham, an African-American author, consisted of several writers, artists, actors, and intellectuals, including Howard Fast and Dashiell Hammett. As they picketed the White House, bearing signs that read "Save the Martinsville Seven" and "Make Your Civil Rights Bill Come Alive," word reached them that Governor Battle and Judge Hutcheson had both refused to intervene. At that point, Graham and Jon Randolph, an actor, carried to the White House gate a petition which asked President Truman to invoke federal civil rights legislation and "the great moral and persuasive power of [his] office" to reverse the death sentences. "It would look strange indeed," the petition asserted, "if, while the U.S. Government offers itself as the protector of civil rights on a world scale, the state of Virginia, without objection from the federal government, is allowed to execute seven innocent Negro men." Truman refused to meet any of the picketers, and his secretary instructed them to leave the petition with the guards.[17]

The following morning Martin and Tucker began a last-ditch effort to gain legal relief for their clients. They drove to Charlottesville to ask Judge Armistead M. Dobie of the federal Court of Appeals for the Fourth Circuit for a certificate of probable cause to appeal Hutcheson's ruling. Dobie, a seventy-year-old bachelor, had been appointed to the court of appeals in 1939 after teaching at the University of Virginia School of Law for thirty years, the last seven as dean, and serving less than a year on the federal District Court for the Western District of Virginia. Dobie declined to issue the probable cause order. He did not issue a formal opinion, but the loquacious jurist explained to reporters, "I just decided on the basis of all the facts, I should not interfere."[18]

Because any of the judges in the circuit could issue the order, Martin and Tucker immediately drove to Charlotte, North Carolina, to present their case to Chief Judge John J. Parker. Four years younger than Dobie, Parker had been appointed to the court in 1925 by Calvin Coolidge as a reward for his staunch support of the Republican party in North Carolina. In 1930 Herbert Hoover nominated him for a vacancy on the Supreme Court, but the Senate rejected him after the NAACP and other groups revealed that he had run on an antiblack and antilabor platform during the 1920 North Carolina gubernatorial election. Since then he had ruled in favor of the NAACP in a number of residential segregation and school equalization suits, including several Virginia cases handled by the Hill, Martin, and Robinson firm. He remained, however, a conservative jurist who shunned sociological arguments and deferred to state courts and legislatures in the absence of Supreme Court precedent.[19]

On February 1 at 10:00 A.M., Martin presented to Parker a petition almost identical to the one that had been rejected by Hutcheson and Dobie. Lindsay Almond and his assistant, Henry T. Wickham, also appeared to oppose the petition. At the end of the hearing Parker found "no merit in the contention" that racial discrimination had influenced the juries' sentencing. He noted that the "exhaustive and able opinion" of the Virginia Supreme Court of Appeals had "found that every aspect of the trial in the court below was consonant with the principles of due process." No subsequent court had seen fit to question that ruling. Because the defendants had received a full hearing in state and federal courts, Parker refused to "stay the hands of the sovereign state of Virginia."[20]

As it became apparent that the federal judiciary would not intervene in the cases, the CRC and the Committee to Save the Martinsville Seven stepped up their efforts to convince the governor that justice would best be served by commuting the death sentences. Around 6:00 P.M. on January 31 the CRC initiated a vigil in Richmond's Capitol Square to engage in prayer from dawn to midnight every day until the men had been saved. Aubrey Grossman also encouraged ministers across the nation to organize local prayer vigils. Shifts of volunteers maintained the vigil by chanting, singing hymns, and reading from the Bible, often huddling under umbrellas or crowding around oil-drum fires to escape the chilling rain showers and dense fog that surrounded them. The vigil was usually small because the Richmond police prohibited more than four people at a time from staffing the demonstration. On the morning of the first execution, however, at least seventy-five people swelled its ranks.[21]

Grossman also sent volunteers into the streets and to the telephones to build support for the men. Teams of three or four people distributed leaflets in the Broad Street shopping district and by the gates of the cigarette factories. Others dialed numbers from the local telephone book at random and asked anyone who answered to call or to write the governor. As a result of these and other national publicity campaigns, thousands of letters, telegrams, and petitions flooded the governor's office. Again, some of the correspondence reflected the sentiment that the guilt of the defendants notwithstanding, the evidence of discrimination unearthed by the NAACP merited a reduction in their sentences. Many more of the letters, however, demanded a pardon for the seven, echoing the charges of "legal lynching" and "Jim Crow frame-up" that the CRC had emphasized from the beginning.[22]

The impending executions also received attention beyond Richmond. The *Nation* and *New Republic* featured stories and editorials criticizing "Virginia's Black Justice." African-American celebrities, including Josephine Baker, Ossie Davis, and Ruby Dee, lent their names to publicize the plight of the Martinsville Seven. The American Communist party asked Eleanor Roosevelt to help stop the executions. Robert M. Lovett, a former government official in the Virgin Islands, suggested to Nobel Prize winner and civil rights activist Ralph Bunche that he attend to "this life and death issue which has great national and international implications." Demonstrations also occurred in many major cities. Harry Byrd, leader of Virginia's Democratic party machine, refused to see picketers at his Senate office in Washington. On the eve of the executions, six street corners along Lenox Avenue in Harlem featured picketers carrying signs and distributing leaflets.[23]

Protestors also focused their efforts on the president of the United States. In the week leading up to the executions, President Truman received nearly a hundred cards and letters and over 2,500 telegrams urging clemency for the Martinsville Seven. The following week about 1,700 more telegrams arrived. Picketers from the Council of Arts, Sciences, and Professions continued to brave snow flurries and freezing temperatures to maintain the "death watch" in front of the White House. As the weather worsened and some picketers left to demonstrate in Richmond, the protest dwindled to eight people, but reinforcements soon arrived from New York. On February 1, a delegation led by Mary Church Terrell, an eighty-year-old veteran of the civil rights struggle, attempted to meet with Truman. Phileo Nash, Truman's administrative assistant, informed the group that while the president was "very familiar" with the Martinsville Seven case, "he was not seeing anybody about the case." If they had any new evidence, he added, they should contact the Justice Department. In a letter to Eleanor Roosevelt written the following day, J. Howard McGrath, the attorney general, explained that the president could not intervene because he had no clemency authority over state convictions and "it has not appeared that the violation of any Federal law has occurred."[24]

In addition, the case received considerable international attention. Although foreigners had expressed their concern to Truman and Battle since the previous July, the foreign correspondence increased markedly as the executions approached and the sentencing disparity figures received greater publicity. Letters from Poland and Romania demanded the prisoners' immediate release. A telegram from Moscow, signed by "workers in science, literature and the arts," including Dmitri Shostakovich and Sergei Prokofiev, expressed "deepest indignation at this act of infamy and brutality inspired by race hatred" and urged "all honest men and women to speak up in defense of the innocent youths and save them from the electric chair." A notice from Peking was even more harsh, calling the "barbaric sentence . . . further evidence of [the] type of so-called law and order now prevalent in America which offers protection only to extreme racial hatred, fascist hooliganism, and war-mongering."[25]

Citizens of some of the United States' closest allies also questioned the death sentences. Letters from Israel and West Germany demanded that Governor Battle act immediately. Sixty-two deputies of the French Assembly asked Truman to intervene. The World Federation of Democratic Youth erected billboards in Paris. Another French organization, the Movement against Racism, Anti-Semitism, and for Peace, hung large posters in several cities that reminded "French anti-racists" of their "duty of protesting to the U.S. authorities." Many protests originated in Great Britain. A petition from "the coloured people in London" demanded that Battle repudiate the death sentences. Semahala Mulumbra, head of Uganda's exiled Bataka party, told British prime minister Clement Atlee, "Africans are anxiously watching to see what you will do to help save innocent Martinsville Negro lads condemned to execution." The American Embassy in London also received several inquiries about the executions and monitored the left-wing press for criticisms of the United States arising from interest in the case. Embassy personnel also noticed that many "non-Communists" had expressed concern for the seven, and they asked that the State Department supply "the real facts" so that they could "answer properly" queries about the case.[26]

On the evening of February 1, as Martin and Tucker drove to Washington to seek Supreme Court intervention, Oliver Hill and Spottswood Robinson met with John Battle to seek a commutation or a stay of execution. Following the meeting Battle announced that he would grant no further stays because "every possible opportunity has been afforded for the presentation to the highest court in the land of every phase of these cases." He recognized that "some very sincere and honorable people" had taken an interest in the cases, and he assured them that he had given their requests for executive clemency "the best consideration of which I am capable." However, he complained, the propaganda emanating from the *Daily Worker* and the "so-called" Civil Rights Congress bore "no semblance of truth and [was] designed for no other purpose than to attempt to foment ill feeling between the races and to mislead those who have no knowledge of the true facts of these cases." At the time he denied that the "slanderous statements" had any bearing on his decision, but he admitted several years later that at least two of the younger men probably deserved commutations to life imprisonment. The emphasis on the seven as a unit made special exceptions for individuals difficult, however, because "they were as guilty as the rest." Moreover, Battle had to avoid the appearance that radical protest had swayed him. Finally, as always, Battle hesitated to overrule the decisions of the courts. "I've slept with a clear conscience," he told an interviewer in 1967. "The law had spoken."[27]

Later that night several clergymen made a final effort to save the men. The Reverend Robert S. Anderson, spiritual adviser to John Taylor, sent a telegram to Battle contending that two of the prisoners, Frank Hairston and DeSales Grayson, were protesting their innocence, claiming they had never touched the woman. Anderson asked the governor to authorize lie detector tests, but Battle refused, reportedly because the blood pressure of men facing execution would render the tests inaccurate. A delegation of ministers tried to see the governor personally to make the same request but had to settle for delivering a written statement to his secretary.[28]

Shortly after midnight on February 2, Martin, Tucker, and another NAACP attorney, Frank Reeves, met in Chief Justice Fred M. Vinson's hotel room in Washington, D. C., to argue for a stay of execution. After discussing the case for about an hour and a half, Vinson rejected the plea because the Supreme Court had already twice refused to review the case. Barely six hours before the executions were to begin, the attorneys reported that the NAACP had exhausted all legal avenues without success and "knew of no further possible action that could be taken."[29]

For the most part the seven men confined to death row in the Virginia State Penitentiary were unaware of the last-minute efforts being made on their behalf. During their nineteen months of incarceration, the prisoners' chief contacts with the outside world had been the clergymen who acted as their spiritual advisers. Family members saw them on holidays, but the cost and distance of the trip precluded more than occasional visits. The clerical influence on the men was considerable. Only DeSales Grayson, a Roman Catholic, had professed any religion before the trials; but under the guidance of the ministers, the rest of the men were baptized in prison. In addition to attending a daily prayer service, the men occupied themselves by answering the many letters that they received, most of them from CRC members and some from foreign countries. Joe Henry Hampton asked the Colorado State Civil Rights Congress to write to them regularly, and Booker T. Millner encouraged the Committee to Save the Martinsville Seven to write to their parents. James Hairston told a Chicago woman that he appreciated her comparison of his plight to that of the Scottsboro boys. Grayson also heard periodically from William Patterson, who assured him that "we will not desert you" in the "fight for your freedom and the freedom of the other young men who are there behind bars with you."[30]

Shortly after midnight, February 2, Joe Henry Hampton, Howard Lee Hairston, Booker T. Millner, and Frank Hairston, Jr., said good-bye to their families and ate their last meals. According to the clergymen who were with them, the prisoners spent their last hours singing, praying, and talking to one another. They remained, said the ministers, "calm, composed, and in high spirits to the last minute." At approximately 7:30 A.M. prison guards led George Hailey, a white man convicted on February 3, 1950, of raping and murdering a twelve-year-old girl, to the electric chair. About thirty minutes later the guards returned for Hampton.

The execution chamber, like death row, was housed in the basement of Building A of the penitentiary. Constructed in 1905, Building A was the only structure to survive the renovation of the prison in 1928. The electric chair had been installed in 1908 when the General Assembly ordered the penitentiary to assume responsibility for executions from the local jurisdictions. The chair sat along one of the pastel green walls in the room, which measured about twenty-four feet square. As guards attached electrodes to Hampton's head and left ankle, twelve witnesses, eight of them from Martinsville, took their places in a row of chairs at the opposite end of the room. Hampton offered prayers as the guards strapped him down; the others would do the same when their turns came. The executioner pulled a switch that sent 2,800 volts of electricity through Hampton's body. At 8:12 the prison doctor pronounced him dead.[31]

The other men followed "in an orderly manner," according to Superintendent Frank Smyth. While Howard Hairston was being executed, Millner reached through the bars of his cell, held Frank Hairston's hand, and asked God to "forgive the men who are doing this to us." Howard died at 8:32, and Millner died seventeen minutes later. As the captain of the guard led Frank Hairston to the chair, the Richmond *Afro-American* reported, Hairston shook hands with the officer, who told him, "Frank, you have been a model prisoner." Once fastened to the chair, he looked at the witnesses and told them, "Gentlemen, I want you all to meet me in Heaven." The first jolt of electricity failed to kill him, and Smyth ordered the executioner to pull the switch again. At 9:05 the doctor removed his stethoscope from Hairston's chest and pronounced him dead. In less than two hours five bodies had accumulated on stretchers that lined the walls of the execution chamber, the largest number of men ever executed by the state in one day.[32]

Although no protest took place on the prison grounds, the vigil of prayer continued at Richmond's Capitol Square. The CRC and the Committee to Save the Martinsville Seven, claiming that this case made "the murder of Sacco and Vanzetti seem a trivial act of irresponsible officials," called on several persons of authority to intervene. In New York a delegation at the United Nations sought intervention from the Commission of Human Rights, and a crowd of 2,500 people assembled in Harlem to protest the executions that occurred that morning. Many of these people later met at City Hall to ask Mayor Vincent Impelliterri to persuade Governor Battle "to stop this mass blood-shed." One hundred Chicagoans called on Illinois senator Paul Douglas, one of Truman's staunchest supporters, to demand the president's intervention. In Richmond volunteers distributed handbills and black armbands, while theater and store owners, some of them white, urged their customers to call the governor. Some restaurateurs closed their doors to deliver coffee and food to the freezing demonstrators. On Sunday, February 4, 218 people marched down Broad Street, Richmond's main thoroughfare, to join the vigil.[33]

Protestors also continued the letter and telegram campaign to the governor. Long-distance telephone calls tied up the switchboard at the executive office for hours. Battle refused to accept phone messages, and Western Union briefly halted delivering telegrams to him. Mail continued to pour into the governor's office, the most strident of which informed him that "you white sons of bitches will suffer for crucifying these innocent boys. . . . Soon the glorious Negro race will revolt and rule in your place and you will be strung up from the Courthouse flagpole and your carkass thrown to the dogs. YOU MUST DIE!!!" Battle denounced the bulk of the messages as Communist propaganda and refused to hear any more misguided pleas, leading one man to accuse him of "legalized murder by absenteeism."[34]

In Washington, CRC officials planned a mass demonstration to begin on Sunday with a "big memorial meeting" at the Vermont Avenue Baptist Church and to culminate with a procession in which four coffins would be carried to the White House. However, church officials canceled the meeting after they learned that William Patterson would be one of the speakers. "The church belongs to the people," the Reverend C. T. Murray explained, "and I just cannot have organizations that are on the subversive list using its facilities." Instead between one hundred and three hundred demonstrators marched in a circle in front of the White House. District of Columbia police chief Robert Barrett said the picket line was the longest he had seen and called a hundred extra policemen to "be on the alert." The group included Josephine Grayson and her five children, who tried unsuccessfully to see President Truman and Vice President Alben Barkley.[35]

Later that evening Martin Martin permitted Aubrey Grossman to make a plea for a stay of execution to United States Supreme Court Justice Harold Burton. Martin allowed Grossman the use of his firm's legal records, but he emphasized that he was "not associated with Grossman's organization." At nine o'clock that night Grossman and two Washington attorneys who occasionally represented CRC clients, Belford Lawson and Joseph Forer, met Justice Burton in his chambers. As in the previous appeals, the attorneys argued that Virginia's pattern of death penalty sentencing for rape violated the equal protection clause, but they made two additional arguments. First, they contended that the defendants had been denied their Sixth Amendment right to effective assistance of counsel because "any white lawyer . . . who represented the petitioners vigorously" would have "become an object of hatred in the white community thereby incurring serious consequences to his practice and his social life." In fact, they complained, "the defense of the petitioners by the appointed counsel was apathetic." Second, the lawyers argued that the death sentences constituted cruel and unusual punishment in violation of the Eighth Amendment. This argument was probably inspired by Burton's vigorous dissent three years earlier in *Louisiana ex rel. Francis v. Resweber,* a case involving a botched execution attempt, in which he argued that the cruel and unusual punishment clause applied to the states. In this case, however, Burton reverted to his traditional deference to jury discretion and his reluctance to interfere in state criminal proceedings. He declined to stay the executions because there was no evidence that the juries or the attorneys had acted improperly.[36]

Early in the morning of Monday, February 5, John Clabon Taylor, James Luther Hairston, and Francis DeSales Grayson ate their last meals and silently waited in their cells, listening to the radio. Extra guards were posted outside the prison to counter any protests, but the only observers staring through the prison gates were twenty men who hoped to take the place of any witnesses who failed to appear. At half past seven the prisoners marched to the green chamber, and at 7:41 the prison doctor pronounced Taylor dead. The executions proceeded for the most part "with calm efficiency," although the *Afro-American* reported that the last two prisoners presented some difficulties. Hairston had to be electrocuted twice before he died at 8:00, and Grayson, who died fifteen minutes later, protested that he was innocent before he was strapped into the chair.[37]

As news of the executions reached the lawn of the Capitol, the vigil of prayer disbanded and the demonstrators left. Only one task remained, and that would be completed as soon as the hearses backing out of the penitentiary driveway reached their destinations. After two years, six trials, five stays of execution, ten opportunities for judicial review, and two denials of executive clemency, the legal odyssey of the Martinsville Seven had ended.

Epilogue

On Sunday, February 4, 1951, relatives of Booker T. Millner gathered for his funeral at the First Baptist Church in east Martinsville, while a few dozen miles away the family of Joe Henry Hampton buried him in Pittsylvania County. The following morning services for Frank Hairston were held in the home of his parents. Later that day the bodies of John Taylor and James Hairston arrived at the James T. Allen Funeral Home in Martinsville. Hairston was buried on Tuesday with his half-brother, Howard Lee Hairston, but Taylor's funeral was delayed until Thursday because of cold weather. On Friday, Father Ernest Unterkoefler conducted a requiem mass in St. Joseph's Catholic Church in Richmond for DeSales Grayson, the only man with no family ties in Martinsville.[1]

With these burials the Martinsville Seven quickly faded from the front pages of African-American and radical newspapers, and they disappeared completely from more widely read periodicals. The controversies raised by the case, however, continued to be debated by reformers, attorneys, and public officials. The failure to save the Martinsville Seven from the electric chair led civil rights organizations to reassess their tactics. The strikingly different ways in which the NAACP and the CRC approached the cases prompted many observers to contemplate the appropriate manner of combating racial discrimination in an era of cold war. Most significant, the legal strategies developed to challenge the executions of the Martinsville Seven continued to play a prominent role in efforts to abolish the death penalty.

For a brief period in the 1950s, the case itself provided a rallying cry for civil rights activists. The leaders of the Virginia State Conference proclaimed that "the indefensible tragic result of the Martinsville case will . . . strengthen the determination of the NAACP to continue its fight for equal and exact justice for all under our Constitution." William Patterson and Aubrey Grossman recruited Josephine Grayson to join the Civil Rights Congress's campaign against the executions of Willie McGee and other black defendants. The CRC cited the case eight times in its petition to the United Nations charging the federal and state governments with genocide. Artists used the seven to symbolize the racial antagonism that faced black Americans. In Philadelphia, for example, Ossie Davis produced a dramatic reading of Walter Lowenfels's poem "The Martinsville Chant," while New Mexico artist Ted Egri designed a series of woodcuts and statues in memory of the Martinsville Seven, McGee, "and other lynch victims." The Martinsville incident also continued to affect Virginia politics. As late as 1969 many black voters opposed William C. Battle's gubernatorial bid because of his father's refusal to grant clemency.[2]

Beyond its symbolic value, the Martinsville case led many Americans to consider the effect of changing social and political circumstances on the administration of justice to blacks. Immediate assessments of the case tended to focus on the role of the Civil Rights Congress. Most observers reached the same conclusion: the CRC aided criminal defendants only in cases that served the Communist party's immediate interests. To the Richmond *Times-Dispatch* the "malicious and willful distortions" of the facts by the CRC provided "a perfect illustration of the manner in which Communists operate." *Time* magazine criticized the "well-greased Communist apparatus" that was "making propaganda hay out of the Martinsville Seven—with suitable adjustments in the facts." The delegation to Richmond, according to the Roanoke *World News,* represented "the rankest sort of Red propaganda." The efforts to make martyrs of the seven, declared the Danville *Register,* comprised one small part "of the Red campaign to divide the only powerful foe facing the Kremlin." On the day of the final executions, Senator Clyde R. Hoey of North Carolina inserted into the *Congressional Record* an anti-Communist editorial from the Washington *Evening Star* that "present[ed] the facts which are sadly overlooked or ignored in the wild propaganda circulated by Communist newspapers and writers."[3]

Black Virginians ranked among the sharpest critics of the CRC. Lawyers and officers associated with the Virginia State Conference of the NAACP consistently resisted the group's participation in the case. After the executions the Richmond *Afro-American* reported that most of Martinsville's black community believed the men would have been awarded clemency if not for the marches on Richmond and Washington organized by the CRC. Like the white-owned periodicals, the state's leading African-American newspapers explicitly linked the activities of the CRC to the international Communist movement. "The only victor in the whole sordid business of the Martinsville Seven," the *Afro-American* lamented, "was Russian propaganda." The Norfolk *Journal and Guide* agreed, concluding that "the chances for executive clemency would have been better if the national and international crusade had not occurred."[4]

These assessments of the CRC underestimated the organization's depth of concern for the Martinsville Seven. In order to ensure the involvement of the NAACP, the CRC agreed not to represent any of the men, and it adhered to this promise despite occasional requests for legal assistance from the prisoners themselves. Throughout their incarceration William Patterson kept the men abreast of efforts on their behalf, and after the executions he continued to provide assistance to their families. With the aid of churches in New York City, the CRC secured employment and housing for Josephine Grayson and her five children. Critics of the CRC rarely acknowledged these efforts, nor did they draw distinctions between the activities of the CRC and those of more radical groups, often based in foreign countries, that exhibited an interest in the Martinsville case.[5]

Nevertheless, certain actions by the CRC reinforced the impression that the organization only took an interest in the case for its propaganda value. The evident guilt of the defendants led the CRC to fabricate stories of their innocence, confirming to many observers the lengths to which Communists would go to discredit the American legal system. Accusations that the victim "promised to emote the lines written for her" in exchange for payment from Martinsville businessmen rang false because NAACP lawyers had never contested the verdicts of guilt, only the severity of the sentences. The CRC routinely used fund-raising meetings for the seven to introduce churches and labor unions to the party platform and to publicize the plight of Communist defendants being tried for subversion in federal courts. "One cannot separate the execution of these seven Negroes from the conviction of the eleven Communist leaders through an indictment drawn from the Smith Act," wrote author and CRC celebrity Howard Fast. Some of the money raised on behalf of the seven was diverted to support the CRC's other causes, a tactic which bothered even some local CRC branches. The executive secretary of the Civil Rights Congress of Illinois, for instance, sarcastically asked Aubrey Grossman what he should do with money left over from a meeting attended by Josephine Grayson, "other than contributing it to your office." The CRC's concern for the defendants, therefore, was balanced by the potential for publicity, membership, and revenue that a case like the Martinsville affair could generate.[6]

Just as the CRC harbored a variety of altruistic, ideological, and practical motives for aiding the Martinsville Seven, the NAACP's interest in the case extended beyond the welfare of its clients in an effort to link civil rights for African Americans to the cold war liberal agenda. Beginning in the late 1940s, many civil rights activists argued that the most effective way for the United States to promote worldwide democracy and counter Soviet criticism was to guarantee racial equality at home. Accordingly, NAACP leaders tried to alert public officials to the global implications of the Martinsville case. Walter White, executive secretary of the NAACP, complained that "the Martinsville Seven case has already proved to be as generous a gift to Communist propaganda as could be devised." Before the last set of executions, he implored Governor Battle "to see beyond the borders of his own state and political ambitions" by granting executive clemency "not only as an act of mercy, but also in the interest of national security." In a letter to the editors of the *Nation* written shortly after the executions, Martin Martin, Oliver Hill, J. M. Tinsley, and Lester Banks called for the elimination of sentencing disparity in capital cases "if the United States is to retain its leadership in world affairs." Others outside the NAACP echoed these concerns. The *Christian Century*, for instance, recommended the abolition of the death penalty because the "striking difference in the punishment inflicted on members of the two races will certainly be used by Communist propaganda around the globe."[7]

In the immediate context of the Martinsville case, efforts to make the fight against racial discrimination an objective of the Cold War clearly failed. Communism and civil rights activism were too closely linked in the minds of most southerners to permit any capitulation to either the NAACP or the CRC. This was especially the case after the NAACP began advancing its sentencing disparity arguments, because the emphasis on the inequitable treatment of black defendants paralleled radical attacks on the American legal system. The officials with authority over the Martinsville matter shared the beliefs of other southerners. Governor Battle particularly, but also some jurists, such as Judge Doubles of the hustings court, clearly expressed their desire not to appear to be influenced by subversive organizations.[8]

From a broader perspective, however, both the NAACP's appeals to cold war values and the foreign protests inspired by the CRC prompted the federal government to reexamine its civil rights policies, at least from a public relations standpoint. Shortly after the executions Harry Seamans, an information officer in the Department of State's Division of Public Liaison, sought advice from the American Civil Liberties Union about counteracting "unfavorable propaganda abroad in relation to the Martinsville, Virginia incident." Staff attorney Herbert Levy, who had corresponded with Martin Martin and Thurgood Marshall about the case, recommended as a short-term solution that the State Department characterize the executions as an isolated occurrence and emphasize the "great strives that have been made towards . . . equal justice, pointing out that Virginia is a small part indeed of the entire country." Nevertheless, he reminded Seamans, "just as we correctly attack Communism because of its totalitarianism, they can attack us because of the attitude of the South towards the Negro." The most effective way to combat criticism of "what we all know to be unequal administration of justice in the South" would be to "secure some reactivation of the President's civil rights program." In the long run, Levy believed, "enactment of legislation to equalize the rights of Negroes would be one of the strongest blows that could be dealt to Communism."[9]

The State Department actually implemented policies that paralleled Levy's recommendations. American embassies that had received correspondence criticizing the conduct of the Martinsville cases mailed responses that summarized the facts of the cases and reiterated the United States' commitment to due process for all races. Embassy officials generally regarded this tactic as fruitless, since most of the people who bothered to acknowledge receipt of the information "were just spoiling for a word fight." More effective were the State Department's attempts to influence federal civil rights policy because of its concern that international attention to the racial problems of the United States threatened its efforts to export democracy to developing nations that were susceptible to Soviet influence. Although the Martinsville case certainly was not the catalyst for these efforts, it added credence to the State Department's position that racial discrimination was a problem that required federal intervention in order to protect the country's foreign policy interests.[10]

While the cold war aspects of the case dominated contemporary debate about its significance, the Martinsville proceedings had more lasting effects on the internal policies and legal strategies of the NAACP. The difficulties encountered by NAACP attorneys and staff members prompted the national office to reevaluate its relationship to the local branches and its criteria for representing criminal defendants. At the conclusion of the case J. M. Tinsley, president of the Virginia State Conference, and Lester Banks, the conference's executive secretary, complained to Roy Wilkins that "the attitude of the National office has been first hot and then cold." Although the Virginia State Conference had maintained firm control of the case within the state, local branches outside of Virginia could not engage in any publicity or fundraising activity because they received no direction from New York. The Civil Rights Congress "did a mammoth job of arousing the people," Tinsley continued, "all of which could have and should have been done by the NAACP." Had the national office acted more forcefully, "it would not now find itself in the embarrassing position of having to explain and inform its branches as to the NAACP's connection with the case." Tucker and Banks also complained that the national office had not provided any monetary assistance to defray the $4,000 debt incurred in the case, which made it difficult for the conference to pursue its transportation and school desegregation cases. As a result the executive committee of the NAACP Legal Defense and Educational Fund voted to contribute $1,500 toward the Virginia State Conference's debt. At a February meeting of the NAACP's board of directors, the members also agreed that the NAACP should enter rape cases as early as possible "without waiting to take up the matter of expenses or anything else." Some of them speculated that "perhaps because it was felt that these men were guilty, the Board lost sight of the larger problem. The issue was not whether the men were guilty of rape but whether a Negro should die for rape when no white man dies for it."[11]

The revelation of capital sentencing disparity in Virginia was by far the most significant legacy of the Martinsville case. The trial court's attention to due process requirements had forced attorneys for the seven to develop other grounds for appeal. The Martinsville case was thus the first time that attorneys presented in court equal protection arguments that challenged the racial disparity of death sentences for rape.[12]

For opponents of capital punishment the statistics gathered by Martin, Tucker, and Ealey provided compelling evidence for the abolition of the death penalty. "When it comes to inflicting the death penalty," an editorial in the *Christian Century* opined, "members of the two races simply are not equal before the law. . . . The majesty of the law would be better upheld and the pretensions of democracy more convincingly defended if capital punishment were dropped entirely." Even people who supported capital punishment, however, expressed dismay at the inequality of sentences. Virginius Dabney, editor of the Richmond *Times-Dispatch,* opposed clemency for the Martinsville Seven because of the brutality of their crime, but he confessed that "there are things about the statistic . . . which disturb me." A New York man informed Dabney that "even the most reactionary and right wing of my friends were shocked by the severity of the sentence."[13]

The evidence of unequal capital sentencing also caught the attention of other attorneys. Despite the failure of the sentencing disparity arguments in the Martinsville proceedings, civil rights lawyers seized on the equal protection strategy in capital cases as the next logical step in the pursuit of equal justice for African Americans. Frank Donner, counsel for the Congress of Industrial Organizations (CIO), publicized the Martinsville lawyers' findings in his *Civil Liberties Reporter.* Although the death of the Martinsville Seven was "an accomplished fact and for them the case is closed," Donner wrote, "the issues involved in this criminal proceeding have not at all been finally disposed of." Recognizing the relevance of the case to emerging equal protection jurisprudence, he argued that the sentencing disparity arguments "warrant the attention of the Federal courts if constitutional protections, as set forth in the Fourteenth Amendment are to have any meaning in life, particularly for the Negro people." Concurring in this judgment, the ACLU assigned an attorney to research the sentencing disparity argument so that it would be available when a similar case arose. Its Legal Survey Group, comprised of law students at Columbia University, also investigated whether federal civil rights statutes created a cause of action for the families of the Martinsville Seven to seek damages based on the state's unequal treatment of black defendants.[14]

Sentencing disparity arguments soon found their way into state and federal courtrooms. After the executions attorneys from around the country sought advice from the Hill, Martin, and Robinson firm on collecting, organizing, and presenting data related to executions. Martin shared his files with Ralph Powe, an attorney for the Civil Rights Congress who was preparing appeals for Willie McGee in Mississippi and Ocie Jugger and Paul Washington in Louisiana. All three men had been sentenced to death for raping white women. Powe was familiar with the evidence gathered by the firm of racial discrimination in sentencing by Virginia juries, and he enlisted a group of lawyers and academics to develop comparable statistics for Mississippi and Louisiana. CRC attorneys presented this evidence to courts in both states in unsuccessful attempts to block the executions.[15]

Equal protection challenges to capital punishment persisted throughout the 1950s. The most comprehensive effort was undertaken by Ernest D. Jackson, a Jacksonville lawyer and graduate of Howard law school who advanced the argument twice before the Supreme Court of Florida and once in federal appeals court. Florida law at that time prescribed death as the punishment for rape unless a majority of the jury recommended mercy. Jackson examined Florida sentencing practices since 1925 and discovered that thirty-three African Americans and only one white defendant had been executed for rape. Furthermore, he pointed out that Florida juries had never recommended mercy when a defendant was black and his victim white. As in Virginia, Mississippi, and Louisiana, however, the Florida courts were unpersuaded by this evidence because it did not take into account variations in the particular facts of the cases, the autonomous nature of jury deliberations, or the special character of legal evidence. "To a sociologist or a psychologist in some fields of research [the arguments] would no doubt have validity," Justice Glenn Terrell admitted, "but in a court of law as presented they are devoid of force or effect."[16]

Equal protection challenges to the death penalty returned to the Virginia Supreme Court of Appeals in the 1960s. Attorneys for the defendant in *Wansley v. Commonwealth* (1964) did not introduce statistical evidence of sentencing disparity but contended instead that the Virginia rape statute was unconstitutional because it maintained the antebellum distinctions between punishments for white and black defendants. In arguments that closely paralleled those raised by Martin Martin and Samuel Tucker in the Richmond hustings court fourteen years earlier, Wansley's attorneys argued that although the statute no longer prescribed specific punishments for different races, it informally maintained two tiers of punishment—the death penalty for blacks and a maximum of twenty years in prison for whites—that had existed before the Civil War. The Supreme Court of Appeals refused to consider this argument, finding other grounds to reverse the conviction.[17]

Four years later the court explicitly addressed the sentencing disparity argument in two cases arising from the rape of a white woman in Norfolk. Attorneys for Bernard Fogg and Elvin Brickhouse, Jr., presented the justices with statistics from Donald Partington's article in the *Washington and Lee Law Review* showing that of the fifty-six men executed for rape or attempted rape since 1908, all had been African Americans. This evidence had not been introduced at trial, however, and the court refused to take judicial notice of the penitentiary records that Partington had utilized. Citing the decision in *Hampton v. Commonwealth* (1950), the justices held that the defendant bore the burden of proving discrimination at trial.[18]

In the early 1960s attorneys for the NAACP Legal Defense and Educational Fund (LDF) launched a national campaign to abolish the death penalty for rape. The catalyst for this undertaking was United States Supreme Court Justice Arthur Goldberg's dissent from a denial of certiorari in *Rudolph v. Alabama* (1963). Goldberg urged attorneys to litigate various issues associated with the imposition of capital punishment for rape. Although he did not mention racial discrimination as one of the issues, the LDF decided to focus on sentencing disparity, drawing on the experiences of lawyers who had raised equal protection arguments throughout the previous decade. Jack Greenberg, director of the LDF, later identified the Martinsville and Florida cases as significant precursors to the LDF's organized attack.[19]

Reviewing the earlier cases, the LDF concluded that more sophisticated social science evidence would be necessary to convince intransigent judges. It enlisted Marvin Wolfgang, a criminologist at the University of Pennsylvania, to collect and evaluate data on 3,000 capital rape cases from eleven states. Wolfgang controlled for variables such as the degree of violence and the prior criminal record of the defendant, which judges in earlier cases had blamed for the disparities, and concluded that none of those factors diminished the statistical connection between the presence of a black defendant and a white victim and the imposition of the death penalty. Lawyers for the LDF introduced these findings in dozens of cases, but each time the courts rejected the statistical evidence as inconclusive.[20]

The disposition of *Maxwell v. Bishop,* the most publicized case in the LDF campaign, revealed that judicial suspicion of statistical arguments against the death penalty had not abated twenty years after Martinsville. William Maxwell, a black man, had been sentenced to death by an Arkansas jury for the rape of a white woman. In a habeas corpus proceeding, Maxwell's attorneys, led by Anthony Amsterdam, a law professor and architect of the LDF's capital punishment campaign, presented evidence from Wolfgang's work to demonstrate that black defendants convicted of raping white women in Arkansas were more than four times as likely to be sentenced to death than black or white defendants convicted of raping women of their own race.

Judges in the district and circuit courts questioned the relevance of the Wolfgang study because Maxwell's attorneys had presented no evidence that the jury in his particular case had harbored discriminatory motives. Judge Harry Blackmun, who wrote the opinion for the eighth circuit, was also distressed by Amsterdam's admission that the court's acceptance of Wolfgang's statistics would make it unconstitutional for the state of Arkansas to sentence African Americans to death for rape while leaving open the possibility that whites could still be executed. When pressed during oral arguments, Amsterdam replied that "once the negro situation was remedied the white situation 'would take care of itself.'" Blackmun was unwilling, however, to accept a constitutional doctrine of equality which explicitly favored one racial group and protected the other "only through assumed and hoped-for day-to-day practicalities."[21]

The most significant objections to the sentencing disparity argument in *Maxwell* focused on the validity of the statistical evidence. Some of the reservations concerned the applicability of the Arkansas data, since the county in which Maxwell was prosecuted had not been included in Wolfgang's sample. But the judges also expressed broader concerns about the usefulness of empirical evidence in legal proceedings. "Statistics are elusive things at best, and it is a truism that almost anything can be proved by them," declared district judge J. Smith Henley. "We are not certain," wrote Judge Blackmun for the eighth circuit, "that, for Maxwell, statistics will ever be his redemption." In 1970 the Supreme Court vacated the judgment on other grounds, but it declined even to hear arguments on the equal protection issue.[22]

By 1970 the LDF had virtually abandoned the equal protection strategy, in part because of its failure in the courts and in part because other abolitionist organizations, especially the ACLU, had defined capital punishment as a general civil liberties issue which affected defendants of all races who had been convicted of all manner of capital crimes. Attorneys for the LDF still included equal protection arguments in their appellate briefs, but they began emphasizing other constitutional provisions, particularly the cruel and unusual punishment clause of the Eighth Amendment. When the Supreme Court invalidated existing death penalty statutes as unconstitutionally arbitrary in *Furman v. Georgia* (1972), which involved one African American sentenced to death for murder and two sentenced for rape, only justices Thurgood Marshall and William O. Douglas explicitly acknowledged evidence of racial discrimination in capital sentencing, while Justice Potter Stewart alluded to the potential for racial bias created by the lack of clear standards in state laws. The most telling illustration of the Court's disregard for sentencing disparity arguments appeared in *Coker v. Georgia* (1977). In declaring the death penalty for rape unconstitutional, which was the initial goal of the equal protection campaign, the majority opinion did not mention race at all, focusing instead on the disproportionality of a death sentence for a crime which did not take a life.[23]

In 1987 the United States Supreme Court directly addressed for the first time the issue of racial disparity in capital sentencing. In *McClesky v. Kemp*, a case involving a black man sentenced to death in Georgia for the murder of a white police officer, LDF lawyers presented evidence culled from an exhaustive report, commissioned by the LDF, on Georgia homicide sentencing since *Furman*. Utilizing extensive multivariate analysis, researchers David Baldus, George Woodworth, and Charles Pulaski found no significant link between capital sentencing and the race of a defendant, but they discovered that, even when they controlled for variables other than race, murderers of whites were about four times more likely to receive the death penalty than murderers of nonwhites. Moreover, these disparities occurred most often in cases that lacked extreme aggravating or mitigating circumstances, increasing the discretion of prosecutors and juries.[24]

Although the majority of the Supreme Court presumed that the Baldus study was statistically valid and conceded that it "indicates a discrepancy that appears to correlate with race," the Court held that a condemned person had to show overt bias either by the state legislature in passing the death penalty provisions or by the jury in deciding his particular case. Justice Lewis Powell's majority opinion, like the rulings of judges in numerous earlier cases, betrayed a skepticism of the role of statistical methods in legal analysis, emphasized the primacy of state legislatures in formulating death penalty policy, and placed great faith in jurors' abilities to render decisions based on the relevant facts of a case. Indeed, Justice Powell, who had once professed that his "understanding of statistical analysis . . . ranges from limited to zero," had tried to convince his colleagues to deny certiorari in the *McClesky* case because the Baldus study "tends to show that the system operates rationally as a general matter: The death penalty was most likely in those cases with the most severe aggravating factors and the least mitigating factors, and least likely in the opposite cases. The pattern suggests precisely the kind of careful balancing of individual factors that the Court required."[25]

After *McClesky*, efforts to end racial discrimination in capital sentencing shifted to the legislative arena, but elected representatives proved as reluctant as judges to limit the discretionary powers of prosecutors and jurors. In 1994, for example, the United States Congress considered a $30 billion crime bill. The House version of the bill contained a Racial Justice Act that would have allowed federal and state prisoners on death row to use statistical evidence to prove that their sentences furthered a pattern of racial discrimination in capital sentencing. Conservative senators threatened to filibuster if the "quota for murderers" provision passed, because they feared that it would effectively abolish the death penalty. The Congressional Black Caucus, in turn, threatened to block passage of the entire bill if the "racial justice" provisions did not remain intact. The black caucus briefly stalled the bill in the House by joining Republicans and conservative Democrats who opposed the gun control elements of the bill. The caucus relented, however, under pressure from black mayors who coveted the funds for crime prevention and social programs that the bill would allocate to urban areas. In August 1994 both houses of Congress approved a crime bill, signed into law by President Bill Clinton on September 13, that did not include the Racial Justice Act.[26]

Despite the failure of equal protection attacks on capital punishment, the Martinsville case stands as a significant episode in the legal history of civil rights. In 1985 Samuel Tucker rated the Martinsville case as one of the most influential cases with which he had been associated, placing it just behind his work for educational equality. The ranking is significant because the strategies developed on behalf of the Martinsville Seven represented an attempt to link the NAACP's criminal litigation efforts to the more conventional aspects of the civil rights movement, such as the desegregation of schools, transportation, and public facilities. The attorneys for the seven decided against using arguments based on the Eighth Amendment, Roland Ealey explained, because they wanted to emphasize equal protection and due process, "the bedrock of legal rights."[27] It was no coincidence that Tucker, Ealey, and Martin Martin formulated their attack on the discriminatory application of the death penalty at the same time that Thurgood Marshall, Oliver Hill, and Spottswood Robinson mounted a direct assault on the "separate but equal" doctrine. Both instances constituted the beginning of a unified campaign to challenge directly the unequal treatment of African-American citizens in every facet of the social, political, and legal institutions of the United States.

NOTES

BIBLIOGRAPHY

INDEX

NOTES

Abbreviations

ACLU Papers	Papers of the American Civil Liberties Union, Seeley G. Mudd Library, Princeton University, Princeton, N.J.
Appellants' Brief	Petition for Writ of Error, record no. 3635, *Hampton v. Commonwealth*, Virginia State Law Library, Richmond
Battle Papers	Executive Papers of Governor John S. Battle, 1950–54, Virginia State Library and Archives, Richmond
BF-NAACP Papers	Branch Files, Papers of the National Association for the Advancement of Colored People, Library of Congress, Washington, D.C.
Burton Papers	Harold Hitz Burton Papers, Library of Congress, Washington, D.C.
Change of Venue Testimony	Transcript of Testimony, Motion for Change of Venue, *Commonwealth v. Joe Henry Hampton*, Martinsville Circuit Court
Commonwealth's Brief	Brief on Behalf of the Commonwealth, record no. 3640, *Taylor and Hairston v. Commonwealth*, Virginia State Law Library, Richmond
Communism File	File 350.21: Communism, Records of the Foreign Service Posts of the Department of State, Record Group 84, Washington National Records Center, National Archives and Records Administration, Suitland
CRC Papers	Papers of the Civil Rights Congress, Schomburg Center for Research in Black Culture, New York
Dabney Papers	Virginius Dabney Papers, University of Virginia Library, Charlottesville
Frank Hairston Transcript	Transcript of Testimony, *Commonwealth v. Frank Hairston, Jr.*, Martinsville Circuit Court
GO-NAACP Papers	General Office Files, Papers of the National Association for the Advancement of Colored People, Library of Congress, Washington, D.C.

Grayson Transcript	Transcript of Testimony, *Commonwealth v. Francis DeSales Grayson*, Martinsville Circuit Court
Hampton Transcript	Transcript of Testimony, *Commonwealth v. Joe Henry Hampton*, Martinsville Circuit Court
Howard Hairston Transcript	Transcript of Testimony, *Commonwealth v. Howard Hairston*, Martinsville Circuit Court
LF-NAACP Papers	Legal Files, Papers of the National Association for the Advancement of Colored People, Library of Congress, Washington, D.C.
MCC	Clerk's Office, Martinsville Circuit Court, Martinsville, Va.
Millner Transcript	Transcript of Testimony, *Commonwealth v. Booker T. Millner*, Martinsville Circuit Court
Nash Files	Phileo Nash Files, Harry S. Truman Library, Independence, Mo.
Patterson Papers	William L. Patterson Papers, Moorland-Spingarn Research Center, Howard University, Washington, D.C.
Preliminary Hearing Transcript	Transcript of Preliminary Hearing, *Commonwealth v. Joe Henry Hampton*, Feb. 17, 1949, copy in file a128, box 7, CRC Papers
Reply Brief	Reply Brief for Plaintiffs in Error, record nos. 3635–40, *Hampton v. Commonwealth*, Virginia State Law Library, Richmond
Spingarn Papers	Arthur Spingarn Papers, Library of Congress, Washington, D.C.
Taylor and Hairston Transcript	Transcript of Testimony, *Commonwealth v. John Clabon Taylor and James Luther Hairston*, Martinsville Circuit Court
Truman Papers	Harry S. Truman Papers, Harry S. Truman Library, Independence, Mo.
Tuck Papers	Executive Correspondence of Governor William M. Tuck, 1946–50, Virginia State Library and Archives, Richmond
Wilkins Papers	Roy Wilkins Papers, Library of Congress, Washington, D.C.

Introduction

1. Bowers, *Legal Homicide*, App. A, is the most accessible compilation of state-imposed executions between 1864 and 1982 but it includes only those executions

carried out by state prison authorities. Schneider and Smykla, "Summary Analysis," is a brief description of a more comprehensive machine-readable database, M. Watt Espy and John Ortiz Smykla, *Executions in the United States, 1608–1987: The Espy File* (Ann Arbor, Mich., 1987), which contains information on nearly 15,000 executions performed by federal, state, and local authorities.

Descriptions of reported lynchings appear in National Association for the Advancement of Colored People, *Thirty Years of Lynching*, 43–105; Ames, *Changing Character of Lynching*, 34–50; Guzman, *Negro Year Book, 1941–1946*, 304–6.

2. Wright, *Racial Violence in Kentucky*, is an excellent analysis of the transformation from mob rule to institutionalized violence. But see Brundage, *Lynching in the New South*, 255–57, which notes important distinctions between the rituals of the mob and the rituals of the courtroom.

3. See Martin, "Oklahoma's 'Scottsboro' Affair," 175–88; Cortner, *"Scottsboro" Case in Mississippi;* and Carter, *Scottsboro*. For a catalog of innocent defendants, white and black, who were wrongfully convicted of murder or capital rape between 1900 and 1985, see Bedau and Radelet, "Miscarriages of Justice," 91–172.

4. Two recent interpretations of the Martinsville case place it squarely in the tradition of "legal lynchings" like Scottsboro. See Simmons, "Virginia Justice and the Martinsville Seven," and Horne, *Communist Front?* 213–23.

5. *Virginia Code Annotated*, ch. 173, § 4414 (1942).

6. Change of Venue Testimony, 47–58, 88; *Martinsville Bulletin*, April 19, 1949.

7. Brundage, *Lynching in the New South*, 15, 140, 186–90; Ames, *Changing Character of Lynching*, 34–50; National Association for the Advancement of Colored People, *Thirty Years of Lynching*, 41; Bowers, *Legal Homicide*, App. A; Chamberlain, *Negro and Crime in Virginia*, 73.

8. Walker, *Popular Justice*, 194–97, 201–5, 208–13. For a discussion of the tension between crime control and due process ideals, see Packer, *Limits of the Criminal Sanction*, 158–63.

9. Powell v. Alabama, 287 U.S. 45 (1932); Brown v. Mississippi, 297 U.S. 278 (1936); Chambers v. Florida, 309 U.S. 227, 237–38 (1940); Bodenhamer, *Fair Trial*, 101–5. On the Supreme Court's role in *Powell* and *Brown*, see Carter, *Scottsboro*, 160–65, and Cortner, *"Scottsboro" Case in Mississippi*, chap. 6.

10. Schneider and Smykla, "Summary Analysis," 11–13.

11. No comprehensive account of the NAACP's criminal due process campaign exists. Mark Tushnet devotes some attention to the subject in *Making Civil Rights Law*, chap. 4. An excellent study of the NAACP's role in an early criminal case is Cortner, *A Mob Intent on Death*, which examines the Supreme Court's ruling in Moore v. Dempsey, 261 U.S. 86 (1923). *Moore* held that mob-dominated legal proceedings violated due process. Kluger, *Simple Justice*, 144–54, and Tushnet, *NAACP's Legal Strategy*, 38–42, examine the effect of the association's criminal litigation experience on its desegregation campaign.

12. The rivalry between the NAACP and the Communist party is discussed in

Record, *Race and Radicalism;* and Carter, *Scottsboro,* chap. 3. On the relationship between anticommunism and racism, see Horne, *Black and Red,* and Clark, "Analysis of the Relationship between Anti-Communism and Segregationist Thought."

1. A Rape in Martinsville

1. *Daily Worker,* May 31, 1949; Harold C. Woodruff to Charles P. Chew, June 7, 1949, box 115, Battle Papers; Frank Hairston Transcript, 23–24.

2. Woodruff to Chew, 1–2; Frank Hairston Transcript, 110–15; Grayson Transcript, 61–62; Taylor and Hairston Transcript, 98–105.

3. Frank Hairston Transcript, 117–18, 126–27; Millner Transcript, 76–78, 99.

4. Hampton Transcript, 32, 92–93; Frank Hairston Transcript, 118, 130–32; Millner Transcript, 78.

5. Grayson Transcript, 55–60; Taylor and Hairston Transcript, 64–68, 114–15.

6. Hampton Transcript, 36–37, 68–72, 111–17; Frank Hairston Transcript, 89–103.

7. Hampton Transcript, 39–40, 52–54; Frank Hairston Transcript, 149–51; Howard Hairston Transcript, 34, 48–50.

8. Hampton Transcript, 72–74; Frank Hairston Transcript, 82–86; Millner Transcript, 43–45; Taylor and Hairston Transcript, 96–97.

9. Frank Hairston Transcript, 66, 84–85; Millner Transcript, 40–41.

10. *Daily Worker,* June 3, 1949; Woodruff to Chew, p. 5; "A Petition to His Excellency John S. Battle, Governor of Virginia, for Commutation of Sentence," n.d., p. 3, box 115, Battle Papers.

11. Frank Hairston Transcript, 67; Millner Transcript, 40–41.

12. Hampton Transcript, 78–80, 82–83; Frank Hairston Transcript, 104–5; Millner Transcript, 57–58.

13. Millner Transcript, 46–48, 80. Unlike most other states, incorporated cities in Virginia maintained a judiciary independent of the judicial system of the counties in which they were physically located. Like many of the state's smaller cities, however, the city of Martinsville shared jail facilities with the surrounding county. See Bain, *"A Body Incorporate",* 27; Virginia Department of Corrections, *Annual Report* (Richmond, 1949), 110.

14. Salmon, *Guide to State Records,* 39–40. On the development of state police departments in general, see Johnson, *American Law Enforcement,* 155–66, and Smith, *Rural Crime Control,* chap. 5.

15. Hampton Transcript, 60; Frank Hairston Transcript, 69–71.

16. Hairston Transcript, 71–72, 122–23; Millner Transcript, 48, 80–81.

17. Statement of Frank Hairston, Jr., file 149-607, MCC.

18. Millner Transcript, 48–50, 80–81; Statement of Booker T. Millner, file 149-606, MCC.

19. *Martinsville Bulletin,* Jan. 9, 1949; Grayson Transcript, 39–40; Taylor and Hairston Transcript, 42–46.

20. Woodruff to Chew, p. 6; Petition for Commutation, 3; *Daily Worker,* June 3, 1949.

21. Taylor and Hairston Transcript, 44–47, 55.

22. Ibid., 44–49; Petition for Commutation, 3; *Daily Worker,* June 3, 1949; Statement of James Luther Hairston, file 149-609, MCC.

23. Statement of Howard Hairston, file 149-610, MCC; Howard Hairston Transcript, 56–59; Petition for Commutation, 3; *Daily Worker,* June 3, 1949.

24. Woodruff to Chew, 6; Petition for Commutation, 3; *Daily Worker,* June 3, 1949.

25. Grayson Transcript, 42–45; Statement of Francis DeSales Grayson, Jan. 9, 1949, file 149-611, MCC.

26. Change of Venue Testimony, 84–85, 90; Taylor and Hairston Transcript, 56.

27. Taylor and Hairston Transcript, 56.

28. Statement of John Clabon Taylor, file 149-608, MCC.

29. Millner Transcript, 45; Grayson Transcript, 86–88; Taylor and Hairston Transcript, 97.

30. Frank Hairston Transcript, 105–6; Millner Transcript, 58–59; Howard Hairston Transcript, 38–39; Grayson Transcript, 80.

31. Woodruff to Chew, p. 5; *Daily Worker,* June 3, 1949; Order Book, Martinsville Circuit Court, Jan. 14, 1947, 1:27.

32. Hampton Transcript, 54–58, 61–62, 74–75.

33. Statement of Joe Henry Hampton, file 149-612, MCC.

34. Change of Venue Testimony, 74, 79, 92–93; Woodruff to Chew, p. 3.

35. Woodruff to Chew, p. 3; *Martinsville Bulletin,* Jan. 10, 1949.

36. *Martinsville Bulletin,* Jan. 28, 1949, Feb. 2, 1949.

37. Ibid., Jan. 17, 1949; Richmond *Afro-American,* Jan. 29, 1949.

38. Hampton Transcript, 81–86; Frank Hairston Transcript, 106; Millner Transcript, 59–60; Howard Hairston Transcript, 39–40; Grayson Transcript, 81.

39. *Martinsville Bulletin,* Feb. 18, 1949; Richmond *Times-Dispatch,* Feb. 18, 1949.

40. Hoffer, Mann, and House, *Jails of Virginia,* 222–23.

41. Preliminary Hearing Transcript, 2–8.

42. Ibid., 22–40.

43. Rosett and Cressey, *Justice by Consent,* 17–19; LaFave and Israel, *Criminal Procedure,* 765–72.

44. Preliminary Hearing Transcript, 15–17, 20–21.

45. Ibid., 41–47; *Martinsville Bulletin,* Feb. 18, 1949.

46. Preliminary Hearing Transcript, 45–51.

47. Ibid., 49–53.

48. See Cleary, *McCormick on Evidence,* 83–85.

49. Preliminary Hearing Transcript, 54–55; Richmond *Times-Dispatch,* Feb. 18, 1949.

50. Order Book, Martinsville Circuit Court, April Term 1949, 1:466; *Daily Worker,* Feb. 1, 1951.

51. No one has undertaken a comprehensive analysis of the criminal justice system in Martinsville. However, Frankie Yvonne Bailey has studied the administration of justice in Danville, Martinsville's nearest urban neighbor. Bailey concludes that between 1900 and 1930 efforts to maintain the racial status quo in the legal system were subsumed within a broader concern for the maintenance of order and social stability. Bailey, "Boundary Maintenance," 189–91.

52. *Daily Worker*, May 31, 1949.

53. Smith, *Rural Crime Control*, 153–55; Johnson, *American Law Enforcement*, 115–17.

54. Richmond *Afro-American*, Feb. 26, 1949.

2. A Matter for the Jury to Decide

1. *Henry County: A Proud Look Back*, 34; Mitchell, "Political and Social History of Henry County," 12–13; United States Department of Labor, *Statistical Summary of the Martinsville Area*, [5]; Bureau of Population and Economic Research, *Economic and Social Summary*, 3, 7; Dodson, *Cities of the Commonwealth of Virginia*, s.v. "Martinsville."

2. Cleal and Herbert, *Foresight, Founders, and Fortitude*, 4–5, 17–18, 35, 71, 74–75, 135, 142; *Statistical Summary*, [8, 12]; Edwards, *Farm Family Income*, 13; Edwards, *Youth in a Rural Industrial Situation*, 8; *Martinsville Bulletin*, July 3, 1939, "Industry" sec.; *Economic and Social Summary*, 19; Crawley, "Governorship of William M. Tuck," map 4.

3. *Economic and Social Summary*, 7–8, 22–27; Chamberlain, *Negro and Crime*, 26–27.

4. Wilkinson, *Harry Byrd*, 9–11; Buni, *Negro in Virginia Politics*, 72; Chalmers, *Hooded Americanism*, 230–33; Ramsey, "Public Schools of Henry County," 88, 110; Pittsburgh *Courier*, May 21, 1949.

5. Martinsville–Henry County Woman's Club, *Martinsville and Henry County*, 89, 91; Hill, *History of Henry County*, 28–29; *Henry County: A Proud Look Back*, 34; Mitchell, "Political and Social History of Henry County," 18; *Daily Worker*, June 1, 1949.

6. On the traditional approach to interracial rape in Virginia courts, see Pincus, "Virginia Supreme Court," 243, 350. Cleal and Herbert, *Foresight, Founders, and Fortitude*, examines the development of industry in Martinsville. On the emerging standards of fair trial, see Bodenhamer, *Fair Trial*, 101–5.

7. "Memorial: Honorable Kennon Caithness Whittle," 209 Va. ci, ci–cvii (1968); *Martinsville Bulletin*, July 4, 1976, "People" sec.; Liebman, *Directory of American Judges*, s. v. "Whittle, Kennon C.;" *Daily Worker*, June 1, 1949.

8. Order Book, Martinsville Circuit Court, January Term 1949, 1:456; Harold C. Woodruff to Charles Chew, 7 June 1949, Battle Papers; *Martindale-Hubbell Law Direc-*

tory, 82d ed., 2:1732, 1740, 1756; Crawley, "Governorship of William M. Tuck," 429; Clarence P. Kearfott, letter to author, July 15, 1986.

9. Woodruff to Chew, p. 4; *Martinsville Bulletin,* Jan. 28, 1949; *Daily Worker,* Jan. 14, 1951; *Martindale-Hubbell Law Directory,* 82d ed., 2:2860; ibid., 96th ed., 3:6696.

10. Change of Venue Testimony, 2–4.

11. Ibid., 2.

12. *Martinsville Bulletin,* July 3, 1939, city sec.; Pittsburgh *Courier,* May 21, 1949. This pattern of limited racial tolerance was not unique to Martinsville. See, for example, Chafe, *Civilities and Civil Rights,* 138, and Myrdal, *An American Dilemma,* 30–31.

13. *Martinsville Bulletin,* Jan. 14, 1930, July 3, 1939, city sec., July 4, 1976, "History" sec.; Buni, *Negro in Virginia Politics,* 126; Ramsey, "Public Schools of Henry County," 129; Armour G. McDaniel to NAACP, Nov. 11, 1941, box C206, Application for Charter of Martinsville, Virginia, Branch, Oct. 24, 1941, box C246, Annual Report of Branch Activities—1944, Martinsville, Virginia, and Annual Report of Branch Activities—1948, Martinsville, Virginia, both in box C278, BF-NAACP Papers. On the importance of fraternal organizations in African-American life, see Dittmer, *Black Georgia,* 55–59.

14. Petition to Move for Change of Venue, file 149-612, MCC; Change of Venue Testimony, 265.

15. Change of Venue Testimony, 47–54.

16. Ibid., 67–71.

17. Ibid., 66–67, 102–3.

18. *Martinsville Bulletin,* July 4, 1976, "History" sec., June 4, 1989, sec. D.

19. Change of Venue Testimony, 63. On the response of southern black community leaders to racial crisis, see Bailey, "Boundary Maintenance," 106, 159–60, and Wright, *Racial Violence in Kentucky,* 295–96.

20. Change of Venue Testimony, 103–6, 115–16, 119–20.

21. Ibid., 82–88.

22. All of the affidavits are contained in file 149-162, MCC.

23. Change of Venue Testimony, 255–59.

24. Ibid., 259–65.

25. Ibid., 265–66.

26. Ibid., 266–67.

27. Hampton Transcript, 7–8. On the law and strategy of severance, see LaFave and Israel, *Criminal Procedure,* 765–72.

28. Woodruff to Chew, p. 4.

29. Frank Hairston Transcript, 12–13.

30. Ibid., 7–23; Hampton Transcript, 9–30; Millner Transcript, 7–17; Howard Hairston Transcript, 9–26; Grayson Transcript, 8–22; Taylor and Hairston Transcript, 10–41.

31. Hampton Transcript, 30–34.

32. Ibid., 35.

33. Frank Hairston Transcript, 30; Millner Transcript, 25; Howard Hairston Transcript, 33.

34. Hampton Transcript, 35–39; Frank Hairston Transcript, 25–32.

35. Order Book, Martinsville Circuit Court, April Term 1949, 1:484.

36. Frank Hairston Transcript, 32–46; Howard Hairston Transcript, 38; *Martinsville Bulletin*, April 21, 27, 28, 1949.

37. Frank Hairston Transcript, 32–46; Taylor and Hairston Transcript, 81–88, 103–4; *Martinsville Bulletin*, April 22, 1949.

38. Hampton Transcript, 50–59.

39. Frank Hairston Transcript, 48–53; Millner Transcript, 33–34.

40. Grayson Transcript, 56–57; Taylor and Hairston Transcript, 66.

41. Millner Transcript, 57–61; Frank Hairston Transcript, 65–68, 104–7; Hampton Transcript, 72–78, 82–86.

42. Grayson Transcript, 32–32a; Frank Hairston Transcript, 90–97; Howard Hairston Transcript, 70–84.

43. Hampton Transcript, 68–72, 111–17.

44. *Virginia Code Annotated* (1942), ch. 173, § 4414.

45. Hampton Transcript, 91–92; Frank Hairston Transcript, 117–18, 130–32.

46. Frank Hairston Transcript, 118–21, 132–33; Millner Transcript, 178–79.

47. Millner Transcript, 80, 93–95; Frank Hairston Transcript, 141–42.

48. Taylor and Hairston Transcript, 116–17, 123–34.

49. Hampton Transcript, 94–95; Millner Transcript, 81, 93–94; Taylor and Hairston Transcript, 132; Frank Hairston Transcript, 124, 132.

50. See, for example, Frank Hairston Transcript, 71–83.

51. Ibid., 147–48; Howard Hairston Transcript, 62–63, 94; Hampton Transcript, 105.

52. Millner Transcript, 48–50, 54, 81, 95. At both the preliminary hearing and the trial Barnes read, ". . . he took her up the ridge." Ibid., 52–53; Preliminary Hearing Transcript, 30.

53. Grayson Transcript, 44–55.

54. Hampton Transcript, 268–69; Howard Hairston Transcript, 93–94; Taylor and Hairston Transcript, 139–41; Frank Hairston Transcript, 159; Millner Transcript, 99–100; *Martinsville Bulletin*, April 26, 1949.

55. *Martinsville Bulletin*, May 3, 1949.

56. Ibid., April 27, 28, May 3, 1949.

57. Ibid., April 28, May 2, 1949.

58. Hampton Transcript, 119–24; Howard Hairston Transcript, 95–101; Grayson Transcript, 103–14.

59. *Martinsville Bulletin*, April 22, 27, 28, May 3, 1949.

60. Pittsburgh *Courier,* May 14, 1949; Richmond *Times-Dispatch,* June 20, 1993; Simmons, "Virginia Justice," 35–36.

61. Ibid., May 4, 1949; Richmond *Times-Dispatch,* May 4, 1949.

62. *Martinsville Bulletin,* May 4, 1949; Richmond *Afro-American,* May 14, 1949.

63. Richmond *Times-Dispatch,* May 4, 1949; Woodruff to Chew, p. 4; *Daily Worker,* June 2, 1949.

64. Hampton Transcript, 41–42, 67–68; Taylor and Hairston Transcript, 51–63, 81–88, 98–100; Frank Hairston Transcript, 36–39; *Martinsville Bulletin,* April 22, 27, 1949. Michael Meltsner discusses the difficulties of representing a defendant in a capital case in *Cruel and Unusual,* 69. On the importance of preserving the record for appeal, see Kaplan and Waltz, *Cases and Materials on Evidence,* chap. 1.

65. *Martinsville Bulletin,* April 28, 1949; Grayson Transcript, 7–8, 24–28, 34–36; Millner Transcript, 7–9; Taylor and Hairston Transcript, 8–9.

66. Hall, *Revolt against Chivalry,* 145–57, 201–6; Williamson, *Crucible of Race,* 115–30, 183–89, 306–10; Painter, "'Social Equality,'" 47–67; Brundage, *Lynching in the New South,* 70–72. Michael Grossberg describes a similar shift from patriarchy to judicial administration in the field of family law in *Governing the Hearth,* especially pp. 300–307. See also Berry, "Judging Morality," 837–38, 855.

67. Bessie G. Osby to John Battle, May 27, 1950, box 115, Battle Papers; Mrs. Robert Lee House to William Tuck, Aug. 29, 1949, box 116, Tuck Papers; Brownmiller, *Against Our Will,* 231–32; Hall, "'The Mind That Burns in Each Body,'" 335–36. References to the victim's mental breakdown appear in Richmond *Afro-American,* Feb. 10, 1951, and press release, Feb. 13, 1951, file a233, box 11, CRC Papers. On the treatment of Jehovah's Witnesses, see Penton, *Apocalypse Delayed,* 130–45.

68. E. A. Sale to Tuck, May 9, 1949, John P. Smith to Tuck, May 25, 1949, box 116, Tuck Papers; Danville *Bee,* May 3, 1949.

3. Arrangement in Red and Black

1. Pittsburgh *Courier,* May 7, 1949.

2. *Louisiana Weekly,* May 21, 1949, clipping in file a228, box 11, CRC Papers.

3. *Daily Worker,* May 9, 31, June 1, 2, 3, 1949. On the history of the *Daily Worker,* see Buhle, Buhle, and Georgakas, *Encyclopedia of the American Left,* s.v. "Daily Worker (and successors)."

4. Glazer, *Social Basis of American Communism,* 170–71. The best history of the Communist movement in the United States is Howe and Coser, *American Commu- nist Party.* On the Communist Party of the United States during the 1920s, see two books by Theodore Draper: *The Roots of American Communism* and *American Commu- nism and Soviet Russia.* Harvey Klehr, *The Heyday of American Communism,* covers the 1930s but focuses almost exclusively on institutional developments within the

party. On the relationship between the party and African Americans, see Naison, *Communists in Harlem,* and Kelley, *Hammer and Hoe.*

5. In addition to the works by Naison and Kelley, see Meier and Rudwick, "Origins of Nonviolent Direct Action," 332–44.

6. Martin, "International Labor Defense," 167–70.

7. Martin, *The Angelo Herndon Case;* Herndon v. Lowry, 301 U.S. 242 (1937). On the "clear and present danger" test, see Strong, "Fifty Years of 'Clear and Present Danger,'" 41–80.

8. Glazer, *Social Basis of American Communism,* 134; Carter, *Scottsboro,* 161–63, 318–24; Powell v. Alabama, 287 U.S. 45 (1932) (due process requires the appointment of counsel in capital cases); Norris v. Alabama, 294 U.S. 587 (1935) (exclusion of blacks from jury pools cannot be justified by an official's assertion of good faith). On the use of the legal system to promote radical causes, see Hakman, "Old and New Left Activity in the Legal Order," 105–21.

9. Mouledous, "From Browderism to Peaceful Co-Existence," 83–84; Horne, *Communist Front?* 29–40, 108–23; Martin, "Civil Rights Congress and Southern Black Defendants," 25–29; Martin, "Civil Rights Congress and the Second Red Scare," 7–10; Belknap, *Cold War Political Justice,* 58–73; Record, *Negro and the Communist Party,* 232, 254–56; Civil Rights Congress, *Civil Rights Congress Tells the Story,* 1.

10. Horne, *Communist Front?* 29.

11. Ibid., 31–37; Patterson, *Man Who Cried Genocide,* chaps. 4, 5; Naison, *Communists in Harlem,* 15–16; Smith, *Emancipation,* 403.

12. *Civil Rights Congress Tells the Story,* 1.

13. Glazer, *Social Basis of American Communism,* 134; Kennedy and Leary, "Communist Thought on the Negro," 120. The most complete account of the tension between the NAACP and the CPUSA, although excessively critical of leftist organizations, is Record, *Race and Radicalism.*

14. Kellogg, *NAACP* 1:9–19.

15. Ibid., 183–87, 205–8, 241–45; Horne, *Communist Front?* 34; Kluger, *Simple Justice,* 98–100, 102–4, 108–9, 112–15, 122–23; Wright, "NAACP and Residential Segregation," 49–51; Cortner, *Mob Intent on Death,* chap. 7; Hine, *Black Victory,* chap. 4. The citations for the Supreme Court decisions are Guinn v. United States, 238 U.S. 347 (1915); Buchanan v. Warley, 245 U.S. 60 (1917); Moore v. Dempsey, 261 U.S. 86 (1923); and Nixon v. Herndon, 273 U.S. 536 (1927).

16. Kluger, *Simple Justice,* 131–33; Cortner, *Mob Intent on Death,* 192–95; Carter, *Scottsboro,* chap. 3; Tushnet, *NAACP's Legal Strategy,* 1–13; Goings, *NAACP Comes of Age,* 18.

17. McNeil, *Groundwork,* 82–85; Tushnet, *NAACP's Legal Strategy,* 100–101; Roland D. Ealey, attorney, interview with author, Richmond, Aug. 13, 1991.

18. Record, *Race and Radicalism,* 6–10; Tushnet, *NAACP's Legal Strategy,* 37–38. On the Hollins and Crawford cases, see Martin, "Oklahoma's 'Scottsboro' Affair," 175–88; Tucker, "Racial Discrimination in Jury Selection," 739; Tushnet, *NAACP's*

Legal Strategy, 39–42; Kluger, *Simple Justice*, 147–54, 161. Hollins, after successfully appealing two death sentences, accepted a third jury's sentence of life imprisonment. Crawford also accepted a life sentence rather than appeal and risk the death penalty on remand. The ILD, convinced that legal action accompanied by mass protest would ultimately exonerate the men, criticized the NAACP for not carrying the appeals to their conclusion.

19. Wilkins, *Standing Fast*, 210–11; Horne, *Communist Front?* 134–48; Martin, "Civil Rights Congress and Southern Black Defendants," 34–39, 45–52; St. James, *National Association for the Advancement of Colored People*, 151–54; Martin, "Race, Gender, and Southern Justice," 256–61, 267–68; Record, *Race and Radicalism*, 152–56. McAuliffe, "Politics of Civil Liberties," 152–70, and Walker, *In Defense of American Liberties*, 208–11, discuss the ACLU's expulsion of Communist members. On the effect of anticommunism on southern racial attitudes see Horne, *Black and Red*, and Clark, "Analysis of the Relationship between Anti-Communism and Segregationist Thought."

20. Richmond *News Leader*, May 13, 1949; Richmond *Afro-American*, May 14, 1949, secs. 1, 2; Pittsburgh *Courier*, May 14, 1949; news release, May 13, 1949, box C211, BF-NAACP Papers.

21. Richmond *News Leader*, May 13, 1949; news release, May 13, 1949, box C211, BF-NAACP Papers. On the NAACP's policy regarding criminal representation, see memorandum, Thurgood Marshall to Legal Staff, Feb. 16, 1949, box B99, LF-NAACP Papers; Carter, *Scottsboro*, 52–53; St. James, *National Association for the Advancement of Colored People*, 50; Greenberg, *Crusaders in the Courts*, 102.

22. Richmond *Afro-American*, May 14, 1949, secs. 1, 2; Tushnet, *NAACP's Legal Strategy*, 39; interview with Roland Ealey, Aug. 13, 1991. On June 21, 1946, three black men from Princess Anne County had been executed for murder. Bowers, *Legal Homicide*, App. A, 512.

23. *Daily Worker*, May 30, 1949; Richmond *Afro-American*, June 4, 1949. On the Progressive party, see Record, *Negro and the Communist Party*, 278–85, and Markowitz, *Rise and Fall of the People's Century*, 266–311.

24. Patterson, *Man Who Cried Genocide*, 161–64; Horne, *Communist Front?* 21, 33–34; Patterson to Roy Wilkins, June 7, 1950, box A361, GO-NAACP Papers.

25. Richmond *Times-Dispatch*, June 13, 1949. For a complete account of the Trenton Six case, see Horne, *Communist Front?* chap. 5.

26. Richmond *News Leader*, June 9, 1949; Richmond *Times-Dispatch*, June 13, 1949; Richmond *Afro-American*, June 18, 1949; announcement of June 12 meeting, n.d., file a231, box 11, CRC Papers.

27. Richmond *News Leader*, May 14, 1949; *Martinsville Bulletin*, June 12, 1949.

28. Richmond *Times-Dispatch*, June 14, 1949; Richmond *Afro-American*, June 25, 1949, sec. 2. The attorney general listed the Civil Rights Congress as a "Communist," not "subversive," organization on October 21, 1948. See 13 Fed. Reg. 6135, 6137 (1948).

29. Oliver Hill, attorney, interview with author, Richmond, Aug. 13, 1991; program of the Annual Meeting of the Virginia State Conference of Branches, Richmond, Oct. 1951, box C212, BF-NAACP Papers; Sherman, *Case of Odell Waller,* 16–18, 34–37, 53, 64, 90–91.

30. Richmond *News Leader,* June 14, 1949.

31. Ibid., June 14, July 7, 1949, sec. B; Richmond *Times-Dispatch,* July 5, 1949; William Patterson to Roy Wilkins, June 7, 1950, box A361, GO-NAACP Papers; Tom Buchanan, D. C. Executive Secretary, CRC, to Patterson, June 20, 1949, Patterson to Buchanan, June 21, 1949, p. 3, file p50, box 80, CRC Papers.

32. Richmond *Times-Dispatch,* July 5, 1949; Richmond *Afro-American,* July 2, 1949; Patterson to Tom Buchanan, June 21, 1949, p. 3, file p50, box 80, CRC Papers.

33. Horne, *Communist Front?* 21–22, 47–49; Martin, "Race, Gender, and Southern Justice," 256–57; Record, *Negro and the Communist Party,* 260–62.

34. Record, *Race and Radicalism,* 153–54; W. Lester Banks to Roy Wilkins, Aug. 8, 1949, box C211, BF-NAACP Papers; memorandum, Thurgood Marshall to Wilkins, Nov. 16, 1949, box A193, GO-NAACP Papers.

35. Marshall to Patterson, June 9, 1950, box A361, GO-NAACP Papers.

36. Martin, "International Labor Defense," 187–89; Martin, "Oklahoma's Scottsboro Affair," 188; Martin, "Race, Gender, and Southern Justice," 256–57; Martin, "Civil Rights Congress and the Second Red Scare," 23.

37. Patterson, *Man Who Cried Genocide,* 161–62; Richmond *Afro-American,* June 18, 1949; Patterson to Wilkins, June 7, 1950, box A361, GO-NAACP Papers; *Civil Rights* (information bulletin of the St. Louis Chapter, CRC), May 1949, p. 3, copy located in file p121, box 83, CRC Papers.

38. Kellogg, "Civil Rights Consciousness," 18–41, describes how sensitivity to foreign criticisms of American racism affected American attitudes toward civil rights. For a convincing analysis of the relation between cold war ideology and civil rights in the context of school desegregation, see Dudziak, "Desegregation as a Cold War Imperative," 61–120. On the relationship between anticommunism and racism, see Clark, "Analysis of the Relationship between Anti-Communism and Segregationist Thought," 74–75, 115–16, 199–200.

39. W. Lester Banks to Roy Wilkins, Aug. 8, 1949, box C211, BF-NAACP Papers; Horne, *Communist Front?* 217.

4. Appealing the Judgments

1. Morgan v. Virginia, 328 U.S. 373 (1946).

2. Interview with Roland Ealey, Aug. 13, 1991; interview with Oliver Hill, Aug. 13, 1991; program of the Annual State Conference Meeting, Oct. 12–14, 1951, copy in box C212, BF-NAACP Papers; Higginbotham, "Conversations," 15; Hudson, "Hill v. Board of Education," 32; Wallenstein, "Oliver W. Hill versus Jim Crow,"

13–15; Barnes, *Journey from Jim Crow,* 41–48; Tushnet, *Making Civil Rights Law,* 72–75; Freeman, *Style of a Law Firm,* 260–61 n. 48; Pratt, *Color of Their Skin,* 16–17; Segal, *Blacks in the Law,* 187–88; Kluger, *Simple Justice,* 471–72. On the intellectual climate of Howard University in the 1930s, see McNeil, *Groundwork,* 82–85.

3. Interview with Oliver Hill, Aug. 13, 1991; Higginbotham, "Conversations," 11–14; Tushnet, *Making Civil Rights Law,* 10; Wallenstein, "Oliver W. Hill versus Jim Crow," 5–7; Buni, *Negro in Virginia Politics,* 153–57; Hudson, "Hill v. Board of Education," 32; Freeman, *Style of a Law Firm,* 267 n. 80; Segal, *Blacks in the Law,* 188; Kluger, *Simple Justice,* 471–72.

4. Tushnet, *NAACP's Legal Strategy,* 110; Kluger, *Simple Justice,* 472–73; Segal, *Blacks in the Law,* 187–88; Greenberg, *Crusaders in the Courts,* 118.

5. Baltimore *Afro-American,* May 11, 1963; interview with Roland Ealey, Aug. 13, 1991; interview with Oliver Hill, Aug. 13, 1991; Wallenstein, "Oliver W. Hill versus Jim Crow," 11; Sherman, *Case of Odell Waller,* 53, 90–92, 174; Smith, *Emancipation,* 236.

6. Interview with Oliver Hill, Aug. 13, 1991; Oliver Hill, interview by Richard Kluger, April 4, 1971, quoted in Wallenstein, "Oliver W. Hill versus Jim Crow," 27 n. 54; Barnes, *Journey to Jim Crow,* 63, 83, 144–45; Segal, *Blacks in the Law,* 188.

7. Interview with Oliver Hill, Aug. 13, 1991; interview with Roland Ealey, Aug. 13, 1991; Higginbotham, "Conversations," 38; Segal, *Blacks in the Law,* 188; Ralph Powe to Roland "Ealy," file a320, box 16, CRC Papers. Ealey declined the CRC's invitation.

8. Richmond *Afro-American,* May 14, 1949, sec. 2; Richmond *News Leader,* June 30, 1949; W. Lester Banks to Roy Wilkins, Aug. 8, 1949, box C211, BF-NAACP Papers.

9. Richmond *News Leader,* June 30, 1949; "A Petition for Re-Trial," n.d., telegram, Communist Club to Tuck, May 31, 1949, petition, "Free the Martinsville Seven," n.d., James Lionel Mack to Tuck, n.d., Ruth Frank to Tuck, June 14, 1949, Angus MacDonald to Tuck, June 4, 1949, box 116, Tuck Papers. On the activities of the CRC's Miami branch, see Martin, "Civil Rights Congress," 30–31.

10. Rev. John Maselink to Tuck, May 10, 1949, Henry Hannan to Tuck, n.d., Mrs. Robert Lee House to Tuck, Aug. 29, 1949, Sgt. George Temp to Tuck, May 22, 1949, Ellen Steger Groseclose to Tuck, May 5, 1949, and "An Interested Citizen" to Tuck, n.d., box 116, Tuck Papers.

11. Richard B. Poythress to Tuck, June 3, 1949, Ellen Boaz McManaway to Tuck, June 4, 1949, John W. Holloran III, to J. Lindsay Almond, Attorney General, June 21, 1949, ibid.

12. Ray E. Williams to Tuck, July 4, 1949, Everett Edwards to Tuck, July 11, 1949, James W. Mullins to Tuck, n.d., Tuck to Ray Williams, July 7, 1949, ibid.; Richmond *News Leader,* June 30, 1949.

13. Crawley, *Bill Tuck,* 50–53, 69–70, 184, 221–26; Wilkinson, *Harry Byrd,* 25–30, 60; Dabney, *Virginia,* 516–20; Richmond *News Leader,* June 30, 1949.

14. Richmond *Afro-American,* June 11, 1949; Danville *Bee,* Aug. 27, 1949; Tuck to Gertrude English, Aug. 5, 1949, box 116, Tuck Papers; Crawley, "Governorship of William M. Tuck," 604–5; Dabney, *Virginia,* 420.

15. Richmond *News Leader,* July 5, 1949, sec. B; Richmond *Times-Dispatch,* July 6, 1949; Richmond *Afro-American,* July 9, 1949.

16. Richmond *News Leader,* Aug. 2, 3, 1949; Richmond *Afro-American,* Aug. 13, 1949; Tuck to Kennon C. Whittle et al., Aug. 3, 1949, box 116, Tuck Papers.

17. St. James, *National Association for the Advancement of Colored People,* 120–21.

18. Richmond *Afro-American,* July 23, 1949; news release, May 13, 1949, Banks to Wilkins, Aug. 8, 1949, box C211, BF-NAACP Papers.

19. Richmond *Afro-American,* July 23, 1949; James P. Spencer to "Dear Pastor and Congregation," July 14, 1949, box C211, BF-NAACP Papers.

20. Banks to Roy Wilkins, Aug. 8, 1949, news release, Aug. 22, 1949, box C211, BF-NAACP Papers.

21. News release, Aug. 22, 1949, ibid.; Norfolk *Journal and Guide* (home ed.), Sept. 10, 1949; Richmond *Afro-American,* Sept. 10, 1949; Norfolk *Journal and Guide* (peninsula ed.), Sept. 17, 1949.

22. Wilkins, *Standing Fast,* 190; Buni, *Negro in Virginia Politics,* 127, 177; Dowdal H. Davis, president of the Negro Newspaper Publishers Association, to Wilkins, Jan. 8, 1950, pp. 2–3, box 3, Wilkins Papers; interview with Oliver Hill, Aug. 13, 1991.

23. Banks to Wilkins, Aug. 8, 1949, Banks to Moon, Aug. 9, 1949, Moon to Banks, Sept. 7, 1949, box C211, BF-NAACP Papers; Agenda, NAACP Legal Defense and Educational Fund, Inc., Dec. 19, 1949, box 44, Spingarn Papers.

24. Interview with Roland Ealey, Aug. 13, 1991; Appellants' Brief, passim. In their petition to the Virginia Supreme Court of Appeals, the attorneys also objected to the presence in the courtroom of police officers who were witnesses for the prosecution and to Judge Whittle's ruling on evidentiary motions in chambers without the defendants being present. These arguments, however, were not important to the disposition of the appeal.

25. Richmond *Afro-American,* Sept. 3, 10, 1949; Dec. 3, 1949; Richmond *News Leader,* Sept. 6, 1949. On the appellate process in Virginia, see Morris, *Virginia Supreme Court,* 69–72.

26. Richmond *Times-Dispatch,* Jan. 10, 1950; Richmond *Afro-American,* Jan. 14, 1950. The attorneys submitted six separate briefs in the case, each indicating which procedural errors specifically applied to the six trials.

27. Appellants' Brief, 10, quoting 56 Am. Jur. *Venue* sec. 69 (1947), and Wormeley v. Commonwealth, 51 Va. (10 Gratt.) 658 (1853).

28. Appellants' Brief, 6, 13; Pittsburgh *Courier,* Jan. 21, 1950; Richmond *Times-Dispatch,* Jan. 10, 1950.

29. Appellants' Brief, 7–10, 13; Reply Brief, 4.

30. Appellants' Brief, 6–7, 13; Reply Brief, 5.

31. Appellants' Brief, 15–16; Reply Brief, 11–12. Moore v. Dempsey, 261 U.S. 86 (1923), declared that mob-dominated criminal proceedings violated a defendant's due process rights under the Fourteenth Amendment.

32. See, for example, Brown v. Mississippi, 297 U.S. 278 (1936) (confessions obtained through physical torture are not voluntary and therefore violate due process); Chambers v. Florida, 309 U.S. 227 (1940) (psychological coercion violates due process); Malinski v. New York, 324 U.S. 401 (1945) (the admission into evidence of an involuntary confession violates due process even in the face of other overwhelming evidence of guilt); and Haley v. Ohio, 332 U.S. 596 (1947) (conviction of a black teenager who confessed after being held incommunicado for five hours overturned because his youth and lack of legal or parental counsel rendered his confession involuntary). On the development of the voluntariness test, see Nissman, Hagan, and Brooks, *Law of Confessions*, chap. 1.

33. Appellants' Brief, 19–21; Reply Brief, 9–10.

34. *Virginia Code Annotated*, ch. 173, § 4899 (1942).

35. Reply Brief, 7–9.

36. Appellants' Brief, 17–19. On the legislative history of capital punishment for rape in Virginia, see Partington, "Incidence of the Death Penalty," 50–51, and "Capital Punishment in Virginia," 101–12.

37. Ely, *Crisis of Conservative Virginia*, 51–54; Wilkinson, *Harry Byrd*, 133–37; Kluger, *Simple Justice*, 480–82; *New York Times*, Nov. 6, 1957; interview with Oliver Hill, Aug. 13, 1991. In 1957, at the height of Virginia's "massive resistance" against desegregated schools, Almond succeeded Thomas B. Stanley of Martinsville as governor of Virginia. Although Almond remained committed to the principle of segregation, he opposed state interposition and in 1959 convinced the General Assembly to accept token integration. See Ely, *Crisis of Conservative Virginia*, 122–33; Wilkinson, *Harry Byrd*, 138–49; Pratt, *Color of Their Skin*, 9–11; Bartley, *Rise of Massive Resistance*, 322–25.

38. Commonwealth's Brief, 7, 10–13; Richmond *Times-Dispatch*, Jan. 10, 1950.

39. Commonwealth's Brief, 15–16, 20–21, 23.

40. Ibid., 14–15, 23–24; Brief on Behalf of the Commonwealth, p. 23, record no. 3639, *Grayson v. Commonwealth*, Virginia State Law Library.

41. Commonwealth's Brief, 33; Richmond *Times-Dispatch*, Jan. 10, 1950.

42. Morris, *Virginia Supreme Court*, 38, 48–49, 53, 73, 77–78, 98–99, 176; Wilkinson, *Harry Byrd*, 24; interview with Roland Ealey, Aug. 13, 1991. For biographical information on the justices, see Richmond *Times-Dispatch*, July 30, 1958 (Hudgins), March 10, 1951 (Gregory), May 19, 1976, sec. B (Eggleston), Oct. 26, 1976, sec. B (Spratley), May 5, 1979, sec. B (Buchanan), Aug. 29, 1947, Jan. 12, 1951 (Staples), Dec. 21, 22, 1960 (Miller). Additional information as well as assessments of the justices' contributions to the state's jurisprudence can be found in the records of memorial proceedings contained in the *Virginia Reports*. See 200 Va. lxxxv (1959)(Hudgins); 193 Va. lxxix (1952)(Gregory and Staples); 217 Va. vii (1976) (Eg-

gleston); 218 Va. viii (1977)(Spratley); 223 Va. ix (1980) (Buchanan); 202 Va. cliii (1961) (Miller).

43. Morris, *Virginia Supreme Court*, 72–73; *Martinsville Bulletin*, March 14, 1950.

44. Morris, *Virginia Supreme Court*, 77, 109; Richmond *Times-Dispatch*, July 30, 1958; 200 Va. lxxv, cii–civ.

45. Hampton v. Commonwealth, 190 Va. 531, 544–45, 549–51 (1950); Morris, *Virginia Supreme Court*, 77.

46. *Hampton*, 557–58, 561–62.

47. Ibid., 554–57.

48. Interview with Roland Ealey, Aug. 13, 1991; Richmond *Times-Dispatch*, March 14, 24, 1950; Richmond *Afro-American*, April 1, 1950; Martin to Kennon C. Whittle, April 5, 1950, Joe Henry Hampton File, MCC; Martin to Herbert M. Levy, March 30, 1950, vol. 61 (1951), ACLU Papers.

49. Richmond *Times-Dispatch*, April 12, May 20, 23, 1950; M. M. Poindexter to Battle, May 22, 1950, Battle to Poindexter, May 23, 1950, box 115, Battle Papers.

50. Because the CRC could not always control the actions of local branches, some lapses occurred. For instance, in July 1949 the Wisconsin Civil Rights Congress organized a demonstration to persuade the mayor of Milwaukee to join the protests against the "Martinsville frameup." Most branches also participated, with the approval of the national office, in the letter-writing campaign to Governor Tuck. *Daily Worker*, July 12, 1949; Mrs. Bobby Graff, Miami Civil Rights Congress, to William Patterson, July 9, 1949, file p53, box 80, CRC Papers.

51. Press release, March 14, 1950, file a232, box 11, CRC Papers.

52. Richmond *Afro-American*, April 1, June 3, 1950; Norfolk *Journal and Guide*, June 3, 1950; *Daily Worker*, March 26, May 29, 1950; announcement of protest meeting, "They Must Not Die!," n.d., file a231, box 11, CRC Papers.

53. Conference list, June 3, 1950, *Papers of Felix Frankfurter* (microfilm), pt. 1, reel 45, frame 0741; Harper and Rosenthal, "What the Supreme Court Did Not Do in the 1949 Term," 293. On the procedure for appealing a case to the Supreme Court, see Prettyman, "Petitioning the United States Supreme Court," 582–603.

54. Cert. Memorandum, no. 538 Misc., 1949 Term, *Papers of Felix Frankfurter* (microfilm), pt. 1, reel 45, frames 0268–69; Richmond *Times-Dispatch*, May 20, 1950; interview with Roland Ealey, Aug. 13, 1991.

55. Hampton v. Commonwealth, 339 U.S. 989, no. 538 Misc., *cert. denied;* Cert. Memorandum, *Papers of Felix Frankfurter* (microfilm), pt. 1, reel 45, frames 0268–69.

56. Danville *Register*, June 6, 1950.

57. Hagan, "Patterns of Activism," 103, 113; Morris, *Virginia Supreme Court*, 77–78. Hagan believes that "the Virginia Supreme Court of Appeals is very close to being an ideal reflection of" a nonactivist court. Hagan, "Patterns of Activism," 113.

58. Davis v. Allen, 157 Va. 84 (1931); Morris, *Virginia Supreme Court*, 97–98.

59. Nelson, *Study of Judicial Review,* chap. 7; Partington, "Incidence of the Death Penalty," 44, 48, 60, 64–70; interview with Roland Ealey, Aug. 13, 1991. The single reversal occurred in a case in which the testimony of the alleged victim and her husband was judged so incredible "as to be unbelievable even to the most incredulous and naive." Legions v. Commonwealth, 181 Va. 89, 92 (1943).

60. Interview with Oliver Hill, Aug. 13, 1991. Some representative cases include Shelley v. Kraemer, 334 U.S. 1 (1948); Sweatt v. Painter, 339 U.S. 629 (1950); McLaurin v. Oklahoma State Regents, 339 U.S. 637 (1950); Chambers v. Florida, 309 U.S. 227 (1940); Ashcraft v. Tennessee, 322 U.S. 143 (1944); and Haley v. Ohio, 332 U.S. 596 (1948). On the Vinson Court's record on civil rights and criminal procedure, see Currie, *Constitution in the Supreme Court,* 358–64; Bolner, "Chief Justice Vinson and Racial Discrimination," 29–43; Gorfinkel, "Fourteenth Amendment and State Criminal Proceedings," 682–91.

61. Gorfinkel, "Fourteenth Amendment and State Criminal Proceedings," 690; Murphy, *Constitution in Crisis Times,* 263–64, 276–77, 303; Stephens, *Supreme Court and Confessions of Guilt,* 100–102; Harper and Etherington, "What the Supreme Court Did Not Do during the 1950 Term," 408–9.

5. "A More Novel, Innovative Strategy": Challenging the Death Penalty

1. Lawson, Colburn, and Paulson, "Groveland," 16–17; Martin, "Race, Gender, and Southern Justice," 256–57, 263–64; Martin, "Civil Rights Congress and Southern Black Defendants," 45–50; Horne, *Communist Front?* 74–98, 192–95, 205–12.

2. Patterson to Wilkins, June 7, 1950, box A361, GO-NAACP Papers.

3. Marshall to Patterson, June 9, 1950, ibid. Roy Wilkins later informed Patterson, "I have nothing to add to Mr. Marshall's letter, which expresses substantially what I would have said had I been in the city." Wilkins to Patterson, June 16, 1950, ibid.

4. Patterson to Anne Shore, June 14, 1950, file p92, box 82, CRC Papers; Patterson to Marshall, June 15, 1950, box A361, GO-NAACP Papers.

5. *Daily Worker,* June 12, 19, 1950; press release, June 16, 1950, file a232, box 11, CRC Papers; Herman Katzen to Marshall, June 23, 1950, box A369, and Marshall to Katzen, July 5, 1950, box A361, GO-NAACP Papers.

6. Bowers, *Legal Homicide,* 22; Baldus, Woodworth, and Pulaski, *Equal Justice and the Death Penalty,* 248–50; Johnson, "The Negro and Crime," 93–104; Garfinkel, "Research Notes," 369–81; Johnson and Johnson, *Research in Service to Society,* 140–41; Civil Rights Congress, *We Charge Genocide,* 160.

7. Partington, "Incidence of the Death Penalty," 68–70; interview with Roland Ealey, Aug. 13, 1991.

8. Richmond *Times-Dispatch,* June 21, 1950; Norfolk *Journal and Guide,* July 1,

1950; Battle to Rep. Burr P. Harrison, June 23, 1950, "A Petition to His Excellency John S. Battle, Governor of Virginia, for Commutation of Sentence," n.d., box 115, Battle Papers.

9. *Daily Worker,* July 5, 1950; John H. Marion to Virginius Dabney, June 22, 1950, box 8, Dabney Papers.

10. Richmond *Afro-American,* June 24, 1950; *Daily Worker,* June 30, July 5, 1950; Norfolk *Journal and Guide,* July 1, 1950; Program, "Civil Rights Congress—Madison Square Garden Meeting," June 28, 1950, file a181, box 9, CRC Papers.

11. *Daily Worker,* June 15, 1950; press release, Feb. 13, 1951, file a233, box 11, CRC Papers; Martin, "Civil Rights Congress and Southern Black Defendants," 41; Horne, *Communist Front?* 43, 46. Susan Brownmiller asserts that radical organizations often blamed the victims of rape in order to support the dogma that charges of interracial rape were invariably concocted to control unruly blacks. Brownmiller, *Against Our Will,* 227–29.

12. Approximately 90 letters asking Governor Battle for clemency on behalf of the Martinsville Seven are extant in box 115, Battle Papers.

13. Lillie Thomas to Battle, June 6, 1950, Arthur Hirshfield to Battle, June 13, 1950, box 115, Battle Papers. The form letter from the Council of Churches is attached to a letter from Frank D. Daniel to Battle, June 22, 1950, ibid. See also John H. Marion to Virginius Dabney, June 22, 1950, box 8, Dabney Papers. The facts of the Richmond police case are summarized in Davis v. Commonwealth, 186 Va. 936 (1943). Editorials in the Richmond *Afro-American,* July 15, 1950, Aug. 5, 1950, and the Norfolk *Journal and Guide,* July 8, 1950, also mentioned the case.

14. Morris U. Schappes to Battle, June 7, 1950, Gerda Lerner to Battle, June 8, 1950, Hanah Levin to Battle, June 8, 1950, box 115, Battle Papers.

15. Frank Daniel to Battle, June 22, 1950, Mr. and Mrs. Brown to Battle, June 8, 1950, and Aaron Holmes to Battle, n.d., ibid.

16. Bernard M. Dabney, Jr., to Battle, June 6, 1950, Bessie G. Osby to Battle, May 27, 1950, Carrie Shelton to Battle, May 3, 1950, ibid.

17. Hampton to Battle, June 21, 1950, Millner to Battle, n.d., Hairston to Battle, n.d., Grayson to Battle, June 21, 1950, ibid.

18. Battle to Grayson, June 23, 1950, ibid.

19. Anderson to Battle, June 27, 1950, ibid.; Richmond *Afro-American,* Feb. 10, 1951.

20. Henriques, "John S. Battle," 22–25, 38–40, 69, 177, 187, 188–93, 203–6, 316–17; Wilkinson, *Harry Byrd,* 91–99; Abramowitz and Paget, "Executive Clemency in Capital Cases," 141–42 n. 27, 178; Battle to Clara J. Napper, June 12, 1950, box 115, Battle Papers.

21. See Lawes, *Life and Death in Sing Sing,* chap. 8.

22. Richmond *Times-Dispatch,* July 8, 1950; Petition for Commutation, n.d., box 115, Battle Papers.

23. Richmond *Times-Dispatch,* July 8, 1950.

24. Ibid.

25. M. Elizabeth Kline to "Dear Friend," July 13, 1950, box A369, GO-NAACP Papers; press release, July 12, 1950, file a232, box 11, CRC Papers; *Daily Worker*, July 14, 17, 23, 1950.

26. Norfolk *Journal and Guide*, July 8, 1950; Suggs, "Black Strategy and Ideology," 190; Suggs, *P. B. Young*, 152–53.

27. Richmond *Afro-American*, July 15, 22, 1950.

28. Statement of Governor Battle re: Joe Henry Hampton et al., July 24, 1950, box 115, Battle Papers.

29. Ibid.

30. Richmond *Afro-American*, July 29, Aug. 5, 1950.

31. On the factors persuading state governors to commute death sentences, see Abramowitz and Paget, "Executive Clemency in Capital Cases," 159–77, and Johnson, "Selective Factors in Capital Punishment," 165–69.

32. *Daily Worker*, July 26, 1950.

33. Ibid.; flyer, "Save the Martinsville Seven from Death," [July 1, 1950], Official File, Truman Papers; Frost, *The Mooney Case*, 285–319; Dinnen, *The Purple Shamrock*, 307.

34. Interview with Roland Ealey, Aug. 13, 1991; Petition for Writ of Habeas Corpus, *Hairston v. Smyth*, Hustings Court of the City of Richmond, Part II, July 26, 1950, and Order, *Hairston v. Smyth*, July 26, 1950, copies located in file a230, box 11, CRC Papers.

35. Richmond *Afro-American*, Aug. 26, 1950; Norfolk *Journal and Guide*, Aug. 26, 1950; *Daily Worker*, Aug. 23, 1950.

36. Telegram, Patterson to White, July 27, 1950, and White to Patterson, July 31, 1950, box A361, GO-NAACP Papers.

37. Russell Meek, executive secretary of the Harlem CRC, to "Dear Friend," Sept. 7, 1950, box A369, ibid.; John Pittman, "Power Shown in the McGee Case," *Daily Worker*, Aug. 1, 1950, p. 6.

38. Norfolk *Journal and Guide* (Virginia ed.), Sept. 9, 1950; Richmond *Afro-American*, July 29, Sept. 9, 1950.

39. Miller et al., *Criminal Justice Administration*, 1235–36, 1245–46; interview with Oliver Hill, Aug. 13, 1991.

40. Bowers, *Legal Homicide*, 10–14; Meltsner, *Cruel and Unusual*, 18; Mackey, *Voices against Death*, xli; Bohm, "American Death Penalty Opinion," 118.

41. Wiecek, *Liberty under Law*, 157–58; Plessy v. Ferguson, 163 U.S. 537 (1896). Justice Holmes's comment appears in Buck v. Bell, 274 U.S. 200, 208 (1927).

42. Richmond *Times-Dispatch*, July 28, 1950; Norfolk *Journal and Guide* (Virginia ed.), Aug. 5, 1950.

43. Kluger, *Simple Justice*, 474–79; Tushnet, *NAACP's Legal Strategy*, 136–46; Ware, "Invisible Walls," 746–48, 757–61, 765–68. The Supreme Court declared restrictive covenants unconstitutional in Shelley v. Kraemer, 334 U.S. 1 (1948).

44. Kluger, *Simple Justice*, 472–75; Pratt, *Color of Their Skin*, 16–17; Wallenstein, "Oliver W. Hill versus Jim Crow," 27–28; interview with Oliver Hill, Aug. 13, 1991.

45. Memorandum, H. M. Levy to P. M. Malin, July 28, 1950, vol. 61 (1951), ACLU Papers.

46. Herbert Levy to Grace Rhoads, Feb. 16, 1951, ibid.; Muller, "Legal Defense Fund's Capital Punishment Campaign," 161–62; Walker, *In Defense of American Liberties*, 127–33, 162–64, 208–11, 237–39; Record, *Race and Radicalism*, 162–64.

47. Levy to Thurgood Marshall, Aug. 14, 1950, memorandum, George Soll to file, Jan. 4, 1951, Levy to Rhoads, Feb. 16, 1951, vol. 61 (1951), Levy to Thomas Elliston, May 1, 1951, vol. 47 (1951), ACLU Papers.

48. Liebman, *Directory of American Judges*, s.v. "Doubles, Malcolm Ray;" interview with Roland Ealey, Aug. 13, 1991; Act of June 25, 1948, Pub. L. 773, ch. 646, 62 *Statutes at Large* 869, 967. On the exhaustion doctrine, see Duker, *Constitutional History of Habeas Corpus*, 203–10.

49. Richmond *Times-Dispatch*, Oct. 1, 1950, sec. B. The editorial appeared in the Richmond *News Leader*, Sept. 22, 1950.

50. Joint Brief on Behalf of Petitioners, *Hampton v. Smyth*, pp. 2–3, and Petition for Writ of Habeas Corpus, *Hairston v. Smyth*, p. 2, copies located in file a230, box 11, CRC Papers.

51. Joint Brief, 4–7; Supplement to Joint Brief on Behalf of the Petitioners, *Hampton v. Smyth*, Appendix, copy in file a230, box 11, CRC Papers.

52. Richmond *Times-Dispatch*, Oct. 1, 1950, sec. B; Sherman, *Case of Odell Waller*, 64, 90–91.

53. Strauder v. West Virginia, 100 U.S. 303 (1879); Neal v. Delaware, 103 U.S. 370 (1881); Norris v. Alabama, 294 U.S. 587 (1935); Supplement to Joint Brief, 2–5. On the development of constitutional doctrine on jury exclusion, see Carter, *Scottsboro*, 320–24.

54. Civil Rights Cases, 109 U.S. 3 (1883); Yick Wo v. Hopkins, 118 U.S. 356 (1886); Richmond *Times-Dispatch*, Oct. 1, 1950, sec. B; Supplement to Joint Brief, 4–5; Petition for Writ of Habeas Corpus, 2. On state action and "color of law," see Tribe, *American Constitutional Law*, 1147–74.

55. Richmond *Times-Dispatch*, Oct. 1, 1950, sec. B; Richmond *Afro-American*, Oct. 7, 1950. On the career of W. Frank Smyth, see Keve, *History of Corrections in Virginia*, 122–23, 181, 278.

56. Richmond *Times-Dispatch*, Oct. 1, 1950, sec. B; Supplement to Joint Brief, 5.

57. Opinion, *Hampton v. Smyth*, pp. 3, 5, copy located in file 149-612, MCC.

58. Between 1908 and 1919, 11.3 percent of the African Americans convicted of rape in Virginia were sentenced to death. Between 1940 and 1950 that figure fell to 1.8 percent. Ibid., 4.

59. Ibid., 5–7.

60. Ibid., 5–6.

61. Richmond *Times-Dispatch*, Oct. 20, 28, 1950; Richmond *Afro-American*, Oct. 28, Nov. 4, 1950.

62. Richmond *Times-Dispatch*, Nov. 4, 1950.

63. Ibid.

64. "A Call for a Crusade against Jim Crow Justice in Virginia," Oct. 28, 1950, file a229, press release, Nov. 6, 1950, file a227, box 11, CRC Papers; *Daily Worker*, Oct. 12, 1950; Richmond *Afro-American*, Nov. 11, 1950.

65. "Why the Crusade on the Martinsville Seven?" Nov. 8, 1950, file a234, box 11, CRC Papers; *Daily Worker*, Oct. 24, Nov. 22, 1950; Norfolk *Journal and Guide*, Oct. 14, Dec. 2, 1950; Suggs, *P. B. Young*, 152–53.

66. *Daily Worker*, Nov. 8, 24, 1950.

67. Arthur McPhaul, executive secretary of the Civil Rights Congress of Michigan, to "Dear Pastor," Oct. 27, 1950, "Report of Campaign around Martinsville Seven, Detroit Civil Rights Congress," Nov. 1950, Shore to Aubrey Grossman and Patterson, Nov. 11, 1950, file p92, box 82, Lester Davis, executive secretary of the Civil Rights Congress of Illinois, to Grossman, Nov. 17, 1950, file p62, box 80, CRC Papers.

68. Minutes of the Membership and Annual Meeting of NAACP Legal Defense and Educational Fund, Inc., Nov. 13, 1950, box 44, Spingarn Papers; Norfolk *Journal and Guide*, Nov. 18, 1950.

69. "Proposed Rules for Delegation," file a233, box 11, CRC Papers.

70. Richmond *Times-Dispatch*, Nov. 11, 1950; Richmond *Afro-American*, Nov. 18, 1950.

71. Press release, "Martinsville Crusade Cancelled When Governor Grants Stay," n.d., file a227, Elaine Ross to Oliver Martin, Nov. 8, 1950, file a229, poster, "They Shall Not Die!!" n.d., file a234, box 11, CRC Papers; *Daily Worker*, Nov. 19, 1950; Taylor to Patterson, Nov. 18, 1950, folder 37, box 9, Patterson to Taylor, Nov. 22, 1950, folder 38, box 2, Patterson Papers.

72. Richmond *Afro-American*, Nov. 18, 25, 1950; Norfolk *Journal and Guide*, Nov. 25, 1950.

73. Norfolk *Journal and Guide*, Nov. 25, 1950; Pittsburgh *Courier*, Dec. 2, 1950.

74. Richmond *Afro-American*, Dec. 30, 1950.

75. Hampton v. Smyth, 340 U.S. 914, no. 245 Misc. (1951), *cert. denied;* Conference List, Dec. 29, 1950, *Papers of Felix Frankfurter* (microfilm), pt. 1, reel 54, frames 0659–60; Cert. Memorandum, no. 245 Misc. 1950 Term, box 220, Burton Papers.

76. Meltsner, *Cruel and Unusual*, 27–28; Tushnet, *NAACP's Legal Strategy*, 117–19; Kluger, *Simple Justice*, 128.

77. Tushnet, *NAACP's Legal Strategy*, 161; Dorin, "Two Different Worlds," 1671–90; Rosen, *Supreme Court and Social Science*, 202–3, 212–13; Morris, *Virginia Supreme Court*, 77–78; Murphy, *Constitution in Crisis Times*, 276–78.

78. Partington, "Incidence of the Death Penalty," 56–57; Rosen, *Supreme Court and Social Science*, 218–19; Gross and Mauro, *Death and Discrimination*, 120–21.

79. See, for example, Louisiana ex rel. Francis v. Resweber, 329 U.S. 459 (1947), in which the Court held that a second trip to the electric chair after a mechanical failure aborted the first attempt did not constitute cruel and unusual punishment or violate the double jeopardy clause of the Fifth Amendment.

80. Meltsner, *Cruel and Unusual*, 24; Partington, "Incidence of the Death Penalty," 63; Morris, *Virginia Supreme Court*, 158–60.

6. The Eleventh Hour

1. Richmond *Afro-American*, Feb. 3, 1951.

2. *Daily Worker*, Jan. 2, 12, 1951; chapter bulletin, Jan. 8, 1951, file j19, box 40, Patterson to "Dear Reverend," Jan. 8, 1951, memorandum, Aubrey Grossman to Chapter Secretaries, Jan. 9, 1951, file a229, box 11, CRC Papers.

3. Horne, *Communist Front?* 32; Grossman to Chapter Secretaries, Jan. 9, 1951, file a229, "The Case of the Martinsville Seven—Fact Sheet," Jan. 11, 1951, file a227, box 11, chapter bulletin, Jan. 22, 1951, file j19, box 40, CRC Papers.

4. Grossman to Josephine Grayson, Dec. 15, 1950, file a229, form letter from Grossman, Dec. 16, 1950, file a227, box 11, Grossman to Lester Davis, executive secretary of the Chicago CRC, Jan. 7, 1951, Davis to Grossman, Jan. 10, 1951, file p63, box 80, CRC Papers; flyer, "Seven Martinsville Negroes Railroaded!" n.d., box 115, Battle Papers; *Daily Worker*, Jan. 18, 1951.

5. Press release, Jan. 29, 1951, file a233, box 11, Alma Foley to Civil Rights Congress, Jan. 12, 1951, file p110, box 83, Katherine [Hyndman] to Grossman, Jan. 14, 1951, file p74, box 81, Yetta Land to Civil Rights Congress, Jan. 23, 1951, file p2, box 77, CRC Papers; *Daily Worker*, Jan. 29, 1951.

6. *Daily Worker*, Jan. 12, 17, 22, 25, 29, 1951; chapter bulletin, Jan. 22, 1951, file j19, box 40, CRC Papers; Horne, *Communist Front?* 218–19, 293.

7. Memorandum, Grossman to Chapter Secretaries, Jan. 9, 1951, file a229, Jemison to Patterson [copy of letter to Battle], Jan. 15, 1951, file a233, box 11, CRC Papers; Walker to Battle, Jan. 30, 1951, copy in box 77, Burton Papers; petition, "Must They Die?" n.d., petition, "Free the Martinsville Seven," n.d., "Emergency Petition to Save the Martinsville Seven," n.d., Harlin Talbert to Battle, Jan. 26, 1951, box 115, Battle Papers.

8. *Daily Worker*, Jan. 18, 1951; Roy Wilkins to Thurgood Marshall, Jan. 26, 1951, box 3, Wilkins Papers; Nancy [Kleinbord] to Aubrey [Grossman] and Pat [William Patterson], Feb. 14, [1951], file p42, box 79, CRC Papers; Horne, *Communist Front?* 63.

9. Norfolk *Journal and Guide*, Jan. 6, 1951; Norfolk *Journal and Guide* (Virginia ed.), Jan. 27, 1951; Richmond *Afro-American*, Jan. 27, 1951.

10. Patterson to Battle, Jan. 25, 1951, box 11, Battle Papers.

11. Danville *Register,* Jan. 26, 1951; Norfolk *Journal and Guide* (Virginia ed.), Feb. 3, 1951; Roy Wilkins to Thurgood Marshall, Jan. 26, 1951, box 3, Wilkins Papers; memorandum, Gloster Current to NAACP Branch Officers, Jan. 30, 1951, box A361, GO-NAACP Papers; Richmond *Afro-American,* Feb. 3, 1951.

12. *Martinsville Bulletin,* Jan. 30, 1951; Richmond *Afro-American,* Feb. 3, 1951; Pittsburgh *Courier,* Feb. 10, 1951; William Patterson to Clyde O. Jackson, Jan. 31, 1951, file m36, box 58, CRC Papers.

13. *Martinsville Bulletin,* Jan. 30, 1951; *Daily Worker,* Jan. 31, 1951; Pittsburgh *Courier,* Feb. 10, 1951; Henriques, "John S. Battle," 181–82.

14. Norfolk *Virginian-Pilot,* Feb. 1, 1951; *Daily Worker,* Jan. 31, 1951; Pittsburgh *Courier,* Feb. 10, 1951.

15. Richmond *Afro-American,* Feb. 3, 1951. On Sterling Hutcheson, see Peltason, *Fifty-Eight Lonely Men,* 212–13, and Kluger, *Simple Justice,* 486–87.

16. Norfolk *Journal and Guide* (Virginia ed.), Feb. 3, 1951; Richmond *Afro-American,* Feb. 3, 1951.

17. *Daily Worker,* Jan. 29, 30, 31, 1951; Norfolk *Journal and Guide* (Virginia ed.), Feb. 3, 1951.

18. Richmond *Afro-American,* Feb. 3, 1951; Richmond *Times-Dispatch,* Feb. 1, 1951; Kluger, *Simple Justice,* 485–86; Bryson, *Legal Education in Virginia,* 197–202.

19. Peltason, *Fifty-Eight Lonely Men,* 22–23; Kluger, *Simple Justice,* 141–44; Goings, *NAACP Comes of Age,* 21–24, 73–90.

20. Summary of Parker's Ruling, n.d., box 115, Battle Papers; Richmond *Times-Dispatch,* Feb. 1, 1951; Richmond *News Leader,* Feb. 1, 1951.

21. Richmond *Times-Dispatch,* Feb. 1, 2, 3, 1951; Richmond *News Leader,* Feb. 2, 1951; Mandel, "Vigil in Richmond," 7.

22. Mandel, "Vigil in Richmond," 6; Richmond *Times-Dispatch,* Feb. 2, 1951; Richmond *News Leader,* Feb. 1, 1951.

23. Caplan, "Virginia's Black Justice," 17; "The Shape of Things," 71; press release, Feb. 5, 1951, file a233, box 11, CRC Papers; handwritten recollections of Ossie Davis and Ruby Dee, n.d., folder 91, box 9, Patterson Papers; Richmond *Times-Dispatch,* Feb. 2, 1951; *Daily Worker,* Feb. 2, 1951.

24. Mail log for the week ending Feb. 2, 1951, memorandum, D. E. Long to Mr. Hopkins, Feb. 6, 1951, memorandum, Telegraph Office to Mr. Hopkins, Feb. 10, 1951, Official File, Truman Papers; Attorney General to Eleanor Roosevelt, Feb. 2, 1951, copy in Nash Files; press release, "Virginia Execution of Four of 'Martinsville Seven' Negroes Shocks World," n.d., file a233, box 11, CRC Papers; Richmond *Times-Dispatch,* Feb. 1, 1951; *Daily Worker,* Feb. 2, 1951.

25. Telegram, Soviet Workers to Battle, Jan. 31, 1951, box 115, Battle Papers; Richmond *News Leader,* Feb. 1, 1951; Richmond *Times-Dispatch,* Feb. 1, 1951.

26. *Daily Worker,* Jan. 18, 1951; Richmond *News Leader,* Feb. 1, 1951; petition, postmarked Jan. 15, 1951, box 115, Battle Papers; chapter bulletin, Jan. 29, 1951, p. 2, file j19, box 40, press release, "West German, French Youth, East Africans, Protest

Martinsville Seven Death Sentences," n.d., file a233, box 11, CRC Papers; telegram, American Embassy, London, to Department of State, Jan. 24, 1951, telegram to Secretary of State, Feb. 1, 1951, and telegram, American Embassy, London, to Department of State, Feb. 27, 1951, Communism File.

27. Statement by Governor Battle, Feb. 1, 1951, p. 2, box 115, Battle Papers; Henriques, "John S. Battle," 185–86; Dabney, *Virginia*, 527.

28. Richmond *Afro-American*, Feb. 10, 1951.

29. Norfolk *Journal and Guide*, Feb. 10, 1951; Richmond *Times-Dispatch*, Feb. 2, 1951.

30. Richmond *Afro-American*, July 29, Dec. 9, 1950, Feb. 10, 1951; *Daily Worker*, July 14, Nov. 8, 1950; Booker T. Millner to John Battle, n.d., Frank Hairston to Battle, n.d., Hampton to Battle, June 21, 1950, Grayson to Battle, June 24, 1950, box 115, Battle Papers; press release, "Xmas Greetings from France Pour in to 'Martinsville 7,'" Dec. 18, 1950, file a233, box 11, Nancy [Kleinbord] to Aubrey Grossman, Jan. 6, 1951, file p42, box 46, Patterson to Grayson, Jan. 2, 1951, file a227, box 11, CRC Papers.

31. Richmond *News Leader*, Feb. 2, 1951; Richmond *Afro-American*, Feb. 10, 1951; Keve, *History of Corrections in Virginia*, 118, 147–48, 180–81; Woodzell, "Electrocution and the Death Penalty in Virginia," 15–16.

32. Richmond *News Leader*, Feb. 2, 1951; Richmond *Afro-American*, Feb. 10, 1951; Pittsburgh *Courier*, Feb. 10, 1951; Mandel, "Vigil in Richmond," 5. Superintendent W. F. Smyth, Jr., sent separate letters indicating the date and time of death of each prisoner to Jesse D. Clift, clerk of the Martinsville Circuit Court. See Booker T. Millner file, no. 149-606, Frank Hairston, Jr., file, no. 149-607, Howard Lee Hairston file, no. 149-610, Joe Henry Hampton file, no. 149-612, Martinsville Circuit Court.

33. Mandel, "Vigil in Richmond," 8; Richmond *Times-Dispatch*, Feb. 5, 1951; "Statement: The Virginia Execution of Four of the Martinsville Seven," Feb. 2, 1951, "An Appeal to the Mayor of New York," Feb. 2, 1951, press release, "Richmond People Out in Front in Martinsville Defense Campaign," Feb. 10, 1951, file a233, box 11, CRC Papers.

34. Richmond *Times-Dispatch*, Feb. 3, 1951; Booker Carver Washington III to Battle, Feb. 5, 1951, box 115, Battle Papers.

35. Richmond *Afro-American*, Feb. 10, 1951; Richmond *Times-Dispatch*, Feb. 4, 5, 1951; *Daily Worker*, Feb. 5, 1951.

36. Petition for a Writ of Habeas Corpus, *Grayson v. Smyth*, box 77, and Diary of Harold Burton, Feb. 4, 1951, microfilm reel 3, Burton Papers; Louisiana ex rel. Francis v. Resweber, 329 U.S. 452 (1947); Berry, *Stability, Security, and Continuity*, 59–66, 145–46; Marquardt, "The Judicial Justice," 156–60, 173–74, 260–61.

37. Richmond *Times-Dispatch*, Feb. 6, 1951; Richmond *News Leader*, Feb. 5, 1951; Richmond *Afro-American*, Feb. 10, 1951; Norfolk *Journal and Guide*, Feb. 10, 1951; *Martinsville Bulletin*, Feb. 6, 1951. For dates and times of death, see letters from

W. F. Smyth, Jr., to Jesse D. Clift, Feb. 5, 1951, in Francis DeSales Grayson file, no. 149-611, and John Taylor and James Hairston file, no. 149-608/609, MCC.

Epilogue

1. Richmond *Afro-American*, Feb. 17, 1951; *Martinsville Bulletin*, Feb. 6, 1951.

2. Richmond *Afro-American*, Feb. 10, 1951; Grossman to Josephine Grayson, Feb. 16, 1951, Patterson to Josephine Grayson, March 19, 1951, file a229, box 11, Egri to Patterson, June 1, [1951], file m34, box 58, CRC Papers; Lowenfels, "Martinsville Chant," copy in file 57, box 2, Patterson Papers; Civil Rights Congress, *We Charge Genocide*; Henriques, "John S. Battle," 187 n. 20.

3. Richmond *Times-Dispatch*, Feb. 1, 1951; *Time*, Feb. 12, 1951, p. 21; Roanoke *World News*, Feb. 1, 1951; Danville *Register*, Jan. 26, 1951; Washington *Evening Star*, Feb. 4, 1951, reprinted in *Congressional Record*, 82d Cong., 1st sess., 1951, 97, pt. 11: A574.

4. Richmond *Afro-American*, Feb. 17, 1951; Norfolk *Journal and Guide*, Feb. 10, 1951.

5. William Patterson to John Taylor, Nov. 22, 1950, folder 38, box 2, Patterson Papers; Patterson to Mrs. Hairston, Feb. 27, 1951, file a229, box 11, Patterson to Josephine Grayson, Aug. 27, 1951, file m49, box 58, James Malloy to John Saunders, Oct. 31, 1951, file p137, box 84, CRC Papers.

6. *Daily Worker*, Feb. 1, 1951; advertisement, "An Open Letter to the Chief Justice of the United States Supreme Court," *Daily Compass*, Feb. 22, 1951, clipping in file j110, box 45, "Report of Campaign around Martinsville Seven," Detroit Civil Rights Congress, Nov. 1950, file p92, box 82, Patterson to Frances Damon, Nov. 17, 1950, file a227, box 11, Lester Davis to Grossman, Nov. 17, 1950, file p62, box 80, CRC Papers.

7. Walter White, typescript of syndicated column, Feb. 8, 1951, box 34, Wilkins Papers; Report of the Executive Secretary, NAACP, Jan. 1951, box A145, GO-NAACP Papers; *Nation*, Mar. 3, 1951, p. 212; "Equality before the Law," *Christian Century*, Feb. 21, 1951, p. 227; Dudziak, "Desegregation as a Cold War Imperative," 75–76.

8. Conservative southern attitudes toward communism and civil rights are explored in Clark, "Analysis of the Relationship between Anti-Communism and Segregationist Thought," 24–26, 74–75, 172, 199–200, and Fried, "Electoral Politics and McCarthyism," 195–200.

9. Levy to Seamans, Feb. 8, 1951, Seamans to Levy, Feb. 12, 1951, vol. 61 (1951), ACLU Papers.

10. Memorandum, American Embassy, London, to Department of State, Feb. 27, 1951, Communism File; Dudziak, "Desegregation as a Cold War Imperative," 98–102, 118.

11. Tinsley and Banks to Roy Wilkins, Feb. 8, 1951, Tinsley and Banks to Gloster Current, Feb. 8, 1951, box C212, BF-NAACP Papers; Meeting of the NAACP Board of Directors, Feb. 13, 1951, box A135, GO-NAACP Papers; Meeting of the Executive Committee of the Board of Directors, NAACP Legal Defense and Educational Fund, Inc., March 19, 1951, box 44, Spingarn Papers; Anne Shore to Aubrey Grossman and William Patterson, Nov. 11, 1950, file p92, box 82, CRC Papers.

12. Greenberg and Himmelstein, "Varieties of Attack," 113–14; Muller, "Legal Defense Fund's Capital Punishment Campaign," 165.

13. "Equality before the Law," *Christian Century*, Feb. 21, 1951, p. 228; James Pollard to Virginius Dabney, Feb. 7, 1951, box 10, Dabney to Gerald F. Harris, Feb. 13, 1951, box 6, Dabney Papers; Henry S. Smith to Harold Burton, Feb. 28, 1951, box 77, Burton Papers.

14. "The Case of the Martinsville Seven," *Civil Liberties Reporter*, Feb. 27, 1951, pp. 6, 8–11, copy in file v135, box 98, CRC Papers; George Soll to Robert Carter, Feb. 9, 1951, Herbert Levy to Nanette Dembitz, July 13, 1951, vol. 61 (1951), George Soll to Ralph Felsten, Feb. 15, 1951, vol. 57 (1952), ACLU Papers.

15. Interview with Roland Ealey, Aug. 13, 1991; Martin to Powe, Oct. 6, 1950, file a180, Box 9, CRC Papers; Johnson, "New Orleans Story," 216–18; McGee v. State, 51 So. 2d 783 (Miss. 1951); State v. Jugger, 47 So. 2d 46 (La. 1952). For more detailed examinations of the McGee, Jugger, and Washington cases, see Martin, "The Civil Rights Congress and Southern Black Defendants," 45–50, and Horne, *Communist Front?* 74–98, 199–201.

16. State ex rel. Copeland v. Mayo, 87 So. 2d 501, 503 (Fla. 1956); Thomas v. State, 92 So. 2d 621 (Fla. 1957); Florida ex rel. Thomas v. Culver, 253 F. 2d 507 (5th Cir. 1958). The Supreme Court of Florida also rejected similar arguments in Williams v. State, 110 So. 2d 654 (Fla. 1959), an appeal brought by attorney Fred Minnis of St. Petersburg, another graduate of Howard law school.

17. Wansley v. Commonwealth, 205 Va. 412, 137 S.E.2d 865 (1964); Partington, "Incidence of the Death Penalty," 54–56.

18. Brickhouse v. Commonwealth, 208 Va. 533, 159 S.E.2d 611 (1968); Fogg v. Commonwealth, 208 Va. 541, 159 S.E.2d 616 (1968); Partington, "Incidence of the Death Penalty," 64–70; "Capital Punishment in Virginia," 135–36.

19. Rudolph v. Alabama, 375 U.S. 889 (1963); Greenberg and Himmelstein, "Varieties of Attack," 113.

20. Muller, "Legal Defense Fund's Capital Punishment Campaign," 165–68; Greenberg and Himmelstein, "Varieties of Attack," 114–16; Meltsner, *Cruel and Unusual*, chap. 5; Baldus, Woodworth, and Pulaski, *Equal Justice and the Death Penalty*, 250–51; Wolfgang and Riedel, "Race, Judicial Discretion, and the Death Penalty," 126–33. For summaries of cases that raised the equal protection issue, see Annotation, "Racial Discrimination in Punishment for Crime," 40 A.L.R. 3d 227 (1971).

21. Maxwell v. Bishop, 398 F. 2d 138, 148 (8th Cir. 1968).

22. Ibid.; Maxwell v. Bishop, 257 F. Supp. 710, 720 (E.D. Ark. 1966); Maxwell v. Bishop, 398 U.S. 262 (1970).

23. Meltsner, *Cruel and Unusual*, 106–8; Dorin, "Two Different Worlds," 1668; Acker, "Social Science in Death Penalty Cases," 431–33; Muller, "Legal Defense Fund's Capital Punishment Campaign," 168–70, 182; Furman v. Georgia, 408 U.S. 238, 249–51 (Douglas, J., concurring), 310 (Stewart, J., concurring), 364–66 (Marshall, J., concurring) (1972); Coker v. Georgia, 433 U.S. 584 (1977).

24. McClesky v. Kemp, 481 U.S. 279 (1987). For a comprehensive account of the Baldus study and its place in the *McClesky* litigation, see Baldus, Woodworth, and Pulaski, *Equal Justice and the Death Penalty*.

25. *McClesky*, 312; Acker, "A Different Agenda," 74–79; Jeffries, *Justice Lewis F. Powell*, 437–40. In 1991, four years after Powell retired from the Court, he told his biographer that he would change his vote in *McClesky* because he had come to believe that inconsistent enforcement of the death penalty "brings discredit on the whole legal system." Jeffries, *Justice Lewis F. Powell*, 451–52.

26. *Washington Post*, July 14, Aug. 3, 10, 12, 22, 26, Sept. 14, 1994; *New York Times*, July 14, 1994; *Newsweek*, Aug. 1, 1994, p. 24.

27. Higginbotham, "Conversations," 40; interview with Roland Ealey, Aug. 13, 1991.

BIBLIOGRAPHY

Primary Sources

Manuscripts

American Civil Liberties Union. Archives. Seeley G. Mudd Manuscript Library, Department of Rare Books and Special Collections, Princeton University Libraries, Princeton, N.J.

Battle, John S. Executive Papers, 1950–54. Archives and Records Division, Virginia State Library and Archives, Richmond.

Burton, Harold Hitz. Papers. Manuscript Division, Library of Congress, Washington, D.C.

Civil Rights Congress. Papers. Manuscripts, Archives, and Rare Books Division, Schomburg Center for Research in Black Culture, New York Public Library, Astor, Lenox, and Tilden Foundations, New York.

Dabney, Virginius. Papers. Manuscript Division, Special Collections Department, University of Virginia Library, Charlottesville.

Foreign Service Posts of the Department of State. Records, 1936–63. Record Group 84. Washington National Records Center, National Archives and Records Administration, Suitland, Md.

The Papers of Felix Frankfurter (microfilm). Frederick, Md.: University Publications of America, 1986.

Nash, Phileo. Files. Harry S. Truman Library, Independence, Mo.

National Association for the Advancement of Colored People. Papers. Manuscript Division, Library of Congress, Washington, D.C.

Patterson, William. Papers. Manuscript Division, Moorland-Spingarn Research Center, Howard University, Washington, D.C.

Reed, Stanley F. Papers. Division of Special Collections and Archives, Margaret I. King Library, University of Kentucky, Lexington.

Spingarn, Arthur. Papers. Manuscript Division, Library of Congress, Washington, D.C.

Truman, Harry S. Papers. Harry S. Truman Library, Independence, Mo.

Tuck, William M. Executive Correspondence, 1946–50. Archives and Records Division, Virginia State Library and Archives, Richmond.

Vinson, Fred M. Papers. Division of Special Collections and Archives, Margaret I. King Library, University of Kentucky, Lexington.

Wilkins, Roy. Papers. Manuscript Division, Library of Congress, Washington, D.C.

Legal Documents

Clerk's Office, Martinsville Circuit Court, Martinsville City Hall, Martinsville, Va.
   Miscellaneous Documents, Martinsville Seven File.
   Order Book, vol. 1, Martinsville Circuit Court.
   Transcript, *Commonwealth v. Francis DeSales Grayson,* file no. 149-611.
   Transcript, *Commonwealth v. Frank Hairston, Jr.,* file no. 149-607.
   Transcript, *Commonwealth v. Howard Lee Hairston,* file no. 149-610.
   Transcript, *Commonwealth v. Joe Henry Hampton,* file no. 149-612.
   Transcript, *Commonwealth v. Booker T. Millner,* file no. 149-606.
   Transcript, *Commonwealth v. John Clabon Taylor and James Luther Hairston,* file
      nos. 149-608 and 149-609.
Virginia State Law Library, Supreme Court Building, Richmond.
   Briefs on Behalf of the Commonwealth, *Hampton v. Commonwealth,* record
      nos. 3635–40.
   Petitions for Writs of Error, *Hampton v. Commonwealth,* record nos. 3635–40.
   Reply Brief for Plaintiffs in Error, *Hampton v. Commonwealth,* record nos.
      3635–40.

Cases

Ashcraft v. Tennessee, 322 U.S. 143 (1944).
Boynton v. Virginia, 364 U.S. 454 (1960).
Brickhouse v. Commonwealth, 208 Va. 533, 159 S.E.2d 611 (1968).
Brown v. Mississippi, 297 U.S. 278 (1936).
Buchanan v. Warley, 245 U.S. 60 (1917).
Buck v. Bell, 274 U.S. 200 (1927).
Chambers v. Florida, 309 U.S. 227 (1940).
Civil Rights Cases, 109 U.S. 3 (1883).
Coker v. Georgia, 433 U.S. 584 (1977).
Davis v. Allen, 157 Va. 84 (1931).
Florida ex rel. Thomas v. Culver, 253 F. 2d 507 (5th Cir. 1958).
Fogg v. Commonwealth, 208 Va. 541, 159 S.E.2d 616 (1968).
Furman v. Georgia, 408 U.S. 238 (1972).
Guinn v. United States, 238 U.S. 347 (1915).
Haley v. Ohio, 332 U.S. 596 (1947).
Hampton v. Commonwealth, 190 Va. 531, 58 S. E. 2d 288 (1950).
Hampton v. Commonwealth, 339 U.S. 989, Misc. No. 538 (1950).
Hampton v. Smyth, unpublished decision, Oct. 5, 1950, Hustings Court of the City
      of Richmond, Part II, Richmond.
Hampton v. Smyth, 340 U.S. 914, Misc. No. 245 (1951).
Herndon v. Lowry, 301 U.S. 242 (1937).
Legions v. Commonwealth, 181 Va. 89 (1943).

Louisiana ex rel. Francis v. Resweber, 329 U.S. 459 (1947).

Malinski v. New York, 324 U.S. 401 (1945).

Maxwell v. Bishop, 257 F. Supp. 710 (E.D. Ark. 1966).

Maxwell v. Bishop, 398 F. 2d 138 (8th Cir. 1968).

Maxwell v. Bishop, 398 U.S. 262 (1970).

McClesky v. Kemp, 481 U.S. 279 (1987).

McGee v. State, 51 So. 2d 783 (Miss. 1951).

McLaurin v. Oklahoma State Regents, 339 U.S. 637 (1950).

Moore v. Dempsey, 261 U.S. 86 (1923).

Morgan v. Virginia, 328 U.S. 373 (1946).

Neal v. Delaware, 103 U.S. 370 (1881).

Nixon v. Herndon, 273 U.S. 536 (1927).

Norris v. Alabama, 294 U.S. 587 (1935).

Plessy v. Ferguson, 163 U.S. 537 (1896).

Powell v. Alabama, 287 U.S. 45 (1932).

Rudolph v. Alabama, 375 U.S. 889 (1963).

Shelley v. Kraemer, 334 U.S. 1 (1948).

State ex rel. Copeland v. Mayo, 87 So. 2d 501 (Fla. 1956).

State v. Jugger, 47 So. 2d 46 (La. 1952).

Strauder v. West Virginia, 100 U.S. 303 (1879).

Sweatt v. Painter, 339 U.S. 629 (1950).

Thomas v. State, 92 So. 2d 621 (Fla. 1957).

Wansley v. Commonwealth, 205 Va. 412, 137 S.E.2d 865 (1964).

Williams v. State, 110 So. 2d 654 (Fla. 1959).

Wormeley v. Commonwealth, 51 Va. (10 Gratt.) 658 (1853).

Yick Wo v. Hopkins, 118 U.S. 356 (1886).

Government Documents

Bureau of Population and Economic Research. University of Virginia. *Economic and Social Summary, Martinsville, Virginia.* Charlottesville, Feb. 1948.

Congressional Record. Washington, D.C., 1949–51.

Edwards, Allen D. *Farm Family Income and Patterns of Living: An Analysis of Original Census Schedules and Land Classification of Henry County, Virginia, 1940.* Population Study Report no. 3. Richmond, 1944.

——. *Youth in a Rural Industrial Situation: Spencer-Penn Community, Henry County, Virginia.* Virginia Rural Youth Survey Report no. 2. Blacksburg, Va., 1940.

Federal Register. Washington, D. C., 1948.

Garnett, W. E. *Some Virginia Population Trends of General Significance.* Mimeo Report no. 3. Blacksburg, Va., Aug. 1939.

——, and Charles G. Burr. *Virginia Faces Its Population Future.* Rural Sociology Mimeo Report no. 10. Blacksburg, Va., Oct. 1939.

Salmon, John S., comp. *A Guide to State Records in the Archives Branch, Virginia State Library.* Richmond, 1985.

U.S. Department of Labor. Bureau of Labor Statistics. *A Statistical Summary of the Martinsville Area, Virginia.* Industrial Area Statistical Summary no. 19. Washington, D.C., Jan. 1944.

Virginia Department of Corrections. *Annual Reports.* Richmond, 1946–51.

Newspapers

Baltimore *Afro-American*
Daily Compass (New York)
Daily Worker (New York)
Danville *Bee*
Danville *Register*
Lynchburg *News*
Martinsville Bulletin
New York Times
Norfolk *Journal and Guide*
Norfolk *Virginian-Pilot*
Pittsburgh *Courier*
Richmond *Afro-American*
Richmond *News Leader*
Richmond *Times-Dispatch*
Roanoke *World News*
Washington Post

Interviews

Ealey, Roland D. Interview with author. Richmond, Aug. 13, 1991.
Hill, Oliver W. Interview with author. Richmond, Aug. 13, 1991.

Secondary Sources

Books and Articles

Abramowitz, Elkan, and David Paget. "Executive Clemency in Capital Cases." *New York University Law Review* 39 (Jan. 1964): 136–92.

Acker, James R. "A Different Agenda: The Supreme Court, Empirical Research Evidence, and Capital Punishment Decisions, 1986–1989." *Law and Society Review* 27 (1993): 65–88.

———. "Social Science in Supreme Court Death Penalty Cases: Citation Practices and Their Implications." *Justice Quarterly* 8 (Dec. 1991): 421–46.

Ames, Jessie Daniel. *The Changing Character of Lynching: Review of Lynching, 1931–1941.* Atlanta, 1942.

Annotation. "Racial Discrimination in Punishment for Crime." 40 A.L.R. 3d 227 (1971).

Atkinson, David N. "American Constitutionalism under Stress: Mr. Justice Burton's Response to National Security Issues." *Houston Law Review* 9 (Nov. 1971): 271–88.

Bain, Chester W. *"A Body Incorporate": The Evolution of City-County Separation in Virginia.* Charlottesville, Va., 1967.

Baldus, David C., George Woodworth, and Charles A. Pulaski, Jr. *Equal Justice and the Death Penalty: A Legal and Empirical Analysis.* Boston, 1990.

Barnes, Catherine A. *Journey from Jim Crow: The Integration of Southern Transit.* New York, 1983.

Bartley, Numan V. *The Rise of Massive Resistance: Race and Politics in the South during the 1950s.* Baton Rouge, La., 1969.

Bedau, Hugo Adam, ed. *The Death Penalty in America.* 3d ed. New York, 1982.

——, and Michael Radelet. "Miscarriages of Justice in Potentially Capital Cases." *Stanford Law Review* 40 (Nov. 1987): 21–179.

Belknap, Michal. *Cold War Political Justice: The Smith Act, the Communist Party, and American Civil Liberties.* Westport, Conn., 1977.

Berman, William C. *The Politics of Civil Rights in the Truman Administration.* Columbus, Ohio, 1970.

Berry, Mary Frances. "Judging Morality: Sexual Behavior and Legal Consequences in the Late Nineteenth-Century South." *Journal of American History* 78 (Dec. 1991): 835–56.

——. *Stability, Security, and Continuity: Mr. Justice Burton and Decision-Making in the Supreme Court, 1945–1958.* Westport, Conn., 1978.

Bodenhamer, David J. *Fair Trial: Rights of the Accused in American History.* New York and Oxford, 1992.

Bohm, Robert M. "American Death Penalty Opinion, 1936–1986: A Critical Examination of the Gallup Polls." In *The Death Penalty in America: Current Research,* ed. Robert M. Bohm, pp. 113–45. Cincinnati, 1991.

Bolner, James. "Mr. Chief Justice Fred M. Vinson and Racial Discrimination." *Register of the Kentucky Historical Society* 64 (Jan. 1966): 29–43.

Bowers, William J. *Legal Homicide: Death as Punishment in America, 1864–1982.* Boston, 1984.

Brownmiller, Susan. *Against Our Will: Men, Women, and Rape.* New York, 1975.

Brundage, W. Fitzhugh. *Lynching in the New South: Georgia and Virginia, 1880–1930.* Urbana, Ill., and Chicago, 1993.

Bryson, W. Hamilton, ed. *Legal Education in Virginia, 1779–1979: A Biographical Approach.* Charlottesville, Va., 1982.

Buhle, Mari Jo, Paul Buhle, and Dan Georgakas, eds. *Encyclopedia of the American Left.* New York and London, 1990.

Buni, Andrew. *The Negro in Virginia Politics, 1902–1965.* Charlottesville, Va., 1967.

"Capital Punishment in Virginia." *Virginia Law Review* 58 (Jan. 1972): 97–142.

Caplan, Marvin. "Virginia's Black Justice." *New Republic,* Jan. 29, 1951, p. 17.

Carter, Dan T. *Scottsboro: A Tragedy of the American South.* Baton Rouge, La., 1969.

Case, Lewis H., and John A. Van Etten. "Due Process—Criminal Confessions in Capital Cases Arising in the State Courts." *Albany Law Review* 14 (June 1950): 149–72.

"The Case of the Martinsville Seven." *Civil Liberties Reporter,* Feb. 27, 1951, pp. 8–11.

Chafe, William H. *Civilities and Civil Rights: Greensboro, North Carolina, and the Black Struggle for Freedom.* New York and Oxford, 1980.

Chalmers, David M. *Hooded Americanism: The History of the Ku Klux Klan.* 2d ed. New York and London, 1981.

Chamberlain, Bernard Peyton. *The Negro and Crime in Virginia.* Phelps-Stokes Fellowship Papers no. 15. Charlottesville, Va., 1936.

Civil Rights Congress. *Civil Rights Congress Tells the Story.* New York, n.d.

———. *We Charge Genocide.* New York, 1951.

Cleal, Dorothy, and Hiram H. Herbert. *Foresight, Founders, and Fortitude: The Growth of Industry in Martinsville and Henry County, Virginia.* Bassett, Va., 1970.

Cleary, Edward W. *McCormick on Evidence.* 3d ed. St. Paul, 1984.

Coe, Malcolm Donald, ed. *Our Proud Heritage: A Pictorial History of Martinsville and Henry County, Virginia.* With narrative history by Irene Harlan. Bassett, Va., 1969.

Cortner, Richard C. *A Mob Intent on Death: The NAACP and the Arkansas Riot Cases.* Middletown, Conn., 1988.

———. *A "Scottsboro" Case in Mississippi: The Supreme Court and Brown v. Mississippi.* Jackson, Miss., 1986.

Crawley, William Bryan, Jr. *Bill Tuck: A Political Life in Harry Byrd's Virginia.* Charlottesville, Va., 1978.

Dabney, Virginius. *Virginia: The New Dominion.* Charlottesville, Va., 1971.

Digest of the Public Record of Communism in the United States. New York, 1955.

Dinnen, Joseph F. *The Purple Shamrock: The Honorable James Michael Curley of Boston.* New York, 1949.

Dittmer, John. *Black Georgia in the Progressive Era, 1900–1920.* Urbana, Ill., 1977.

Dodson, E. Griffith, comp. *Cities of the Commonwealth of Virginia as of December 1946.* Richmond, 1947.

Dorin, Dennis D. "Two Different Worlds: Criminologists, Justices, and Racial Discrimination in the Imposition of Capital Punishment in Rape Cases." *Journal of Criminal Law and Criminology* 72 (Winter 1981): 1667–98.

Draper, Theodore. *American Communism and Soviet Russia: The Formative Period.* New York, 1960.

———. *The Roots of American Communism.* New York, 1957.

Dudziak, Mary L. "Desegregation as a Cold War Imperative." *Stanford Law Review* 41 (Nov. 1988): 61–120.

Duker, William F. *A Constitutional History of Habeas Corpus.* Westport, Conn., 1980.

Ely, James W., Jr. *The Crisis of Conservative Virginia: The Byrd Organization and the Politics of Massive Resistance.* Knoxville, Tenn., 1976.

Eminent Judges and Lawyers of the American Bar, 1951. San Francisco, 1950.

"Equality before the Law," *Christian Century,* Feb. 21, 1951, pp. 227–28.

Freeman, Anne Hobson. *The Style of a Law Firm: Eight Gentlemen from Virginia.* Chapel Hill, N. C., 1989.

Fried, Richard M. "Electoral Politics and McCarthyism: The 1950 Campaign." In *The Specter: Original Essays on the Cold War and the Origins of McCarthyism,* ed. Robert Griffith and Athan Theoharis, pp. 190–222. New York, 1974.

Frost, Richard H. *The Mooney Case.* Stanford, Calif., 1968.

Fuller, Hugh N. *Criminal Justice in Virginia.* University of Virginia Institute for Research in the Social Sciences. Monograph no. 19. New York, 1931.

Garfinkel, Harold. "Research Notes on Inter- and Intra-racial Homicides." *Social Forces* 27 (May 1949): 369–81.

Gibson, W. L., Jr. "Industrialization and Rural Land Utilization." *Southern Economic Journal* 11 (April 1945): 353–59.

Glazer, Nathan. *The Social Basis of American Communism.* New York, 1961.

Goings, Kenneth W. *"The NAACP Comes of Age": The Defeat of Judge John J. Parker.* Bloomington and Indianapolis; 1990.

Gorfinkel, John A. "The Fourteenth Amendment and State Criminal Proceedings: 'Ordered Liberty' or 'Just Deserts.'" *California Law Review* 41 (Winter 1953): 672–91.

Greenberg, Jack. *Crusaders in the Courts.* New York, 1994.

——. *Race Relations and American Law.* New York, 1959.

——, and Jack Himmelstein. "Varieties of Attack on the Death Penalty." *Crime and Delinquency* 15 (Jan. 1969): 112–20.

Gross, Samuel R., and Robert Mauro. *Death and Discrimination: Racial Disparities in Capital Sentencing.* Boston, 1989.

Grossberg, Michael. *Governing the Hearth: Law and the Family in Nineteenth-Century America.* Chapel Hill and London, 1985.

Grossman, James R. *Land of Hope: Chicago, Black Southerners, and the Great Migration.* Chicago, 1989.

Guzman, Jessie Packhurst, ed. *Negro Year Book: A Review of Events Affecting Negro Life, 1941–1946.* Tuskegee, Ala., 1947.

Hagan, John Patrick. "Patterns of Activism on State Supreme Courts." *Publius: The Journal of Federalism* 18 (Winter 1988): 97–115.

Hakman, Nathan. "Old and New Left Activity in the Legal Order: An Interpretation." *Journal of Social Issues* 27 (1971): 105–21.

Hall, Jacquelyn Dowd. "'The Mind That Burns in Each Body': Women, Rape, and

Racial Violence." In *Powers of Desire: The Politics of Sexuality,* ed. Ann Snitow, Christine Stansell, and Sharon Thompson, pp. 328–49. New York, 1983.

———. *Revolt against Chivalry: Jessie Daniel Ames and the Women's Campaign against Lynching.* New York, 1979.

Hall, Jerome. "Police and Law in a Democratic Society." *Indiana Law Journal* 28 (Winter 1953): 133–77.

Harper, Fowler V., and Edwin T. Etherington. "What the Supreme Court Did Not Do during the 1950 Term." *University of Pennsylvania Law Review* 100 (Dec. 1951): 354–409.

Harper, Fowler V., and Alan S. Rosenthal. "What the Supreme Court Did Not Do in the 1949 Term—An Appraisal of Certiorari." *University of Pennsylvania Law Review* 99 (Dec. 1950): 293–325.

Harris, Trudier. *Exorcising Blackness: Historical and Literary Lynching and Burning Rituals.* Bloomington, Ind., 1984.

Henry County: A Proud Look Back. Bassett, Va., 1975.

Higginbotham, A. Leon, Jr. "Conversations with Civil Rights Crusaders [Oliver Hill and Samuel Tucker]." *Virginia Lawyer* 37 (Feb. 1989): 11–16, 37–41.

Hill, Judith Parks America. *A History of Henry County, Virginia.* 1925. Rpt. Baltimore, 1976.

Hine, Darlene Clark. *Black Victory: The Rise and Fall of the White Primary in Texas.* Millwood, N. Y., 1979.

Hoffer, Frank William, Delbert Martin Mann, and Floyd Nelson House. *The Jails of Virginia: A Study of a Local Penal System.* University of Virginia Institute for Research in the Social Sciences. Monograph no. 16. New York, 1933.

Horne, Gerald. *Black and Red: W. E. B. Du Bois and the Afro-American Response to the Cold War, 1944–1963.* Albany, 1986.

———. *Communist Front? The Civil Rights Congress, 1946–1956.* Rutherford, N. J., 1988.

Howe, Irving, and Lewis A. Coser. *The American Communist Party: A Critical History, 1919–1957.* New York, 1962.

Hudson, Mike. "Hill v. Board of Education." *Southern Exposure* 17 (Spring 1989): 30–33.

Jack, Robert L. *History of the National Association for the Advancement of Colored People.* Boston, 1943.

Jeffries, John C., Jr. *Justice Lewis F. Powell, Jr.* New York, 1994.

Johnson, David R. *American Law Enforcement: A History.* Arlington Heights, Ill., 1981.

Johnson, Elmer H. "Selective Factors in Capital Punishment." *Social Forces* 36 (Dec. 1957): 165–69.

Johnson, Guy. "The Negro and Crime." *Annals of the American Academy of Political and Social Science* 217 (Sept. 1941): 93–104.

———, and Guion Griffis Johnson. *Research in Service to Society: The First Fifty Years of the Institute for Research in Social Sciences at the University of North Carolina.* Chapel Hill, N. C., 1980.

Johnson, Oakley C. "New Orleans Story." *Centennial Review* 12 (Spring 1968): 193–219.

Kamisar, Yale. *Police Interrogation and Confessions: Essays in Law and Policy.* Ann Arbor, Mich., 1980.

Kaplan, John, and Jon R. Waltz. *Cases and Materials on Evidence.* 6th ed. Mineola, N. Y., 1987.

Kelley, Robin D. G. *Hammer and Hoe: Alabama Communists during the Great Depression.* Chapel Hill, N. C., and London, 1990.

Kellogg, Charles Flint. *NAACP: A History of the National Association for the Advancement of Colored People, 1909–1920.* Vol. 1. Baltimore, 1967.

Kellogg, Peter J. "Civil Rights Consciousness in the 1940s." *Historian* 42 (Nov. 1979): 18–41.

Kennedy, T. H., and T. F. Leary. "Communist Thought on the Negro." *Phylon* 8 (Second Quarter, 1947): 116–23.

Keve, Paul W. *The History of Corrections in Virginia.* Charlottesville, Va., 1986.

Klehr, Harvey. *The Heyday of American Communism: The Depression Decade.* New York, 1984.

Klibaner, Irwin. *Conscience of a Troubled South: The Southern Conference Educational Fund, 1946–1966.* Brooklyn, 1989.

Kluger, Richard. *Simple Justice: The Story of* Brown v. Board of Education *and Black America's Struggle for Equality.* New York, 1975.

LaFave, Wayne R., and Jerold Israel. *Criminal Procedure.* 2d ed. St. Paul, 1992.

Latham, Earl. *The Communist Controversy in Washington: From the New Deal to McCarthy.* Cambridge, Mass., 1966.

Lawes, Lewis E. *Life and Death in Sing Sing.* Garden City, N. Y., 1928.

Lawson, Steven F., David R. Colburn, and Darryl Paulson. "Groveland: Florida's Little Scottsboro." *Florida Historical Quarterly* 65 (July 1986): 1–26.

Lebsock, Suzanne. *"A Share of Honor": Virginia Women, 1600–1945.* Richmond, 1984.

Liebman, Charles. *Directory of American Judges.* Chicago, 1955.

McAuliffe, Mary S. *Crisis on the Left: Cold War Politics and American Liberals, 1947–54.* Amherst, Mass., 1978.

——. "The Politics of Civil Liberties: The American Civil Liberties Union during the McCarthy Years." In *The Specter: Original Essays on the Cold War and the Origins of McCarthyism,* ed. Robert Griffith and Athan Theoharis, pp. 152–70. New York, 1974.

McGovern, James R. *Anatomy of a Lynching: The Killing of Claude Neal.* Baton Rouge, La., 1982.

Mackey, Philip E., ed. *Voices against Death: Classic Appeals Against the Death Penalty in America, 1787–1973.* New York, 1976.

McNeil, Genna Rae. *Groundwork: Charles Hamilton Houston and the Struggle for Civil Rights.* Philadelphia, 1983.

Mandel, William. "Vigil in Richmond." *Jewish Life,* April 1951, pp. 5–8.

Markowitz, Norman. *The Rise and Fall of the People's Century: Henry A. Wallace and American Liberalism, 1941–1948.* New York, 1973.

———. "A View from the Left: From the Popular Front to Cold War Liberalism." In *The Specter: Original Essays on the Cold War and the Origins of McCarthyism,* ed. Robert Griffith and Athan Theoharis, pp. 90–115. New York, 1974.

Martin, Charles H. *The Angelo Herndon Case and Southern Justice.* Baton Rouge, La., 1976.

———. "The Civil Rights Congress and Southern Black Defendants." *Georgia Historical Quarterly* 71 (Spring 1987): 25–52.

———. "The International Labor Defense and Black America." *Labor History* 26 (Spring 1985): 165–94.

———. "Oklahoma's 'Scottsboro' Affair: The Jess Hollins Rape Case, 1931–1936." *South Atlantic Quarterly* 79 (Spring 1980): 175–88.

———. "Race, Gender, and Southern Justice: The Rosa Lee Ingram Case." *American Journal of Legal History* 29 (July 1985): 251–68.

Martindale-Hubbell Law Directory. 82d ed. Summit, N. J., 1950.

———. 96th ed. Summit, N. J., 1964.

Martinsville–Henry County Woman's Club. *Martinsville and Henry County: Historic Views,* ed. Mrs. George B. Adams. Winston-Salem, N. C., 1976.

"The Martinsville Seven." *Time,* Feb. 12, 1951, p. 21.

Meier, August, and Elliott Rudwick. "Attorneys Black and White: A Case Study of Race Relations within the NAACP." *Journal of American History* 62 (March 1976): 913–46.

———. "The Origins of Nonviolent Direct Action in Afro-American Protest: A Note on Historical Discontinuities." In *Along the Color Line: Explorations in the Black Experience,* ed. August Meier and Elliott Rudwick, pp. 307–404. Urbana, Ill., 1976.

———. "Radicals and Conservatives: Black Protest in Twentieth-Century America." In *Old Memories, New Moods,* vol. 2 of *Americans from Africa,* ed. Peter I. Rose, pp. 119–47. New York, 1970.

———, and Francis L. Broderick, eds. *Black Protest Thought in the Twentieth Century.* 2d ed. Indianapolis, 1971.

Meltsner, Michael. *Cruel and Unusual: The Supreme Court and Capital Punishment.* New York, 1973.

Miller, Arthur S., and Jeffrey Bowman. *Death by Installments: The Ordeal of Willie Francis.* New York, 1988.

Miller, Frank W., Robert O. Dawson, George E. Dix, and Raymond I. Parnas. *Criminal Justice Administration.* 4th ed. Westbury, N. Y., 1991.

Moon, Henry Lee. "The Martinsville Rape Case." *New Leader,* Feb. 12, 1951, p. 18.

Morris, Thomas R. *The Virginia Supreme Court: An Institutional and Political Analysis.* Charlottesville, Va., 1975.

Mouledous, Joseph C. "From Browderism to Peaceful Co-Existence: An Analysis of Developments in the Communist Position on the American Negro." *Phylon* 25 (Spring 1964): 79–90.

Muller, Eric L. "The Legal Defense Fund's Capital Punishment Campaign: The Distorting Influence of Death." *Yale Law and Policy Review* 4 (1985): 158–87.

Murphy, Paul L. *The Constitution in Crisis Times, 1918–1969.* New York, 1972.

Murray, Pauli. *States' Laws on Race and Color.* Cincinnati, 1950.

Muse, Benjamin. *Virginia's Massive Resistance.* Bloomington, Ind., 1961.

Myrdal, Gunnar. *An American Dilemma: The Negro Problem and Modern Democracy.* New York, 1944.

Naison, Mark. *Communists in Harlem during the Depression.* Urbana, Ill., 1983.

National Association for the Advancement of Colored People. *Thirty Years of Lynching in the United States: 1889–1918.* 1919. Rpt. New York, 1969.

Nelson, Margaret Virginia. *A Study of Judicial Review in Virginia, 1789–1928.* New York, 1947.

Nissman, Donald M., Ed Hagan, and Pierce R. Brooks. *Law of Confessions.* Rochester, N. Y., 1985.

Nolan, William A. *Communism versus the Negro.* Chicago, 1951.

Packer, Herbert L. *The Limits of the Criminal Sanction.* Stanford, Calif., 1968.

Painter, Nell Irvin. "'Social Equality,' Miscegenation, Labor, and Power." In *The Evolution of Southern Culture,* ed. Numan V. Bartley, pp. 47–67. Athens, Ga., 1988.

Partington, Donald H. "The Incidence of the Death Penalty for Rape in Virginia." *Washington and Lee Law Review* 22 (Spring 1965): 43–75.

Patterson, William L. *The Man Who Cried Genocide: An Autobiography.* New York, 1971.

Pedigo, Virginia G., and Lewis G. Pedigo. *History of Patrick and Henry Counties, Virginia.* 1933. Rpt. Baltimore, 1977.

Peltason, J. W. *Fifty-Eight Lonely Men: Southern Federal Judges and School Desegregation.* New York, 1961.

Penton, M. James. *Apocalypse Delayed: The Story of Jehovah's Witnesses.* Toronto, 1985.

Peters, John O. *Tale of the Century: A History of the Bar Association of the City of Richmond, 1885–1985.* Richmond, 1985.

Powers, Richard Gid. *Secrecy and Power: The Life of J. Edgar Hoover.* New York, 1987.

Pratt, Robert A. *The Color of Their Skin: Education and Race in Richmond, Virginia, 1954–89.* Charlottesville, Va., 1992.

Prettyman, E. Barrett, Jr., "Petitioning the United States Supreme Court—A Primer for Hopeful Neophytes." *Virginia Law Review* 51 (May 1965): 582–603.

Record, Wilson. "The Development of the Communist Position on the Negro Question in the United States." *Phylon* 19 (Fall 1958): 306–26.

——. *The Negro and the Communist Party.* Chapel Hill, N. C., 1951.

——. *Race and Radicalism: The NAACP and the Communist Party in Conflict.* Ithaca, N. Y., 1964.

Rise, Eric W. "Race, Rape, and Radicalism: The Case of the Martinsville Seven, 1949–1951." *Journal of Southern History* 58 (Aug. 1992): 461–90.

Rosen, Paul. *The Supreme Court and Social Science.* Urbana, Ill., 1972.

Rosett, Arthur, and Donald R. Cressey. *Justice by Consent: Plea Bargains in the American Courthouse.* New York, 1976.

St. James, Warren D. *The National Association for the Advancement of Colored People: A Case Study in Pressure Groups.* New York, 1958.

Schneider, Victoria, and John Ortiz Smykla. "A Summary Analysis of *Executions in the United States, 1608–1987: The Espy File.*" In *The Death Penalty in America: Current Research,* ed. Robert M. Bohm, pp. 1–19. Cincinnati, 1991.

Segal, Geraldine R. *Blacks in the Law: Philadelphia and the Nation.* Philadelphia, 1983.

Shannon, David A. *The Decline of American Communism: A History of the Communist Party of the United States since 1945.* New York, 1959.

"The Shape of Things." *Nation,* Jan. 27, 1951, p. 71.

Sherman, Richard B. *The Case of Odell Waller and Virginia Justice, 1940–1942.* Knoxville, Tenn., 1992.

Smead, Howard. *Blood Justice: The Lynching of Mack Charles Parker.* New York and Oxford, 1986.

Smith, Bruce. *Rural Crime Control.* New York, 1933.

Smith, J. Clay, Jr. *Emancipation: The Making of the Black Lawyer, 1844–1944.* Philadelphia, 1993.

Steinberg, Peter L. *The Great "Red Menace": United States Prosecution of American Communists, 1947–1952.* Westport, Conn., 1984.

Stephens, Otis H., Jr. *The Supreme Court and Confessions of Guilt.* Knoxville, Tenn., 1973.

Stouffer, Samuel A. *Communism, Conformity, and Civil Liberties.* New York, 1955.

Strong, Frank R. "Fifty Years of 'Clear and Present Danger': From Schenck to Brandenburg—And Beyond." *Supreme Court Review* 1969: 41–80.

Suggs, H. Lewis. "Black Strategy and Ideology in the Segregation Era: P. B. Young and the Norfolk *Journal and Guide,* 1910–1954." *Virginia Magazine of History and Biography* 91 (April 1983): 161–90.

——. *P. B. Young, Newspaperman: Race, Politics, and Journalism in the New South, 1910–1962.* Charlottesville, Va., 1988.

Theoharis, Athan. *Seeds of Repression: Harry S Truman and the Origins of McCarthyism.* Chicago, 1971.

Tribe, Laurence H. *American Constitutional Law: A Structure for Liberty.* Mineola, N.Y., 1978.

Tucker, S. W. "Racial Discrimination in Jury Selection in Virginia." *Virginia Law Review* 52 (May 1966): 736–50.

Tushnet, Mark V. *Making Civil Rights Law: Thurgood Marshall and the Supreme Court, 1936–1961.* New York and Oxford, 1994.

——. *The NAACP's Legal Strategy against Segregated Education, 1925–1950.* Chapel Hill, N. C., and London, 1987.

Van Zanten, John W. "Communist Theory and the Negro Question." *Review of Politics* 29 (Oct. 1967): 435–56.

Walker, Samuel. *In Defense of American Liberties: A History of the ACLU.* New York and Oxford, 1990.

——. *Popular Justice: A History of American Criminal Justice.* New York and Oxford, 1980.

Ware, Leland B. "Invisible Walls: An Examination of the Legal Strategy of the Restrictive Covenant Cases." *Washington University Law Quarterly* 67 (Fall 1989): 737–72.

Wiecek, William M. *Liberty under Law: The Supreme Court in American History.* Baltimore and London, 1988.

Wilkins, Roy, with Tom Matthews, *Standing Fast: The Autobiography of Roy Wilkins.* New York, 1982.

Wilkinson, J. Harvie, III. *Harry Byrd and the Changing Face of Virginia Politics.* Charlottesville, Va., 1968.

Williamson, Joel. *The Crucible of Race: Black-White Relations in the American South since Emancipation.* New York and Oxford, 1984.

Wolfgang, Marvin E., and Marc Riedel. "Race, Judicial Discretion, and the Death Penalty." *Annals of the Academy of Political and Social Science* 407 (May 1973): 119–33.

Woodward, C. Vann. *The Strange Career of Jim Crow.* 3d rev. ed. New York, 1974.

Wright, George C. "The NAACP and Residential Segregation in Louisville, Kentucky, 1914–1917." *Register of the Kentucky Historical Society* 78 (Winter 1980): 39–54.

——. *Racial Violence in Kentucky, 1865–1940: Lynchings, Mob Rule, and "Legal Lynchings."* Baton Rouge, La., and London, 1990.

Wynn, Daniel Webster. *The NAACP versus Negro Revolutionary Protest: A Comparative Study of the Effectiveness of Each Movement.* New York, 1955.

Zangrando, Robert L. *The NAACP Crusade against Lynching, 1909–1950.* Philadelphia, 1980.

Dissertations, Theses, and Unpublished Papers

Bailey, Frankie Yvonne. "Boundary Maintenance, Interest-Group Conflict, and Black Justice in Danville, Virginia, 1900–1930." Ph.D. diss., State University of New York at Albany, 1986.

Clark, Wayne Addison. "An Analysis of the Relationship between Anti-

Communism and Segregationist Thought in the Deep South, 1948–1964."
Ph.D. diss., University of North Carolina at Chapel Hill, 1976.

Crawley, William Bryan, Jr. "The Governorship of William M. Tuck, 1946–1950:
Virginia Politics in the 'Golden Age' of the Byrd Organization." Ph.D. diss.,
University of Virginia, 1974.

Henriques, Peter Ros. "John S. Battle and Virginia Politics, 1948–1953." Ph.D.
diss., University of Virginia, 1971.

Hoover, Eugene Carl. "Secondary Education in Henry County, Virginia." Master's
thesis, University of Virginia, 1937.

Isaac, Oliver Burns. "A Selected, Annotated Bibliography of Resources on the
History of Franklin, of Henry, and of Patrick Counties in Virginia." Master's
thesis, Catholic University of America, 1964.

Mainwaring, W. Thomas, Jr. "Community in Danville, Virginia, 1880–1963." Ph.D.
diss., University of North Carolina at Chapel Hill, 1988.

Marquardt, Ronald G. "The Judicial Justice: Mr. Justice Burton and the Supreme
Court." Ph.D. diss., University of Missouri, 1973.

Martin, Charles H. "The Civil Rights Congress and the Second Red Scare." Paper
presented at the annual meeting of the Organization of American Histori-
ans, Los Angeles, April 1984.

Mitchell, Dora Willie. "A Political and Social History of Henry County as Dis-
closed in the County Court Records." Master's thesis, University of Virginia, [1935].

Pincus, Samuel Norman. "The Virginia Supreme Court, Blacks, and the Law,
1870–1902." Ph.D. diss., University of Virginia, 1978.

Ramsey, Benjamin Sterling. "History and Analysis of the Public Schools of Henry
County, Virginia." Master's thesis, Duke University, 1946.

Raubach, Elaine Marguerite. "Social Mobility in Henry County, Virginia, from
1850 to 1870." Master's thesis, University of Virginia, 1971.

Sanford, Delacey Wendell. "Congressional Investigation of Black Communism,
1919–1967." Ph.D. diss., State University of New York at Stony Brook, 1973.

Simmons, Charles W., III. "Virginia Justice and the Martinsville Seven." Master's
thesis, Virginia State University, 1985.

Wallenstein, Peter. "'I Went to Law School to Fight Segregation': Oliver W. Hill
versus Jim Crow in Virginia." Paper presented at the annual meeting of the
Southern Historical Association, Atlanta, November 1992.

Woodzell, Stephen Russell, Jr. "Electrocution and the Death Penalty in Virginia."
Master's thesis, George Washington University, 1969.